Levers of Power

How the 1% Rules and What the 99% Can Do about It

Kevin A. Young, Tarun Banerjee,
and Michael Schwartz

VERSO
London • New York

First published by Verso 2020
© Kevin A. Young, Tarun Banerjee, and Michael Schwartz 2020

This book contains excerpts from the following previously published articles: Kevin Young and Michael Schwartz, "Healthy, Wealthy, and Wise: How Corporate Power Shaped the Affordable Care Act," *New Labor Forum* 23, no. 2 (2014): 30–40 © 2014 The Murphy Institute, City University of New York; Kevin Young and Michael Schwartz, "A Neglected Mechanism of Social Movement Political Influence: The Role of Anticorporate and Anti-Institutional Protest in Changing Government Policy," *Mobilization* 19, no. 3 (2014): 239–260 © 2014 *Mobilization: An International Quarterly*; Kevin A. Young, Tarun Banerjee, and Michael Schwartz, "Capital Strikes as a Corporate Political Strategy: The Structural Power of Business in the Obama Era," *Politics and Society* 46, no. 1 (2018): 3–28 © 2018 Sage Publications.

1 3 5 7 9 10 8 6 4 2

Verso
UK: 6 Meard Street, London W1F 0EG
US: 20 Jay Street, Suite 1010, Brooklyn, NY 11201
versobooks.com

Verso is the imprint of New Left Books

ISBN-13: 978-1-78873-096-9
ISBN-13: 978-1-78873-099-0 (LIBRARY)
ISBN-13: 978-1-78873-097-6 (UK EBK)
ISBN-13: 978-1-78873-098-3 (US EBK)

British Library Cataloguing in Publication Data
A catalogue record for this book is available from the British Library

Library of Congress Cataloging-in-Publication Data

Names: Young, Kevin A., author. | Banerjee, Tarun Kumar, 1948– author. |
  Schwartz, Michael, 1942–
Title: Levers of power : how the 1% rules and what the 99% can do about it
  / Kevin A. Young, Tarun Banerjee, and Michael Schwartz.
Description: London ; New York : Verso, 2020. | Includes bibliographical
  references and index. | Summary: "Levers of Power argues that
  corporations' influence ultimately derives from their control over the
  economic resources on which society depends. When business goes on a
  'capital strike' by refusing to invest in particular locations or
  industries, it imposes material hardship on specific groups or even the
  economy as a whole. For this reason, even politicians who are not
  dependent on corporate campaign cash must strive to keep capitalists
  happy"— Provided by publisher.
Identifiers: LCCN 2020006826 (print) | LCCN 2020006827 (ebook) | ISBN
  9781788730969 (paperback) | ISBN 9781788730990 (library binding) | ISBN
  9781788730983 (ebk)
Subjects: LCSH: Business and politics—United States. | Corporate
  power—Political aspects—United States. | Capitalism—Political
  aspects—United States.
Classification: LCC JK467 .Y68 2020 (print) | LCC JK467 (ebook) | DDC
  322/.30973—dc23
LC record available at https://lccn.loc.gov/2020006826
LC ebook record available at https://lccn.loc.gov/2020006827

Typeset in Minion Pro by Hewer Text UK Ltd, Edinburgh
Printed and bound by CPI Group (UK) Ltd, Croydon CR0 4YY

Contents

Tables and Figures

Acknowledgments

This book is the result of more than a decade of research and discussion. The conversations began in late 2009, motivated by an emergent pattern that we began calling The Obama Conundrum. Though the new Obama administration had been elected with a strong mandate for "Change We Can Believe In" and enjoyed filibuster-proof control of Congress, it was not delivering major progressive reforms. We began to see this pattern as reflective of a much bigger theoretical question: what are the obstacles to progressive political change in modern-day societies, and how might we overcome them?

Our answer has been shaped by our research and by an ongoing discussion among the authors, with input from a large circle of friends and colleagues. We wish to acknowledge the help, in one form or another, of Gilbert Achcar, Idil Akin, Ahmad Al-Sholi, Kenneth Andrews, Florencia Arancibia, Diana Baldermann, Fred Block, Vivek Chibber, the late Dan Clawson, Mary Ann Clawson, G. William Domhoff, Barry Eidlin, Louis Esparza, Crystal Fleming, Gabriela González Vaillant, Jeff Goodwin, Sebastián Guzmán, Tiffany Joseph, Wallace Katz, Richard Lachmann, Prita Lal, Clarence Lo, Matt Mahler, John Marciano, Mike Miller, Joya Misra, Aldon Morris, Joshua Murray, Fernanda Page Poma, Joseph Peschek, Frances Fox Piven, Charlie Post, Christopher Rhomberg, S.M. Rodríguez, Magali Sarfatti Larson, Kim Scipes, Diana Sierra Becerra, Marc Steinberg, Juhi Tyagi, Arnout Van de Rijt, Nancy Whittier, the late Jeffrey Young, and Gilda Zwerman; the attendees at conferences of the American Sociological Association, Eastern Sociological Society, Stony Brook University's *How Class Works*, and the NYU Economic and Political Sociology workshop, where we presented early drafts of pieces of the book; and editors and reviewers at the journals *Mobilization, New Labor Forum,* and *Politics and Society,* where some of the material appeared in print. Finally, our argument about social movement strategy is indebted to numerous organizers, most of whom are not famous, who developed keen analyses of power and how oppressed people could reclaim it.

Abbreviations Used in the Text and Footnotes

ACA	Affordable Care Act
AFL	American Federation of Labor
AHIP	America's Health Insurance Plans
CAA	Community Action Agency
CAP	Community Action Program
CBA	Cost-benefit analysis
CDGM	Child Development Group of Mississippi
CFPB	Consumer Financial Protection Bureau
CFR	Council on Foreign Relations
CFTC	Commodity Futures Trading Commission
CIO	Congress of Industrial Organizations
CORE	Congress of Racial Equality
CRP	Center for Responsive Politics
DADT	"Don't Ask, Don't Tell"
DoD	Department of Defense
DoJ	Department of Justice
EPA	Environmental Protection Agency
FCC	Federal Communications Commission
FDIC	Federal Deposit Insurance Corporation
FERC	Federal Energy Regulatory Commission
GM	General Motors
HELP	Senate Committee on Health, Education, Labor, and Pensions
HMO	Health Maintenance Organization
ICE	Immigration and Customs Enforcement
MAP	Mississippi Action for Progress
NAACP	National Association for the Advancement of Colored People

NAFTA	North American Free Trade Agreement
NBCH	National Business Coalition on Health
NCHC	National Coalition on Health Care
NLF	National Liberation Front (Vietnam)
NLRB	National Labor Relations Board
NYPD	New York Police Department
OCC	Office of the Comptroller of the Currency
OEO	Office of Economic Opportunity
OIRA	Office of Information and Regulatory Affairs
OTC	Over-the-counter (derivatives)
PhRMA	Pharmaceutical Research and Manufacturers of America
ROTC	Reserve Officers' Training Corps
SCLC	Southern Christian Leadership Conference
SEC	Securities and Exchange Commission
SFC	Senate Finance Committee
SNCC	Student Nonviolent Coordinating Committee
TARP	Troubled Asset Relief Program
TPP	Trans-Pacific Partnership
UAW	United Auto Workers
USCAP	US Climate Action Partnership

Publications

AB	*American Banker*
AJS	*American Journal of Sociology*
AP	Associated Press
APSR	*American Political Science Review*
ASR	*American Sociological Review*
BW	*Bloomberg Businessweek* ("*Businessweek*" up to 2009)
FT	*Financial Times*
LN	*Labor Notes*
NLF	*New Labor Forum*
NYT	*New York Times*
PAS	*Politics and Society*
TNY	*New Yorker*
WP	*Washington Post*
WSJ	*Wall Street Journal*

Introduction: Shadow and Substance

In 1931, the philosopher John Dewey lamented that "politics is the shadow cast on society by big business." Government "in general is an echo," and at times a direct "accomplice, of the interests of big business."[1] Dewey was writing in the early years of the Great Depression, as unchecked capitalism had plunged the world into crisis and his government was doing nothing to solve the problem. Today, as in Dewey's time, big business's control over the US government is an open secret. We have formally democratic institutions, but the 1% exercises preponderant control over government policymaking. Statistical studies show that the preferences of non-wealthy people have little or no influence on policy.[2] The 99% are well aware of this fact. In polls, over three-quarters of the public consistently says that government is "run by a few big interests looking out for themselves," namely large corporations and the rich. In the years following the economic crash of 2008, around two-thirds agreed that the government's response had benefited "large banks and financial institutions," "large corporations," and "wealthy people," and that the rest of the population had benefited "not too much" or "not at all."[3]

---

1   John Dewey, "The Need for a New Party," in *John Dewey: The Later Works, 1925–1953*, vol. 6, *1931–1932*, ed. Jo Ann Boydston (Carbondale: Southern Illinois University Press, 1985), 163.

2   Martin Gilens, *Affluence and Influence: Economic Inequality and Political Power in America* (Princeton, NJ: Princeton University Press, 2012); Martin Gilens and Benjamin I. Page, "Testing Theories of American Politics: Elites, Interest Groups, and Average Citizens," *Perspectives on Politics* 12, no. 3 (2014): 564–81.

3   Pew Research Center, "Beyond Distrust: How Americans View Their Government," November 23, 2015: 35; and "Most Say Government Policies Since Recession Have Done Little to Help Middle Class, Poor," March 4, 2015: 1. To avoid clutter, we omit URLs for online sources when they are easily locatable via search engines or available by subscription only.

Critiques of plutocracy—rule by the rich—are not new. Even in Dewey's time, the insight was hardly original. Marxists and anarchists had long denounced capitalists' influence over government. Some liberals like Dewey had voiced similar critiques, dating back at least to Adam Smith's complaint in 1776 that England's "merchants and manufacturers" were "the principal architects" of economic policy, their interests "so carefully attended to" by politicians.[4] And as polls suggest, the idea that government is "the shadow cast by big business" is old news to most of the public today.

But Dewey added a further insight: "The attenuation of the shadow will not change the substance."[5] In other words, electing politicians critical of business will not eliminate business's power to shape government policy. History supports Dewey's point. Governments elected with a strong progressive mandate, from Chile in the early 1970s to Venezuela and Greece more recently, have faced massive economic disruption— and often military coups—when their reforms pose a threat to the profits and privileges of capitalists. Less ambitious would-be reformers like Barack Obama have also incurred the wrath of business despite taking enormous pains to accommodate corporate interests.

The Roots of Corporate Power

Why is business so powerful? Most analysts attribute its political influence to campaign donations and lobbying. But campaign finance is just one means by which business influences government. We argue that the problem goes far beyond money in politics, to the very structure of the economy. The political power of banks and corporations ultimately derives from the power that they wield over the economy itself—what some call their "structural power."[6] They control most of the crucial resources on which society depends, including investment capital (and

---

4   Adam Smith, *The Wealth of Nations* (New York: Bantam, 2003), 841.
5   Dewey, "The Need for a New Party," 163.
6   This argument draws upon the work of many prior analysts. For more detail and citations to relevant studies see Kevin A. Young, Tarun Banerjee, and Michael Schwartz, "Capital Strikes as a Corporate Political Strategy: The Structural Power of Business in the Obama Era," *PAS* 46, no. 1 (2018): 3–28; Beth Mintz and Michael Schwartz, *The Power Structure of American Business* (Chicago, IL: University of Chicago Press, 1985). Structural power is often neglected, however, perhaps because it is not easily quantifiable. It forms part of what David Lowery calls "the dark matter of influence"—hard to measure but omnipresent. "Lobbying Influence: Meaning, Measurement and Missing," *Interest Groups and Advocacy* 2, no. 1 (2013): 8.

thus jobs and loans) as well as food, transportation, medicine, health-care services, and countless other things. The investment decisions made in corporate boardrooms help determine employment levels, the location of jobs, the availability of loans, the price of critical goods, and the revenues available to government.

The most potent weapon of banks and employers is the *capital strike*: the withdrawal of investment capital from one or more sectors of the economy, or "disinvestment," in the form of layoffs, offshoring, transfers of financial capital abroad, the tightening of credit, and other disruptive measures. These actions can be carried out by individual firms or entire industries, or when large investors make a collective decision to disinvest.[7] Banks wield this power of disruption through their lending decisions, while non-bank businesses do so by opening, expanding, closing, and relocating their factories, stores, or service areas.

The withholding of capital is not always a deliberate strike by capitalists for political purposes; capitalists may disinvest simply because of market conditions, such as low demand for their products—as when automakers cut production and lay off workers when demand for certain automobiles declines. The capital strike is distinguished from these "normal" instances of disinvestment by capitalists' demands for government policy change and their promises that favorable changes will bring new or renewed investment. In other words, disinvestment constitutes a capital strike when the withholding of capital is accompanied by a promise to invest in exchange for favors from government. The capital strike is not an automatic response to market conditions, but a conscious capitalist strategy for getting what they want from government.[8]

Because business controls most of the resources upon which we all depend, government officials must constantly appease capitalists so

---

7 Some analysts argue that conflicts among corporations prevent them from acting in unison. However, this argument neglects the many mechanisms, from overlapping boards of directors to social clubs, through which businesses can make collective decisions. See Young et al., "Capital Strikes."

8 Expressing a common view, Charles Lindblom argues that business disinvestment is "an automatic punishing recoil" that follows from any threat to maximum profitability. "The Market as Prison," *Journal of Politics* 44, no. 2 (1982): 325. In contrast, the leading US business magazine acknowledges the major subjective element in investment decisions: "Our review of data going back to 1950 considered a host of variables related to investment, including the output gap, business confidence, capital depreciation, and interest rates. It showed that business confidence, or what John Maynard Keynes liked to call 'animal spirits,' along with the basic laws of supply and demand, are more important drivers of investment." Tim Mahedy, "A Lot of Huff for a Little Puff," *BW*, March 11, 2019: 31.

they will continue to productively invest these resources. Only the boldest governments are willing to coerce capitalists into investing, since doing so typically invites deeper capital strikes and leads to a showdown in which the state must either expropriate private enterprise (defying accusations of totalitarianism) or capitulate.[9] Governments everywhere thus invest great energy and public resources in staving off fits by malcontent executives and investors. Most public officials internalize the logic of "business confidence," which means pursuing policies that will boost business leaders' confidence in the government and avoiding big policies that might invite retaliation. Certain policy options are never even contemplated or discussed given the certainty of fierce business opposition. In this context, businesses resort to overt capital strikes only on occasion. Once the disruptive power of the capital strike has been demonstrated, mere threats often do the trick. The possibility of future capital strikes influences the government in myriad ways, from the appointment of regulators to the laws that Congress makes and the way in which the government enforces, or declines to enforce, those laws.[10]

The pages of the business press feature regular examples of this coercion. A manufacturer refuses to invest in the United States until the government cuts taxes and loosens "environmental regulations and hiring rules." A leader on Wall Street threatens that new government regulations on banks will bring a reduction in their rate of lending and thus a drop in economic growth. Apple's CEO warns that the $181 billion stored by the company in an overseas tax haven won't come "back until there's a fair rate" of taxation on corporate income. Amazon uses its promise to construct a second headquarters to promote a bidding war among 238 cities, with each seeking to outdo the others by lavishing the company with billions in public handouts. Despite holding several trillion dollars in reserves, banks and corporations collectively refuse to make loans or hire new employees.[11]

---

9 Some revolutionary governments have opted to radicalize when faced with this choice, for example in Cuba in 1959–1961 or, to lesser extents, Chile in 1970–1973 and Venezuela in the mid-2000s. On Venezuela see Oliver Levingston, "Venezuela: The Political Economy of Inflation and Investment Strikes," *Links*, February 10, 2014.

10 For a more detailed theory of capital strikes and business confidence see Young et al., "Capital Strikes."

11 Emerson Electric CEO David Farr quoted in Elizabeth Williamson and James R. Hagerty, "The New Political Landscape: Executives Await Friendlier Climate," *WSJ*, November 4, 2010: A6 (first quote); Financial Services Forum CEO Rob Nichols quoted in Donna Borak, Victoria Finkle, and Joe Adler, "Consensus Is Elusive on TBTF, Big-Bank Subsidies," *AB*, April 23, 2013; Jena McGregor, "Tim Cook, the

In response, both Republican and Democratic politicians seek to encourage corporate investment by enacting pro-business reforms. Presidents of both parties beg business to add jobs while aggressively pushing pro-corporate trade deals and scrapping regulations that protect the public and the environment. To lure capital back from offshore tax shelters, they propose cutting corporate taxes and reject any measures that would punish or coerce business, culminating in a historic slashing of corporate taxes in 2017.[12] These examples from the recent past demonstrate the power of the capital strike in action. They also demonstrate that while one party may be more extreme in its service to capitalists, both parties are constrained by corporations' stranglehold over the economy.

Business uses a range of everyday tools alongside the capital strike. It has vast resources to spend on electoral campaigns, and its donations dwarf those of all other groups in society.[13] Campaign donations rarely function as straightforward bribes in which a donation buys a specific policy; their more common function is to secure priority access to the policymaking process.[14] They do so, first, by ensuring that business-friendly candidates get elected. Sometimes the candidates come directly from the business world, sometimes not. In either case, they must prove themselves acceptable to business donors. All candidates at the national level undergo a rigorous screening process by wealthy donors before

---

Interview: Running Apple 'Is Sort of a Lonely Job,'" *WP* online, August 13, 2016 (second quote); Julie Creswell, "Cities' Offers for Amazon Base Are Secrets Even to Many City Leaders," *NYT* online, August 5, 2018; Richard Lachmann, "Amazon Is Waging Class War," *Jacobin*, February 20, 2019.

12   Elizabeth Williamson, "Obama Says Tax Breaks Should Now Spur Hiring," *WSJ*, February 8, 2011: A4; White House Office of the Press Secretary, "Press Conference by the President," November 3, 2010; Jackie Calmes, "Obama Offers to Cut Corporate Tax Rate to 28%," *NYT*, February 22, 2012: B1; Elizabeth Williamson and Jonathan Weisman, "Obama Courts Business Support," *WSJ*, January 19, 2011: A4; Jon Schwarz, "Hillary Clinton Hints at Giant, Trump-Like Giveaway to Corporate America," *Intercept*, June 27, 2016.

13   For instance, in the 2018 elections the finance, insurance, and real estate industries alone contributed almost eight times as much to parties and candidates as labor unions did. Even in the 1970s, when organized labor was much stronger than it is today, the business press noted that, unlike labor unions, corporate lobbyists for the Business Roundtable enjoyed "direct access to the highest levels of the federal government" ("Business' Most Powerful Lobby in Washington," *BW*, December 20, 1976: 60). Unless otherwise noted, all campaign finance and lobbying data cited in this book come from the Center for Responsive Politics, opensecrets.org.

14   Dan Clawson, Alan Neustadtl, and Mark Weller, *Dollars and Votes: How Business Campaign Contributions Subvert Democracy* (Philadelphia, PA: Temple University Press, 1998).

being presented to the public, as part of what one historian calls "the hidden primary of the ruling class." Presidential hopefuls typically approach business elites to gauge their support even prior to announcing their candidacies.[15] Once a candidate is elected, the prior donations will be repaid through close consultation with business lobbyists and through the appointment of business-friendly staff, advisers, regulators, and judges. The relationship helps determine what legislation gets introduced, which policies are excluded from consideration, and how existing laws are implemented. Both sides continue to cultivate this relationship over the long term. The donors, however, hold the most power. They are essentially investors who "hold politicians more or less like stocks," investing in those most likely to yield a return—the ones with a track record of pro-business actions—and dumping those who prove disappointing.[16]

If a politician disappoints, and if business fails to get everything it wants from government, the donors have plenty of other weapons of disruption in their arsenal. Threats of capital strikes, and occasionally real capital strikes, help keep politicians and regulators in line. Business also makes full use of the court system, spending immense sums of money on litigation to challenge laws it dislikes. If a law is passed over business opposition, or if zealous regulators pursue disagreeable regulations, business can still greatly weaken or even nullify those actions through an endless stream of lawsuits. For good measure, business often pressures its allies in Congress to cut funding for regulatory agencies, thus ensuring that the targets of business litigation will be underfunded and ill-equipped to defend their actions against deep-pocketed corporations. In this way, many policies become the focus of a never-ending war over implementation, which continues long after the president has signed a new law, and even long after the president has left office.

The battle over the Wall Street Reform and Consumer Protection ("Dodd-Frank") Act of 2010 illustrates how these diverse corporate strategies reinforce each other. First, a combination of Wall Street

---

15   Laurence H. Shoup, "Election 2008: Ruling Class Conducts Its Hidden Primary," *Z Magazine*, February 2008: 31 (quote); Brian Schwartz, "Wall Street Executives Are Hearing from Cory Booker, Kamala Harris and Other Democrats as They Gauge Interest in Possible 2020 Presidential Campaigns," CNBC.com, January 8, 2019. See also G. William Domhoff, *The Powers That Be: Processes of Ruling-Class Domination in America* (New York: Random House, 1978), 129–67.

16   Thomas Ferguson, *Golden Rule: The Investment Theory of Party Competition and the Logic of Money-Driven Political Systems* (Chicago, IL: University of Chicago Press, 1995), 42.

campaign donations and dire warnings about disinvestment in the wake of the 2008 crash ensured that Obama appointed bank-friendly regulators and advisers, and also guaranteed that Wall Street lobbyists would have direct access to the negotiations over reform. Consequently, the administration's initial drafts of legislation were far less radical than most people had expected based on Obama's 2008 campaign rhetoric. Wall Street then used its access within the administration and in Congress to further weaken the bill. The final product signed in July 2010 was mostly congenial to Wall Street, but it did include some potential constraints on banks' power. So the banks responded by aggressively lobbying around the implementation of the bill (spending even more on lobbying after the bill was passed than they had during the legislative process) and flooding the courts with lawsuits against the financial regulators responsible for implementation. Corporations' withholding of trillions of dollars from the economy—a capital strike writ large—helped bolster officials' responsiveness to banks' demands. Meanwhile, the presence of corporate-friendly personnel in government helped ensure that officials would interpret business disinvestment in the "right" way, as a sign that government needed to do more to boost business "confidence." Thus, Wall Street had multiple strategies for shaping policy. The power of campaign donations, lobbyists, and pro-business personnel within government was continuously magnified through the structural power of the capital strike, and vice versa.[17]

Corporate Disruption in the Obama Era

As the example of Wall Street reform suggests, corporations made full use of all these instruments during the Obama administration. Much of our focus in this book will be on the Obama presidency, not because Obama was any more subservient to capitalists than other presidents,

---

17   Here we are speaking to a classic debate about the roots of business's political leverage. Whereas instrumentalists emphasize the origins of individual policymakers, structuralists argue that state institutions and capitalist control of the economy constrain all state officials, irrespective of their platforms or intentions. Both schools are right: individuals and structural relationships both matter. Our contribution to this debate lies in our synthesis of the two camps' insights, our emphasis on the structural power of disruption wielded by capital, and our argument about how mass resistance can alter the balance of forces among elites. For a concise example of the debate see Nicos Poulantzas, "The Problem of the Capitalist State," and Ralph Miliband, "Reply to Nicos Poulantzas," in *Ideology in Social Science: Readings in Critical Social Theory*, ed. Robin Blackburn (New York: Pantheon, 1972), 238–62.

but because there was such a dramatic disjunction between his progressive promises and his actual policies. As a candidate he vowed to confront fossil fuel companies, health insurers, Wall Street banks, and other predatory business interests. In all these areas his promises had overwhelming support among Democratic voters and were also popular with many Republican and independent voters. Yet his policy reforms fell far short of his rhetoric.[18] Particularly puzzling was the fact that some reforms were within reach during the two years of Democratic control of Congress, or achievable using executive powers. The Obama years demonstrate how, despite a president's resounding electoral victory and a strong public mandate for change, corporations may remain in the driver's seat.

For instance, Obama had promised urgently needed environmental reforms, most notably to prevent catastrophic climate change. The public was supportive. In 2008, 78 percent favored an international treaty to reduce greenhouse gas emissions and 66 percent favored government regulations that would force utilities to use more clean energy sources. Upon securing the Democratic nomination that year, Obama predicted that his presidency would be "the moment when the rise of the oceans began to slow and our planet began to heal."[19] Yet his administration's environmental reforms stopped far short of what was scientifically necessary, legally permissible, and popular with the public. US pledges under the 2015 Paris climate accord were not remotely commensurate with US corporations' historic responsibility and capability, and were not enforceable—even before Donald Trump withdrew from the agreement.[20] The rise of the oceans did not slow, the planet did not begin to heal.

---

18 On the Obama administration there is a vast literature of very uneven quality. Some highlights include Paul Street, *The Empire's New Clothes: Barack Obama in the Real World of Power* (Boulder, CO: Paradigm, 2010); Jeffrey St. Clair and Joshua Frank, eds., *Hopeless: Barack Obama and the Politics of Illusion* (Oakland, CA: AK Press, 2012); William F. Grover and Joseph G. Peschek, *The Unsustainable Presidency: Clinton, Bush, Obama, and Beyond* (New York: Palgrave Macmillan, 2014); Paul Street, *They Rule: The 1% vs. Democracy* (Boulder, CO: Paradigm, 2014); Noam Chomsky, *Who Rules the World?* (New York: Metropolitan, 2016).

19 "Obama, McCain Supporters Largely Agree on Approaches to Energy, Climate Change," worldpublicopinion.org, September 23, 2008; "Obama's Nomination Victory Speech in St. Paul," huffingtonpost.com, June 3, 2008.

20 Intergovernmental Panel on Climate Change, *Climate Change 2014: Synthesis Report* (Geneva, 2014); International Energy Agency, *World Energy Outlook 2016* (Paris, 2016); Adrian E. Raftery et al., "Less Than 2°C Warming by 2100 Unlikely," *Nature Climate Change* 7 (2017): 637–41; Climate Action Tracker, "Paris Agreement in Force, But No Increase in Climate Action," November 2016; Clifford Krauss and Keith Bradsher, "Climate Deal Is Signal for Industry to Go Green," *NYT*, December 14, 2015: A1.

Other progressive reforms were likewise much weaker than most people had expected. On healthcare, 77 percent of respondents polled on the eve of the 2008 election (including 57 percent of those who planned to vote for Republican John McCain) said that the government "should be responsible for ensuring" that everyone's "basic need for healthcare" is met.[21] None of the plans debated within Congress or the administration would have met that need. The only policy change that would have, a single-payer system that eliminated the central role of private insurers, was ruled out from the start by the Democratic leadership. The insurers, drug companies, and private providers were invited to help craft the legislation. As a result, the 2010 Affordable Care Act (ACA) preserved the privileges of the most parasitic healthcare interests.[22]

In the case of financial reform, the incoming administration had an even clearer mandate. Unprecedented anger at big banks would have made strong action popular.[23] But no banking tycoons were prosecuted and the 2010 reforms took great care to preserve Wall Street's profits and prerogatives. Options like nationalization or strict limits to the size of banks were either excluded from the 2010 legislation or weakened as the new law was being implemented. The resulting policies were widely criticized as too weak, even before Trump and Congress rolled back much of the law in 2018.[24]

In the realm of jobs policy, the administration pushed through a substantial but inadequate stimulus bill in February 2009, and then took little further action. Polls found strong support for more government spending to reduce unemployment. Job creation, not deficit reduction, was the public's priority. Respondents also consistently said that there was too much inequality in the United States, even while greatly underestimating the actual level of inequality.[25] The

---

21   "Obama, McCain Supporters Agree Government Responsible for Ensuring Basic Healthcare, Food, and Education Needs," worldpublicopinion.org, October 13, 2008. See also the numerous poll results collected by the Western PA Coalition for Single Payer Healthcare: wpasinglepayer.org/learn-about-single-payer/poll-results-on-single-payer.

22   Kevin Young and Michael Schwartz, "Healthy, Wealthy, and Wise: How Corporate Power Shaped the Affordable Care Act," *NLF* 23, no. 2 (2014): 30–40.

23   Lindsay A. Owens, "Confidence in Banks, Financial Institutions, and Wall Street, 1971–2011," *Public Opinion Quarterly* 76, no. 1 (2012): 142–62.

24   For some of the critiques see Young et al., "Capital Strikes," 21–22n3.

25   Christopher Howard and Richard Valelly, "Deficit-Attention Disorder: What Voters Really Think About Deficits, Debts, and Economic Recovery," *The American Prospect*, November 2010: A8–10; Michael I. Norton and Dan Ariely, "Building a Better America—One Wealth Quintile at a Time," *Perspectives on Psychological Science* 6, no. 1 (2010): 9–12.

conservative thrust of fiscal policy under Obama cannot be blamed on public opinion.[26]

In all these areas, corporations' power of economic disruption is essential for understanding why Obama's policies diverged so sharply from his promises. Business used capital strikes, and the threat of even deeper strikes, to scuttle or weaken progressive reform, and to get the administration to pursue pro-business initiatives like free-trade agreements and deregulation.[27]

Barack Obama entered the White House in 2009 in the midst of the most severe episode of disinvestment since World War II. In 2014, the business press reported that "cash on corporate balance sheets has increased almost 70 percent over the past four years," that it was not being invested in the economy, and that this lack of investment constituted a collective decision to avoid productive investment: "Companies that are spending their cash have largely chosen to increase dividends and buy back stock" rather than increase hiring, wages, or productive investments.[28] That is, business was refusing to reinvest its profits—which owed partly to Obama administration policies—back into the economy.

Long after the Great Recession officially ended in 2009, banks and nonfinancial businesses were still hoarding trillions—yes, *trillions*—of dollars in cash. By Obama's last year in office, a total of around $9.25 trillion was "lying fallow," as business observers reported: $1.94 trillion in nonfinancial companies, $2.15 trillion in bank reserves, $2.5 trillion in overseas tax shelters, and $2.66 trillion in zero-yielding money market funds. To put that figure in perspective, $9.25 trillion could end world hunger by 2030 while also funding twenty years of "Green New Deal" investments to transition the US economy away from fossil

---

26   Of course, many analysts refuse to be bound by the evidence. In 2010 sociologist Neil Fligstein argued that "the Obama administration seems to want to attack the problem of income inequality," but the "public has never been that concerned about inequality." Obama himself gave the same excuse for not pursuing a meaningful jobs program: "It's not where the electorate is." Neil Fligstein, "Politics, the Reorganization of the Economy, and Income Inequality, 1980–2009," *PAS* 38, no. 2 (2010): 239–40; Obama quoted in Michael Grunwald, "Why Change Won't Sell," *Time*, September 10, 2012: 47.

27   We use "free trade" as a shorthand, but the term is misleading on two counts: 1) such agreements actually restrict trade in ways that benefit corporations, for instance by tightening restrictions on intellectual property rights, and 2) the agreements are usually focused more on securing international investment privileges than on trade per se.

28   Matthew Philips and Peter Coy, "Choosing Profits over Productivity," *BW*, May 19–25, 2014: 13.

fuels—with more than $1 trillion left over.[29] Capitalist hoarding on this scale is historically unprecedented. And it was not simply dictated by market conditions or the financial theory taught in business schools, which advises businesses to keep about 2 percent of their revenues as cash—as opposed to 31 percent, in Apple's case, or almost 50 percent, in the case of General Motors. Investing the money virtually anywhere would have yielded higher profits than companies were making on the hoarded cash. While traditional economic considerations played a role in the initial accumulation of this stockpile, the decision to forego profitable investment outlets for years on end, and to use the hoarded cash as a bargaining chip to get favors from Washington, was largely political.[30]

The Obama administration hoped that by pursuing pro-business policies it could boost business confidence in the White House, leading executives to release their hoarded cash in the form of new hiring and loans. Reporting on Obama's February 2011 address to the US Chamber of Commerce, the *Wall Street Journal* described his speech as "a call to business leaders to use the $2 trillion in cash on their balance sheets to 'get in the game' and start adding jobs in the U.S." Obama recognized that corporations' disinvestment was a conscious choice, meaning that they might change their minds if he delivered the policies they wanted. As the *Journal* reported, his speech was a call to Chamber members to "stop hoarding cash and start hiring *in return for* tax breaks and other

---

29   Each requires around $4 trillion. Jeff Cox, "US Companies Are Hoarding $2.5 Trillion in Cash Overseas," CNBC.com, September 20, 2016; Joseph D'Urso, "How Much Would It Cost to End Hunger?" World Economic Forum, July 16, 2015; Robert Pollin, Heidi Garrett-Peltier, James Heintz, and Bracken Hendricks, *Green Growth: A U.S. Program for Controlling Climate Change and Expanding Job Opportunities* (Center for American Progress/Political Economy Research Institute, 2014), 19.

30   Adam Davidson, "Why Are Corporations Hoarding Trillions?" *NYT Magazine*, January 24, 2016: MM22; David Cogman and Tim Koller, "The Real Story Behind US Companies' Offshore Cash Reserves," mckinsey.com, June 2017. These and other observers have offered economic explanations, arguing for example that shareholders look favorably on large cash reserves, or that new capital investments made no sense given hoarders' abundance of existing technology and the shortage of investment outlets that would deliver the very high profit rates (often 30 percent or more) to which they were accustomed. These arguments are plausible, but they neglect the political usage of the hoarding. Even if businesses had some "economic" reasons for hoarding, their motives were also political. They used their disinvestment from the US economy to try to obtain corporate tax cuts and other pro-business policies, manifested for instance in their incessant reference to their hoarded cash when making demands on government.

government support for exports and innovation."[31] By promising tax breaks, subsidies, and deregulation, Obama was trying to negotiate a relaxation of the strike. Notably, the policies he was offering had little to do with boosting consumer demand, which was ostensibly the primary reason for continued hoarding. None of these policy reforms would increase demand. They were designed to address not the economic causes of the problem but the political causes: corporations' low confidence in the administration.

In order to boost business confidence and therefore end the capital strike, the Obama administration granted the dominant corporations in each sector virtual veto power over the reforms that might affect them. This dynamic was captured in a 2010 comment by former vice president Al Gore, bemoaning the failure of climate change legislation in the Senate. "The influence of special interests is now at an extremely unhealthy level," Gore said. "And it's to the point where it's virtually impossible for participants in the current political system to enact any significant change without first seeking and gaining permission from the largest commercial interests who are most affected by the proposed change."[32] The following year, the White House scrapped a proposal to limit emissions of ozone, a key ingredient in smog. White House Chief of Staff Bill Daley explained to public health advocates that a "consensus with industry" could not be reached.[33] As a general rule, no significant reform would succeed unless the "most affected" business interests granted "permission."

In many other areas, proposed reforms were so watered down through corporations' input that they became nearly meaningless. A 2016 law requiring the Environmental Protection Agency (EPA) to test and regulate toxic chemicals found in consumer products only passed because, as the New York Times reported, Democratic leaders in the Senate "worked closely with the American Chemistry Council," the leading industry lobby, "to come up with language that would win the support of the industry." Doing so meant that the EPA's rate of testing for some 64,000 toxic chemicals would be significantly reduced in the bill's final version, to what the Times called "a fairly slow pace" of "20

---

31 Elizabeth Williamson, "Obama Says Tax Breaks Should Now Spur Hiring," WSJ, February 8, 2011: A4 (emphasis added); Grover and Peschek, Unsustainable Presidency, 123–5.

32 Quoted in Ryan Lizza, "As the World Burns," TNY, October 11, 2010: 83.

33 Laura Meckler and Carol E. Lee, "White House Regulation Shift Is a Political Bet," WSJ, September 12, 2011: A6.

chemicals at a time, with a deadline of seven years per chemical." At that fairly slow pace, it could take 22,400 years to test all the chemicals—meaning that the vast majority of toxic chemicals would be sold and used without EPA testing. As an added gift, the new law would also prevent individual states from requiring timelier testing.[34]

The power of the capital strike in these cases was amplified by business campaign donations. Corporate money helped ensure that the White House and Congress would interpret corporate threats in the right way: giving in rather than defying the polluters and poisoners. Corporate cash had helped to elect Obama and to disqualify challengers to his left. Long before the 2008 election, media profiles had noted the "deeply conservative" inclinations of Obama "the conciliator," qualities that corporate donors liked and sought to reinforce with their checkbooks.[35] Donations also helped ensure the appointment of pro-business advisers, including a slew of economic officials with close ties to Robert Rubin, the former chairman of Goldman Sachs and Treasury Secretary who had led the deregulation of Wall Street in the late 1990s. On Obama's new National Economic Council alone, Lawrence Summers came from the hedge fund D. E. Shaw, Michael Froman from Citigroup, and Diana Farrell from Goldman Sachs.[36]

By appointing Rubin's henchmen, Obama was not only repaying the donations, but also seeking to boost business confidence and spur new investment. The Rubinites, in turn, would be keenly responsive to business demands and threats of disinvestment in the future. It was a vicious cycle or a virtuous one, depending on one's perspective. Chief of Staff Bill Daley, who had insisted on a "consensus with industry" before any new ozone regulations could go through, was a direct transplant from the corporate world. He came to the White House from JPMorgan Chase and also served on the boards of military contractor Boeing and a leading pharmaceutical company. His appointment was meant to signal the administration's commitment to business confidence. Obama's announcement touted "the breadth of experience that Bill brings to this job," including the fact that "he's led major corporations," giving him "a deep understanding of how jobs are created and how to

---

34   Coral Davenport, "Senate Approves Updating of Rules on Toxic Chemicals," *NYT*, June 8, 2016: A14.

35   Larissa MacFarquhar, "The Conciliator: Where Is Barack Obama Coming From?," *TNY*, May 7, 2007: 52.

36   See for instance Matt Taibbi, "Obama's Big Sellout," *Rolling Stone*, December 10, 2009: 43–5, 47–50.

grow our economy." The Chamber of Commerce president heralded the appointment as "a very, very strong choice." Unsurprisingly, one of Daley's favorite strategies for growing the economy would be eliminating regulations on business.[37]

This example suggests the mutually reinforcing nature of corporations' various strategies for influence. Daley's appointment and the policies he pursued were meant to cajole business investment, in addition to advancing his own class interests. Corporations' control over the economy worked hand-in-hand with other tools.

Obama was not unique. Business clearly called the shots under George W. Bush and has even done so under the erratic narcissist Donald Trump. He may proclaim himself a "hard-driving, vicious cutthroat" leader unfettered by "special interests," but Trump is still strongly bound by capitalist constraints.[38] On the few occasions when he has challenged certain business interests, he has been met with powerful resistance. The same fundamental patterns characterize US politics regardless of who is in office.

The Disruptive Power of Government Institutions

The Obama era also demonstrated that business leaders are not the only elites with the power to thwart policies they dislike. Sometimes, the key interests blocking progressive change are powerful state institutions like military leadership, anti-immigration agencies like the Border Patrol and Immigration and Customs Enforcement (ICE), or local and state police forces. These institutions do not wield the economic power that business does, but they do exercise great control over the process of policy implementation. They too possess various means of disrupting the operation of government and society, and as such they are in a position to thwart policymakers' attempts to cut their budgets or infringe on their privileges. Their permission is typically necessary for successful reforms in their policy domains or even for holding their members

---

37   "Obama's Remarks Introducing His New Chief of Staff," *NYT* online, January 6, 2011; Chamber president Thomas Donohue quoted in Eric Lipton, "In Daley, a Businessman's Voice in Oval Office," *NYT*, January 7, 2011: A1. On Daley and deregulation see Chapter 3.

38   Donald J. Trump, *Time to Get Tough: Making America #1 Again* (Washington, DC: Regnery, 2011), 13; Ian Schwartz, "Trump: Chamber of Commerce Controlled by Special Interests That Don't Care About You," realclearpolitics.com, June 29, 2016.

accountable when they commit crimes.[39] And, like the capital strike, disruptive behavior by these institutions exerts long-term impacts on policymakers' behavior. Just as most policymakers develop an ingrained sensitivity to business confidence, they learn to cultivate the confidence of these powerful government bureaucracies.

The fulfillment of key Obama campaign promises was made subject to approval by elites in the affected state agencies. In the case of the Guantánamo Bay torture camp, which candidate Obama had vowed to close, leaders in the military, intelligence, and law enforcement establishments played key roles in defining the administration's policy. Obama's Guantánamo Review Task Force was composed of "senior military officers, federal prosecutors, FBI agents, intelligence analysts and officers, military prosecutors and investigators," plus a range of legal personnel. The Obama administration shelved its initial plan to transfer Guantánamo prisoners to federal prisons within the United States because local officials were adamantly opposed.[40] Thus, the administration ceded decision-making power on a key campaign promise to military, law enforcement, and local officials. And what the administration didn't grant willingly, those agencies took without asking: despite the administration's announced policy, the Pentagon worked behind the scenes to systematically obstruct the transfer of Guantánamo prisoners to foreign countries.[41] Military and intelligence officials helped determine many other aspects of foreign policy, as well. Tactics like "enhanced interrogation" and assassination via the use of drones continued, and in the latter case increased, under Obama.[42]

---

39   Like capitalists, the most powerful state institutions can usually shift the costs of their crimes onto others. For example, murders by the police or military almost never result in criminal convictions or penalties for the perpetrating institution. The monetary settlement, if any, is made at the expense of taxpayers, with the institution increasing its future budgetary requests accordingly or in some cases even pushing politicians to raise taxes. For an example of the latter pattern in Cleveland, see Tim Jones, Mark Niquette, and James Nash, "Bad Cops Are Bad Business for Cities," *BW*, March 7–13, 2016: 32.

40   Guantánamo Review Task Force, *Final Report* (Washington, DC: 2010), 3; AP, "Graham Doubts Civilian Trials for 911 Suspects," November 28, 2010. Congress later prohibited the transfers.

41   Charles Levinson and David Rohde, "Special Report: Pentagon Thwarts Obama's Effort to Close Guantánamo," Reuters, December 29, 2015.

42   On the military's significant degree of autonomy see Richard Lachmann and Michael Schwartz, "The Life and Times of 'Who Rules America' and the Future of Power Structure Research," in G. William Domhoff et al., *Studying the Power Elite: Fifty Years of Who Rules America* (New York: Routledge, 2017), 75–8.

Different state institutions possess different degrees of disruptive power. The Pentagon wields much more power than an agency like the EPA, for several reasons. It controls a gargantuan budget; it is directly in charge of implementing much of US foreign policy; and its firmly entrenched leadership is only loosely subject to politicians' control. Military leaders often have close ties to defense contractors who share their interest in ever-expanding Pentagon budgets and wars, which reinforces the commanders' sway in policy discussions.[43]

The EPA's position is qualitatively different. Its budget is not commensurate with its enormous legal responsibility. And to the extent that the EPA seeks to protect the public against polluters, it draws ferocious corporate opposition that the military, law enforcement, or other conservative state agencies do not encounter. Anti-pollution measures may get a little support from renewable energy companies, but they lack the same degree of corporate backing that these other agencies enjoy. Only when the EPA acts in clear service to polluters, as it has under Trump, do its initiatives win strong business support.

Discussions of the power of state institutions often refer to a "deep state." The term can be misleading, however, insofar as it implies a far-reaching conspiracy of state officials acting in concert to thwart the aims of elected politicians. The disruptive power of state institutions is usually more mundane, deriving from each entity's ability to shape the enforcement of policies within its own domain. Disruption does not typically require secret coordination across agencies or a centralized cabal of conspirators.

Why Do the 99% Get *Anything*, Then?

Skeptical readers may accuse us of overstating the power of US elites. What about all those instances of successful progressive reform, when new laws or regulations or court rulings have benefited the public while apparently overcoming business opposition? How can we explain the restraints, however modest, that have been imposed on US military violence overseas or on police violence in US cities? Even if elites *usually* get what they want, they don't *always*.

---

43   For example, generals can look forward to lucrative post-military employment in defense firms, which undoubtedly affects their behavior while in the military. See Bryan Bender, "From the Pentagon to the Private Sector," *Boston Globe*, December 26, 2010: A1.

Indeed, any analysis of power must also explain the limits of that power. Elites face constant challenges. Most importantly, they must contend with competing elites and with popular forces.

Not all industries or corporations have the same interests. They tend to agree on basics like tax cuts for the wealthy and the deregulation of business, but other issues may divide them. For example, employers who fund employee health plans have an interest in containing the skyrocketing cost of healthcare, while the drug manufacturers and insurance companies naturally want to maximize their own profits, which means increasing the cost of health plans. Business may also face resistance from state elites. Judges or regulators may side with the public against polluters. The Pentagon may oppose the expansion of coastal oil drilling for fear that drilling would disrupt offshore military exercises. Conversely, state elites often find that businesses oppose policies that hurt their bottom lines, as several of our case studies will demonstrate.

Disagreement among these business and state actors often frustrates the efforts of individual institutions and industries. Sometimes that disagreement even opens the door to progressive reforms. The Obama administration's 2010 healthcare reform and its overhaul of banking regulations both resulted largely from these disagreements among elites. Some business sectors wanted to rein in the health industries and the mega-banks because they themselves were being hurt by their unchecked greed and recklessness. Health costs were threatening employers' profit margins, while the Wall Street crash of 2008 hurt many industries. This business discontent helped generate pressure for change, leading both political parties in the 2008 election to promise healthcare and financial reform.

A divided elite also increases the likelihood that popular pressure will be successful in changing policy. Intra-elite conflicts are not always a prerequisite for popular forces to have an impact—and social movements can actually *create* intra-elite conflicts, as we will discuss later—but they do raise the chances of success.

Popular disruption can take many forms. On the more dramatic end of the spectrum, workers may go on strike, consumers may boycott companies, soldiers may refuse to fight, young people may decide not to enlist in the military, and people everywhere may stage sit-ins, blockade streets, and engage in other kinds of overtly disruptive behavior. These disruptions increase the costs of the status quo from elites' perspective, especially when the actions directly undermine business profits or the functioning of state institutions like the army. The elite institutions most affected by that disruption will often press others to capitulate, as when Southern capitalists pushed Southern politicians to concede to black protesters' demand for desegregation.

Less overtly disruptive are lawsuits against corporations and state institutions. Being taken to court can increase the costs to elites, both in terms of money and public image. Lawsuits can also shift the legal and political terrain on which elites and social movements operate. The Supreme Court's 1954 decision in *Brown v. Board of Education*, making school segregation illegal, was the culmination of years of prior lawsuits. Although the ruling went almost entirely unenforced for over a decade, it was a significant morale-booster for the civil rights movement and altered the terms of the struggle between black activists and white supremacists in the years ahead.

At the less dramatic end of the resistance spectrum are acts like voting, working on an electoral campaign, and calling one's legislators. These are generally less powerful than other forms of resistance, though they too can help put pressure on corporations and state elites. Corporations do not have total power to decide who wins an election; they might have preferred Republican candidates John McCain or Mitt Romney over Obama, but Obama was deemed more appealing to voters and therefore more likely to win, and thus attracted more corporate cash.[44] Election outcomes, in turn, play some role in setting the general policy agenda. For instance, both the Democratic and Republican candidates in the 2008 election spoke of reforming healthcare and Wall Street, but the eventual details of those reforms were probably more progressive given that it was the Obama administration presiding over them. Likewise, the judges appointed by recent Democratic and Republican presidents have differed significantly in ideology. The fact that the two parties have different electoral bases requires victorious candidates to take at least *some* action on certain campaign promises once elected. As a result, there is some difference in policy between Democrats and Republicans, even if the difference is exaggerated by most commentators and by both parties themselves.

But, while elections may help put progressive reforms on the table, they are rarely the most important variable in determining policy. Much more important are the disruptive forces that constrain politicians of

---

44   In the 2012 election, many business donors' "best argument" for supporting Obama over Romney "boiled down to the simplest one: Obama was going to win." Nicholas Confessore, "Obama's Not-So-Hot Date with Wall Street," *NYT Magazine*, May 6, 2012: MM50.

both parties into supporting particular interests. We have mentioned the disruptive power of business and state elites, but popular forces also possess tremendous power of disruption.[45] That power often lies dormant, but the potential is always there. The presence, intensity, and duration of popular disruption is often the most decisive factor in shaping policy. When mass resistance is disruptive and sustained, it greatly expands the potential for progressive reform, often forcing new policy options onto the table. It can compel politicians to pursue legislation they dislike, and can shape how that legislation is implemented. When mass resistance is absent or merely episodic, business and state elites will call the shots. Non-elites may get a few crumbs as a byproduct of intra-elite conflicts or elections, but any progressive reform will be much weaker and more subject to reversal. A major reason why Obama-era progressive reforms were so tepid is that the Obama years lacked the sustained mass disruption present in other eras of US history. There were some notable examples of mobilization like Occupy Wall Street and black resistance to police violence, but they were not nearly as disruptive as the movements of the 1930s and the 1960s. In the chapters that follow, we draw from both the Obama era and from twentieth-century examples to indicate when and how progressive movements have had the greatest impact on government policy.[46]

A Counter-Intuitive Strategy for Social Movements

Our central argument in this regard is that mass resistance is most effective when it directly targets corporations and state agencies. By threatening the profits or the functioning of those institutions, popular

---

45   Our emphasis on mass disruption is informed by the work of many scholars and organizers. Key studies include Frances Fox Piven and Richard A. Cloward, *Regulating the Poor: The Functions of Public Welfare* (New York: Vintage, 1971); William A. Gamson, *The Strategy of Social Protest*, 2nd ed. (Belmont, CA: Wadsworth, 1990 [1975]); Michael Schwartz, *Radical Protest and Social Structure: The Southern Farmers' Alliance and Cotton Tenancy, 1880–1890* (New York: Academic Press, 1976); Frances Fox Piven and Richard A. Cloward, *Poor People's Movements: How They Succeed, Why They Fail* (New York: Vintage, 1979); Frances Fox Piven, *Challenging Authority: How Ordinary People Change America* (Lanham, MD: Rowman & Littlefield, 2006). The influence of Marxism, anarcho-syndicalism, black freedom struggles, and other theoretical traditions will also be apparent in much of our analysis.

46   We limit our focus to progressive movements because right-wing movements' paths to influence tend to be different. To a far greater extent than progressives, corporate and right-wing forces can rely on elite actors inside and outside the state to promote the policies they desire. See *BW*, "Business' Most Powerful Lobby."

disruption can compel their leaders to accept progressive changes in government policy. Since these elites are usually the key roadblocks to change, and since they possess enormous power over what the government does, it makes more sense to target them than to focus on elected politicians. Their responsiveness to movement demands doesn't spring from their goodwill, but from a rational cost-benefit analysis of their interests. If subjected to mass pressures that disrupt their profit-making or their institutional functioning, these leaders will naturally seek to cut their losses. Conceding to movement demands often becomes the lesser-evil option. If movements can force a change in these elites' cost-benefit calculations, progressive government action then becomes much more likely.

This argument is counter-intuitive. The conventional wisdom among scholars and activists is that "collective action will be most productive if it focuses on elected officials," either by pressuring them or trying to elect new ones.[47] After all, modern corporations, militaries, and law enforcement agencies were consciously designed *not* to be accountable to the public, so how could they be more subject to public influence than elected officials are?

Nonetheless, some of the most successful progressive movements in US history have focused their energies mainly on non-electoral targets. Auto companies in the 1930s grudgingly accepted the unionization of their workers because they faced unprecedented strikes and disruptions on the shop floor. Most labor organizers spent far less time trying to get Democrats elected than on organizing their fellow workers to bring their workplaces to a halt. Franklin Roosevelt was elected in 1932 and reelected in 1936, but workers only succeeded in winning effective unionization rights when they completely disrupted industry and forced the bosses to concede those rights. We examine this process in Chapters 1 and 4.

Similarly, racially segregated businesses in the South opted to integrate because a mass movement directly threatened their profits. Many organizers consciously sought to change politicians' behavior by disrupting business. Martin Luther King Jr. himself concluded that protests should target Southern businesses, since "the political power structure listens to the economic power structure." If the movement

---

47 Edwin Amenta, Neil Caren, and Sheera Joy Olasky, "Age for Leisure? Political Mediation and the Impact of the Pension Movement on US Old-Age Policy," *ASR* 70, no. 3 (2005): 522.

could threaten business leaders enough to "pull them around," they would in turn "pull" the political leaders in the South.[48] As in the 1930s, mass pressure catalyzed changes in the calculations of institutional elites, leading in turn to progressive changes in government policy. We analyze the strategy and impact of the civil rights movement in detail in Chapter 4.

The immigrant rights struggle offers a more recent example of this dynamic. In 2010 the state of Arizona became infamous for passing legislation, SB 1070, that legalized racial profiling against Latinos. In response, national organizations began promoting a boycott of the state's businesses, and numerous individual consumers joined in. In March 2011, dozens of corporate executives wrote a letter to Arizona state legislators asking that they refrain from passing additional anti-immigrant bills. The problem, they explained, was that the boycotts were so "harmful to our image" that "Arizona-based businesses saw contracts cancelled or were turned away from bidding," and "sales outside of the state declined." The threat to their profits led them to insist on a change in public policy. Within a week of receiving the letter, the Republican-controlled legislature rejected five bills designed to further criminalize immigrants.[49] As this example suggests, targeting corporations can be a fruitful political strategy even when those corporations are not the main culprits. Arizona-based companies were not the driving force behind the racist policy, but they had the power to stop it.

In each of these instances, ordinary people took advantage of the levers of power that are available in all systems dependent on human participation. People whose cooperation is essential to an institution have the ability to stop the institution from functioning, and can thus wield tremendous leverage by collectively withdrawing their cooperation. This form of power has been given various names: structural power, positional power, or interdependent power.[50] Perhaps the two clearest examples are workers going on strike and consumers boycotting a company. In both cases, the small fish take advantage of the shark's

---

48 Interviewed by Donald Smith in November 1963, quoted in David J. Garrow, *Bearing the Cross: Martin Luther King, Jr., and the Southern Christian Leadership Conference* (New York: Vintage, 1986), 226.

49 Drew Brown et al., to Russell Pearce, March 14, 2011, nytimes.com; Richard A. Oppel, Jr., "Arizona, Bowing to Business, Softens Stand on Immigration," *NYT*, March 19, 2011: A15.

50 Schwartz, *Radical Protest*, 172–3; Luca Perrone, "Positional Power, Strikes and Wages," *ASR* 49, no. 3 (1984): 412–26; Piven, *Challenging Authority*, 19–35.

dependence on them, frustrating the shark's goals. In so doing, the disruptive small fish can alter the shark's behavior toward them as well as the shark's stance on government policies.

Another key to success for the movements we have mentioned was their ability to exploit, or even create, divisions among elites. After US autoworkers forced General Motors and Chrysler to allow unionization in the late 1930s, the notoriously anti-union Henry Ford and leaders in other industries soon followed suit. Black protesters in the 1960s disrupted business, which then confronted the more militant racists in the Southern political establishment. Immigrant rights activists responded to Arizona's SB 1070 with a similar strategy, forcing business leaders to rein in the white supremacists in the state government. In each case disruption gave rise to counter-coalitions of elites that neutralized the influence of the elites responsible for oppressive policies. In the 1930s and 1960s these intra-elite divisions also left a meaningful long-term residue in the structure of the government. They allowed for the formation or strengthening of state agencies dedicated to restricting the power of elites: the National Labor Relations Board (NLRB) and the civil rights enforcement apparatus of the Department of Justice.[51] In both cases, the agencies imposed significant limits on the freedom of other elites, including the president. Election outcomes and electoral coalitions were of secondary importance in determining policy.[52]

---

51   Our analysis throughout this book recognizes the importance of "state capacity," a concept long stressed by Theda Skocpol (e.g., Skocpol and Kenneth Finegold, "State Capacity and Economic Intervention in the Early New Deal," *Political Science Quarterly* 97, no. 2 [1982]: 255–78). However, Skocpol's work overstates state agencies' autonomy from class interests, particularly business and social movements. As we show in Chapter 4, the development of the NLRB and the DoJ civil rights division into real enforcers was the result of movement-induced disruption, which compelled economic elites to support or acquiesce to the agencies' empowerment. Successful enforcement of labor and civil rights laws depended less on the prior existence of "knowledgeable administrative organizations" within the state (ibid., 260) than on sustained movement disruption that created those organizations, emboldened them, and pushed capitalists to empower them.

52   Our argument here differs from Piven's theory of "dissensus," or the rupture of electoral coalitions as a result of mass disruption (*Challenging Authority*). She views electoral realignments as a key variable in producing policy change. We think that targeting corporations and other non-electoral institutions often leads to changes in government policy *with or without* altering those alignments, and that, in any case, targeting non-electoral institutions may contribute indirectly to electoral realignments. People who are organized in progressive social movements like the ones analyzed in this book are highly unlikely to vote Republican, given the experience and education they acquire through their participation. We elaborate on the role of elections in the chapters that follow.

Explosive disruptive behavior is not the only way to foster these divisions. Intra-elite conflicts are often the result of years or decades of low-grade disruption that eventually convinces one or more elite sectors to favor concessions to the movement. The Supreme Court's 1954 *Brown* decision did not result primarily from the initiative of antiracist Supreme Court justices, but from two converging sources of pressure that impelled judges and politicians to concede to black demands. One source was the long history of black resistance, which reached a tipping point in the years following World War II. The juggernaut that became the civil rights movement began with decades of individual resistance to the Jim Crow system, punctuated by innumerable local protests in cities and even in the most violently oppressive cotton plantations, accompanied by growing denunciations of segregation and terror in the black press.[53] The nationally visible part of this rising protest was the thirty-year legal campaign by the National Association for the Advancement of Colored People (NAACP), built on the high-risk action taken by hundreds of courageous black plaintiffs. These lawsuits challenged first the unequal conditions of segregation and, by the early 1950s, segregation itself.[54] Though often unsuccessful in the short run, the lawsuits and the broader black resistance to segregation helped to cultivate sympathizers within parts of the US judiciary. The lawsuits were not directly disruptive in the same way that boycotts and sit-ins were, but they created a latent division within the elite power structure. Portions of the judiciary slowly lined up against local governments and even against the executive branch of the federal government. At key moments they would become an important resource for civil rights activists, especially by constraining Southern law enforcement's freedom to impose draconian punishments on protesters.

A complementary source of pressure came from outside the United States. Widespread international condemnation of US racism worried postwar politicians, who feared that the nonwhite peoples of the "Third World" would not only reject US racism but also embrace socialist revolution. In 1952, this concern led the Truman administration to

---

53   See for instance Robin D. G. Kelley, *Hammer and Hoe: Alabama Communists during the Great Depression* (Chapel Hill: University of North Carolina Press, 1990); Paul Ortiz, *Emancipation Betrayed: The Hidden History of Black Organizing and White Violence in Florida from Reconstruction to the Bloody Election of 1920* (Berkeley: University of California Press, 2006). For a classic personal account see Theodore Rosengarten, *All God's Dangers: The Life of Nate Shaw* (New York: Knopf, 1974).

54   James T. Patterson, *Brown v. Board of Education: A Civil Rights Milestone and Its Troubled Legacy* (New York: Oxford University Press, 2001), 21–45.

urge the Supreme Court to rule against school segregation.[55] The domestic and global challenges to segregation were mutually reinforcing: each inspired the other, and together they pushed some government officials to confront segregationists in the interest of preserving domestic stability and US global dominance. In turn, the *Brown* decision helped energize the more overt black disruption of the early 1960s that would be necessary for the ruling's implementation.

Social movements are most successful when they can find ways to exploit these tensions within the ruling class, by unleashing disruption that targets the right pressure points. Getting some elites to intervene on behalf of the movement does not mean that organizers need to politely request their help—indeed, that approach is usually a dismal failure. Confrontation and disruption are more likely to "pull around" elites, who then intervene to stop the disruption by urging other corporate and state elites to concede to the movement. Disruption can take diverse forms, from workers shutting down a workplace to lawsuits. Different categories of elites may be susceptible to different forms of movement pressures, as these examples suggest.

Figuring out whom to target, and with what tactics, can be difficult. The most successful movements have exhibited a strategic flexibility that allows them to try new things when the old methods are not working. The degree of flexibility depends a great deal on how the movement is structured: do organizations allow for both strategizing and direct action by the rank-and-file, or are strategizing and decision-making reserved for the top leaders? Do organizations regularly engage their members in reflection on the successes or failures of current strategies? Greater internal democracy facilitates learning and adaptation. Democracy may involve contested elections or formal factions within a movement, but it must also be embodied in other organizational structures that allow for autonomy and experimentation by the membership.[56] The boycott

55   Mary L. Dudziak, "Desegregation as a Cold War Imperative," *Stanford Law Review* 41, no. 1 (1988): 61–120. Eisenhower was opposed to the decision, but his Assistant Attorney General Lee Rankin did submit a brief urging the Court to overturn school segregation. Earl Warren, *The Memoirs of Earl Warren* (Garden City, NJ: Doubleday, 1977), 291; Patterson, *Brown v. Board*, 63.

56   For related conceptions of movement democracy and its strategic importance see Schwartz, *Radical Protest*; Judith Stepan-Norris and Maurice Zeitlin, *Left Out: Reds and America's Industrial Unions* (Cambridge: Cambridge University Press, 2003); Marshall Ganz, *Why David Sometimes Wins: Leadership, Organization, and Strategy in the California Farm Worker Movement* (New York: Oxford University Press, 2009); Joshua Murray and Michael Schwartz, "Moral Economy, Structural Leverage, and Organizational Efficacy: Class Formation and the Great Flint Sit-Down Strike, 1936–1937," *Critical Historical Studies* 2, no. 2 (2015): 219–59.

campaigns of the 1950s and 1960s were often initiated by local black organizers, not national leaders, and would have been impossible without the active participation of rank-and-file black supporters. The boycotts also show that democracy and differences of opinion within a movement need not stop a movement from uniting around a particular strategy. The Southern black movement was quite decentralized and ideologically diverse, but it was able to unify at many critical moments.

Disruption, Reform, and Beyond

In the rest of the book we analyze the forces at work in the various steps of the policymaking process, from the election and appointment of officials, through the crafting of legislation, to the implementation period in which laws are interpreted and enforced (or not enforced, as the case may be). Our examination of this process is not comprehensive. Some types of policies are ignored, and some parts of the process are treated in more depth than others. We focus most attention on aspects that receive insufficient attention in other accounts. But we do assert that our conclusions are valid beyond just the cases we examine. By focusing on some of the most important policy changes of the past century, we have tried to avoid cherry-picking examples that fit our argument.

In analyzing the origins and shaping of legislation, we focus primarily on Obama-era initiatives. We consider a variety of legislative proposals, including both progressive reform initiatives and pro-business ones. The dominant forces in the legislative phase tend to be the elite institutions that are "most affected by the proposed change" (in Al Gore's words). We stress the role of disruption, real or potential, in influencing this process. At times mass pressure plays an important role, particularly in the initiation of legislation. That pressure is usually most effective when social movements threaten the stability of the "most affected."

In the second part of the book we examine the often-neglected but crucial phase of policy implementation. Policy is determined not just by the laws themselves, but by how the executive branch with its myriad departments and agencies decides to apply them. We trace the roles of the "most affected" elite institutions in shaping implementation, and then turn to instances in which mass disruption has played a determining role in how laws are implemented. We discuss the workers' movement of the 1930s, black struggles for civil rights and economic justice in the 1960s, and the US withdrawal from Vietnam. In each case, progressive changes in policy implementation resulted from disruption directed at the "most affected" institutions. This chapter may be of particular interest to readers involved in social movements.

In the Conclusion we offer some further reflections on social movement strategy. Here we highlight the inadequacy of reforms alone. While this book focuses on the prospects for winning reforms, reforms are inherently tenuous since they leave intact the basic institutions of elite power: corporations and conservative state agencies. Progressive government laws and institutions that arise as a result of mass disruption will endure for a time after the disruption ends, but over the long run they will be subject to erosion, as the weakening of the NLRB, EPA, and 1960s civil rights legislation demonstrates. Furthermore, reforms by definition do not address the root of the problem. Forcing a business to recognize a union, desegregate, or allow some holes in the glass ceiling is a major accomplishment, but changes of this type do not eliminate the power of private business owners to make decisions that affect everyone else. We may compel the government to end its occupation of a foreign country, but how can we prevent it from invading another in the future? To address these problems, we need to do away with the private and public institutions that are structured to allocate power and wealth to the richest 1% in society. We need to replace them with institutions that answer to the needs and desires of the 99%.

This revolutionary change is not on the immediate horizon. Many more people must first come to believe that achieving a truly humane and democratic society requires a new set of economic and political institutions, not just a new set of politicians—a fundamentally different *substance*, not just a different *shadow*. We propose that targeting powerful institutions directly is not only a good way to win reforms, but is also conducive to building the mass movements that can achieve that revolutionary transformation.

1

Where Laws Come From:
Schoolhouse Rock! Reconsidered

Some folks back home decided they wanted a law passed, so they called their local congressman and he said, "You're right, there oughta be a law." Then he sat down and wrote me out and introduced me to Congress.

"I'm Just a Bill," from the 1970s children's
cartoon series *Schoolhouse Rock!*

How does a bill become a law? Well, you see, we have these things called lobbyists. They work for big corporations and people with a lot of money. When the lobbyist has sufficiently bribed the elected official, a bill is written to benefit the lobbyist's sponsor. If enough votes are purchased, the bill becomes a law.

Internet parody of *Schoolhouse Rock!*, ca. 2011

According to most civics textbooks and media commentators, new laws reflect changing popular sentiments. Politicians follow public opinion, especially when it is organized and clearly communicated to them.

This picture has never been accurate, but it has drawn greater scorn as corporate power has become more visible and inequality has increased. A quick internet search turns up multiple parodies of the famous 1975 *Schoolhouse Rock!* episode, calling attention to how corporate money and lobbying corrode the democratic process portrayed in the cartoon. As we noted in the Introduction, the vast majority of the public believes our government is "run by a few big interests." Bernie Sanders's recent presidential campaigns have drawn their appeal largely from this observation. Donald Trump's election also owed much to the candidate's anti-elite rhetoric, disingenuous though it was.

Here we will examine the origins of bills introduced in Congress, and then trace their fate after being introduced. We distinguish between two types of legislation. The first type involves straightforward interventions by the government on behalf of business. Examples from the Obama administration include its promotion of tax cuts for corporations and wealthy individuals and its aggressive pursuit of pro-corporate trade agreements. In these cases, explanations like the one in the *Schoolhouse Rock!* parody do not adequately account for the administration's actions. Familiar factors like corporate campaign money, lobbying, Republican obstructionism in Congress, and the president's own conservatism were only part of the story. The capital strike that we described in the Introduction—massive corporate disinvestment from the economy and the threat of its continuation—was a central factor. The administration sought to rekindle "business confidence" so that banks and businesses would ameliorate the recession by making more loans and hiring more workers. Pro-business legislation was a quid pro quo: *we'll give you huge public handouts if you start investing in the economy again.*

The second type of legislation that we examine includes reform bills with some progressive thrust, in the sense that they might impinge on elite profits or power. We will examine four examples from Barack Obama's first term as president: the 2010 Affordable Care Act (ACA), or "Obamacare" (passed); the 2010 Wall Street Reform and Consumer Protection Act, or "Dodd-Frank" (passed); the climate policy bills in the House and Senate in 2009–10 (did not pass); and the 2010 bills to repeal the military's "Don't Ask, Don't Tell" (DADT) policy (passed).[1]

The roots of these progressive bills are more complicated than pro-business legislation like corporate tax cuts. They may originate from a variety of sources. For one, elections help to define the legislative agenda. The Democratic victories in the 2008 elections and the strong public opinion in favor of reform played some role in the initiation of these bills. While the Democrats showed relatively little regard for public opinion in determining the *content* of their new bills (as we will

---

1   The DADT example raises a definitional dilemma. Even in their earliest stages, many "progressive" reform bills are a mixed bag: while progressive in its elimination of legal discrimination against LGB (but not transgender) soldiers, the repeal was decidedly unprogressive since it expanded the number of recruits available to a military that violently advances elite interests around the globe. Many on the left, including in the LGBT community, were critical of mainstream LGBT organizations' decision to focus on this issue. The mixed-bag nature of reforms often smooths the way for their enactment by mitigating elite opposition.

demonstrate), they needed to appear to be taking *some* action. They could not afford to completely ignore their core campaign promises.

Public support for reform and Democratic control of government were inadequate in themselves, however. Elite support was essential. As Al Gore noted in regard to the climate bills, "it's virtually impossible" for politicians "to enact any significant change" unless they have "permission from the largest commercial interests who are most affected by the proposed change."[2] For the healthcare and financial reforms, the greatest pressure came from corporations outside those sectors; most health and financial corporations came to the table later, in the hopes of shaping reform to their liking. The climate bills had the support of some large corporations, though fewer than supported the other bills (which was the main reason climate reform failed to pass). In the case of DADT, the military, rather than business, was the "most affected" institution, and the high command had to give its "permission" for repeal before Congress would agree to support it. Without the support of at least some elite sectors, it is unlikely that any of the bills would have been introduced, let alone passed.

Ascertaining elites' preferences is difficult given that their publicly expressed positions often "reflect accommodations to circumstances that constrain what can be achieved."[3] That is, their views on legislative reforms are shaped, in part, by the external threats and prospects they see on the horizon. In the cases just described, they faced strong pressure for progressive reform from public opinion, from other elite sectors, and from certain leaders in Congress. In one case, the DADT fight, they also faced major pressure from a social movement: gay and lesbian military personnel and their supporters, who were undermining the stability of the military through lawsuits and through the discharges resulting from violations of DADT. In these contexts, many business and military leaders decided that "if you're not at the table, you're going to be on the menu."[4] That is, it is better to participate and shape reform in your interest than to oppose it outright, and therefore risk a much larger setback.

---

2   Quoted in Ryan Lizza, "As the World Burns," *TNY*, October 11, 2010: 83.

3   Jacob S. Hacker and Paul Pierson, "Business Power and Social Policy: Employers and the Formation of the American Welfare State," *PAS* 30, no. 2 (2002): 283.

4   Unnamed pharmaceutical CEO paraphrasing Billy Tauzin, the president and CEO of Pharmaceutical Research and Manufacturers of America (PhRMA). Tauzin was referring to negotiating rather than resisting government regulation of the drug industry. Quoted in Steven Brill, *America's Bitter Pill: Money, Politics, Backroom Deals, and the Fight to Fix Our Broken Healthcare System* (New York: Random House, 2015), 50.

The targeted institutions did not just react defensively to external pressures, however. They also possessed formidable power to influence the initial shape of each bill (and, as we'll see in the next chapter, its reshaping in Congress). The most telling display of their power was their ability to exclude certain reform options from consideration. Single-payer healthcare, socialized medicine, bank nationalization, a carbon tax, and many other potential changes were never seriously discussed, even though many of those options had major public support. Being *at* the table allowed business to keep certain options *off* the table. This form of business power is often ignored by political scientists, but it is vitally important for understanding how policy is made.[5] During the Obama administration, the prior exclusion of unfavorable reform proposals was in large part the result of the capital strike/business confidence dynamic, wherein the potential for business disinvestment helps to prevent even the consideration of progressive policy changes. The business representatives involved in the early reform discussions helped communicate that threat to government policymakers, who limited their initial proposals to reforms that would not significantly disrupt business confidence.

The voice of corporations and other elite institutions held particular weight given that, in all of these cases except the DADT fight, there was little collective protest that threatened "business as usual." Significant pockets of activism certainly existed around all these issues, but they were not very disruptive and could hardly qualify as mass phenomena. Progressive reform bills sometimes arise in the absence of mass disruption, but they tend to be more tepid and congenial to elite interests— and still more so after they emerge from the congressional revision process, as we will show in the next chapter.

We close this chapter by examining a contrasting case: the major reforms to US labor law in the 1930s. Legislation ensuring the right of workers to form independent unions was initiated in response to economic disruption, which was largely due to the explosive working-class strikes and protests of the 1930s that targeted employers. This and other New Deal reforms were more robust than any Obama-era reforms. The key variable was the level of disruptive mass mobilization in each epoch. Corporate elites in the 1930s and 2000s were both forced to

---

5   On such "non-decisions" see Peter Bachrach and Morton S. Baratz, "Decision and Non-Decisions: An Analytical Framework," *APSR* 57, no. 4 (1963): 632–42; Steven Lukes, *Power: A Radical View*, 2nd ed. (New York: Palgrave Macmillan, 2005 [1974]).

accept some amount of reform, but the elites of the 1930s experienced far more pressure. This example suggests how disruptive mass movements can force the initiation of strong progressive reform legislation in Congress: not by pressuring politicians but by threatening the elite institutions that control the politicians.

Capital Strikes and Pro-Business Legislation

The Obama administration initiated a host of new legislation designed to advance the interests of business. Often those initiatives contradicted Obama's campaign rhetoric, which had promised that he would tax the wealthy at higher rates, pursue trade deals that benefited workers rather than corporations, and regulate business more closely. The disjunction stemmed less from the new president "selling out" than from the imperative of boosting business investment in the economy. Cultivating businesses' confidence in the administration was essential because the $787 billion government stimulus bill passed in February 2009 was too small, given the magnitude of the crisis, and because the administration was unwilling or unable to take measures that would force investment in Main Street.[6]

President Obama entered office in the throes of a historic disinvestment crisis. The problem was not a lack of money, but the fact that corporations were hoarding trillions of dollars in capital rather than investing it in the economy. Although the Great Recession officially ended in June 2009, the rate of unemployed or underemployed workers was still 17 percent in November 2010, and remained at almost 15 percent as Obama's second term began in January 2013.[7] Thus, Obama's first term and much of his second were dedicated to convincing business leaders to start investing again.

During Obama's first two years, many corporate leaders deemed his policies insufficiently pro-business. Their critique was overblown: from the start, the administration took great pains to accommodate corporate demands. But business was not satisfied. Treasury Secretary Timothy Geithner later wrote in frustration that although "the President

---

6   Such measures might have included, for instance, making government support conditional on new loans and hiring or, more ambitiously, putting the failing banks and the auto giants GM and Chrysler under joint control of their workers and the public.

7   Based on the U6 measure of the Bureau of Labor Statistics (bls.gov).

helped rescue the economy and their bottom lines," many corporate executives believed "that he was relentlessly hostile to their interests."[8] In the November 2010 midterm elections, business made its anger known. Whereas in 2008 the financial industry had favored Democratic congressional candidates by a margin of $124 million, in 2010 it favored Republicans by almost as large a margin.

When Democrats took huge losses in the midterms, White House officials interpreted it as a sign of the need to bolster business confidence in the administration. More consequential than corporate campaign donations was the fact that business was still withholding so much money from the economy, impeding the recovery and contributing to voter disaffection with the Democrats. Noting that unemployment was still "stubbornly high" and that there was "little likelihood" of renewed government stimulus, the *Wall Street Journal* argued in early 2011 that "the key to economic growth—and Mr. Obama's re-election prospects— could lie in corporate treasuries. U.S. non-financial businesses are sitting on nearly $2 trillion in cash and liquid assets, the most since World War II, and Mr. Obama wants them to use it to create more U.S. jobs."[9] This approach was not the only logical one: many outside observers attributed the Democrats' midterm losses to the shortage of progressive reform in Obama's first two years. But the backgrounds of Geithner, Summers, and Obama's other top advisers virtually ensured that the midterm defeat would be attributed to business discontent. Following election day, Obama buckled down in an effort to boost executives' "confidence" in his administration. On the legislative front, Obama's efforts to "repair relations with corporate America," as the *Journal* wrote, took the form of bills that cut taxes for business and amplified investor privileges overseas via free-trade agreements.[10] According to the *Journal*, Obama was proposing a deal with corporate leaders in which they would "stop hoarding cash and start hiring in return for tax breaks and other government support," including free-trade deals and deregulation.[11]

---

8   Timothy F. Geithner, *Stress Test: Reflections on Financial Crises* (New York: Crown, 2014), 404.

9   Elizabeth Williamson, "President Revs Up Campaign to Make Peace with Business," *WSJ*, January 7, 2011: A1.

10   Elizabeth Williamson and James R. Hagerty, "The New Political Landscape: Executives Await Friendlier Climate," *WSJ*, November 4, 2010: A6. Outreach to business also "aimed at putting to rest concerns that there was some grand new wave of [progressive] things coming," in the words of an administration official quoted in Michelle Cottle, "Executive Indecision: Obama and the CEOs: He Loves Them, He Loves Them Not," *New Republic*, September 23, 2010: 21.

11   Elizabeth Williamson, "Obama Says Tax Breaks Should Now Spur Hiring,"

None of these reforms would directly address the economic roots of the crisis. They would do little to boost the low level of domestic demand, which was the main economic cause of continued recession. Doing so would have required putting more money into the hands of consumers and/or greatly increasing government spending. Rather, the reforms sought to address the *political* nature of the economic recession. By granting concessions to business in unrelated realms of policy, the administration hoped to cajole banks into making new loans and employers into hiring new workers. The reforms did not make economic sense, but they had a compelling political logic. They were concessions designed to get business to cease its capital strike.

Corporate leaders were often explicit about their political demands. In November 2010, Emerson Electric CEO David Farr told the *Journal* that "he would expand more in the U.S. only 'if I felt the government was going to get out of the way'" by overhauling the tax code and streamlining "environmental and hiring rules."[12] Taxes and regulation, not the lack of demand, were also key themes in a meeting between CEOs and Obama later that month. Barclays CEO Robert Diamond said that US corporations "don't have the confidence to hire in the United States of America until we can believe that the government, the private sector and financial institutions are working together and connected again." Bausch & Lomb CEO Brent Saunders warned that "we're being a little more tentative on whether or not you want to move a plant, or invest," due to disagreements with the administration over rules governing profit repatriation.[13] A few months later, Joseph Czyzyk, the chairman of the Los Angeles Chamber of Commerce, said that "the thing that bothers us the most is regulatory reform." To unlock the trillions of dollars that businesses were hoarding, Czyzyk said, the administration would have to get serious about dismantling regulations: "It can't be lip service and blue ribbon commissions on that, it's got to be sacred cows."[14]

WSJ, February 8, 2011: A4. We will examine the deregulatory push in Chapter 3 since it did not involve new legislation.

12   Quoted in Williamson and Hagerty, "The New Political Landscape."

13   Quoted in Elizabeth Williamson and Joann S. Lublin, "Obama's Overture to Business Gets Wary Reception from CEOs," *WSJ*, November 17, 2010: A4.

14   Quoted in Elizabeth Williamson, "Obama Reaches for Corporate Support," *WSJ*, February 7, 2011: A4. Capital strike actions were not limited to big business. The owner of "two small companies in Cleveland that make automotive tools, springs and other items" told reporters he was not hiring "despite a recovery in orders," due to the healthcare reform and "such laws as the Americans with Disabilities Act" (Williamson and Hagerty, "The New Political Landscape").

Obama listened. On tax policy, he agreed in December 2010 to renew the tax cuts for the wealthy originally passed under George W. Bush, which he had previously vowed to end. Although he did sign several measures, such as the ACA, that modestly increased taxes on the wealthy, he left the rate on capital-gains income (income from stock market holdings) lower than it had been two decades earlier. Many tax policy experts also argued that Obama could have ended the tax loophole on "carried interest," which benefits hedge funds and private equity managers, but he did not.[15] Most important for business confidence was the tax rate on corporations. In February 2012 the White House released the "President's Framework for Business Tax Reform," which proposed to reduce the top corporate rate from 35 percent to 28 percent, and 25 percent for manufacturing companies.[16] Obama made the quid pro quos explicit. In exchange for his efforts "to give businesses a better deal" through new legislation, he was hoping to cajole new business investments. He also asked congressional Republicans to fund a small fiscal stimulus "to create jobs through education, training, and public works projects."[17]

The most aggressive administration initiatives involved promoting exports and overseas investments by US corporations. Obama's first secretary of state, Hillary Clinton, effectively became "the government's highest-ranking business lobbyist," as the business press noted, directly negotiating foreign deals for Boeing, Lockheed Martin, General Electric, and other companies. She pushed countries to embrace fracking for natural gas and Monsanto's genetically modified seeds. Clinton also reoriented the State Department itself, converting

---

15   Lori Montgomery and Shailagh Murray, "Obama and GOP Strike Tax Accord," *WP*, December 7, 2010: A1; Josh Barro, "Highest Earners' Tax Rates Rose Sharply in 2013," *NYT*, December 31, 2015: B3; Noam Scheiber, "Justice in Taxes, Most Likely Short-Lived," *NYT*, January 1, 2016: B1; Gretchen Morgenson, "Obama Has Power to End Tax Loophole for the Rich," *NYT*, May 8, 2016: B1. In 2009 Obama had abstained from supporting a bill that would have recovered an estimated $100 billion a year from offshore tax havens. He also signed a law that codified corporations' ability to avoid taxes by shifting profits among overseas subsidiaries, "costing the Treasury hundreds of billions of dollars and going back on an Obama campaign pledge." Robert Kuttner, *A Presidency in Peril: The Inside Story of Obama's Promise, Wall Street's Power, and the Struggle to Control Our Economic Future* (White River Junction, VT: Chelsea Green, 2010), 82–3.

16   Elizabeth Williamson, "Obama Woos CEOs as Frictions Ease," *WSJ*, December 13, 2010: A4; Jackie Calmes, "Obama Offers to Cut Corporate Tax Rate to 28%," *NYT*, February 22, 2012: B1.

17   Mark Landler and Jackie Calmes, "Obama Proposes Deal over Taxes and Jobs," *NYT*, July 31, 2013: A11.

it "into a machine for promoting U.S. business." She created the new position of chief economist, hired a former Wall Street banker for the job, and promoted "the embassy economic officers who act as State's liaisons to business." She directed department employees to embrace what she called the "Ambassador-as-CEO" approach to diplomacy, ordering "embassies to make it a priority to help U.S. businesses win contracts."[18]

As Clinton cleared the path for specific companies, the administration responded to the 2010 midterm defeat by trying to open up new markets for all US corporations. Obama had already appointed a delegation of government and corporate leaders to negotiate bilateral trade treaties that would "open up markets so that American businesses can prosper." By the end of the year, passing new trade agreements with South Korea, Colombia, and Panama became a priority, with the goal that these actions would restore corporate confidence and unlock investment. In Obama's words, these initiatives were intended to "make clear to the business community, as well as to the country, that the most important thing we can do is boost and encourage our business sector and make sure that they're hiring."[19] Business loved it, though the public was less enthused. The *Wall Street Journal* reported in January 2011 that "the administration is relying on business groups to take a lead role in passing the trade deals, countering opposition from unions and a skeptical public."[20]

Following the successful passage of these laws in Congress later that year, Obama moved on to the behemoth Trans-Pacific Partnership (TPP). The deal was designed to extend the privileges granted to corporations under other free-trade agreements to twelve Pacific countries. The administration's pursuit of the TPP was a multiyear campaign involving a "war room" of top officials in the West Wing and the targeting of dozens of individual congressional Democrats

---

18   Quotes from Elizabeth Dwoskin and Indira A. R. Lakshmanan, "Secretary of Commerce," *BW,* January 14–20, 2013: 22, 25. See also Tom Philpott, "Taxpayer Dollars Are Helping Monsanto Sell Seeds Abroad," *Mother Jones* online, May 18, 2013; Mariah Blake, "The Chevron Communiqués," *Mother Jones,* September–October 2014: 50–4, 72.

19   Quoted in Williamson and Hagerty, "The New Political Landscape." See also Jonathan Weisman and Elizabeth Williamson, "Trade Moves up White House Agenda," *WSJ,* November 15, 2010: A5; Williamson, "Obama Woos CEOs," "President Revs Up Campaign," and "White House to Revive Latin America Deals," *WSJ,* February 9, 2011: A2.

20   Elizabeth Williamson and Laura Meckler, "President Tries the GE Way," *WSJ,* January 22, 2011: A4; Williamson, "President Revs Up Campaign."

who were on the fence. The administration also took the inclusion of corporate leaders to new levels. It gave nearly six hundred business representatives direct access to the draft text, which it refused to release to the public or Congress, and recruited CEOs to lobby Congress.[21]

For Congress as well, subsidizing the overseas investments and exports of US corporations was a bipartisan policy, as the approval of the bilateral trade deals suggests. Congress members' behavior was heavily shaped by the business-confidence logic that drove the administration to support these proposals. A telling example came late in Obama's second term, when Congress was divided over whether to renew the Export-Import Bank's subsidies to US exporters. The threat of disinvestment created the leverage needed for a congressional majority. As *Bloomberg Businessweek* reported, key manufacturers threatened to migrate overseas if Congress resisted. Boeing's CEO "quietly warned that Boeing might have to move work abroad if it didn't have Ex-Im's help." These threats "alarmed moderate members of Congress," and produced the votes needed to assure the bank's renewal.[22]

There are several noteworthy patterns in these efforts to bolster business confidence. First, representatives of large US corporations were directly involved in administration initiatives: through consultation in formulating tax policy, through the corporate presence on trade delegations and within the State Department, and through the White House's enlistment of CEOs as consultants and lobbyists for the TPP. These business representatives helped design policy and also performed the crucial role of winning over Congress. Victories like the renewal of the Export-Import Bank and Congress's approval of foreign trade deals did not result from negotiations between Republicans and Democrats, but from negotiations between corporate leaders and reluctant members of both parties. The deployment of business lobbyists against one's congressional opponents is a common political strategy utilized by both Democrats and Republicans.

Second, many of the policies initiated after the 2008 economic crash entailed quid pro quos between government and business. The policies were not designed to address the economic roots of disinvestment, nor

21   Jonathan Weisman and Michael D. Shear, "Hard Politicking Behind Democrats' 'Yea' Votes on Trade Bill," *NYT*, June 27, 2015: B1; Elizabeth Palmberg, "The Insider List," *Sojourners* online, June 29, 2012; Carter Dougherty, "Obama's New Best Allies on the Hill: CEOs," *BW*, January 25–February 1, 2015: 28–29.

22   Peter Coy, "Open Season on Big Business," *BW*, February 29–March 6, 2016: 12.

to directly resolve problems like unemployment and slow growth. Rather, they were part of a bargaining process that traded government actions for corporate investment. This disconnect is particularly visible in the pursuit of trade and investment treaties, which were publicly advertised as ways to "make sure" that corporations would expand domestic production and therefore add jobs. But trade agreements can only produce net job gains if they generate increased production, if the increased production takes place domestically, and if that production involves expanding the workforce. In practice, this has generally not occurred.[23] Likewise, as even the business press and most mainstream economists concede, reduced corporate tax rates tend to have "little bearing on economic growth" in industrialized nations. As business analysts would later testify during the 2017 tax cut debate, corporate tax cuts or a tax holiday (designed to allow corporations to repatriate money held in overseas tax shelters at a low tax rate) would not produce significant new investments or jobs.[24] Many CEOs frankly admitted in late 2017 that "tax cut proceeds will go to shareholders." And, as predicted, most of the proceeds of the December 2017 tax cut were indeed used to increase profit levels, stock prices, and shareholder dividends.[25]

23   From the standpoint of the US economy, the principal impact of neoliberal trade agreements has been an increase in direct corporate investment in the economies of treaty partners, disinvestment in the US economy, and the reduction of domestic manufacturing employment. From the standpoint of the treaty partners' economies, the results have included an increase in sweatshop jobs, a (typically larger) increase in agricultural unemployment, and the undermining of national regulatory autonomy. See Robert E. Scott, "No Jobs from Trade Pacts: The Trans-Pacific Partnership Could Be Much Worse Than the Over-Hyped Korea Deal," Economic Policy Institute, Issue Brief #369, July 18, 2013; Mark Weisbrot, Lara Merling, Vitor Mello, Stephan Lefebvre, and Joseph Sammut, Did NAFTA Help Mexico? An Update after Twenty-Three Years (Center for Economic and Policy Research, 2017).

24   Mark Glassman, "Correlations: Taxes and Growth," BW, January 6–12, 2014: 17 (quote); David Cogman and Tim Koller, "The Real Story Behind US Companies' Offshore Cash Reserves," mckinsey.com, June 2017. In 2017, only 2 percent of mainstream US economists—one out of forty-two surveyed—said that US GDP "will be substantially higher a decade from now" as a result of the Trump administration's corporate tax cut. "Tax Reform," Initiative on Global Markets, University of Chicago Booth School of Business, November 21, 2017.

25   Toluse Olorunnipa, "Trump's Tax Promises Undercut by CEO Plans to Help Investors," bloomberg.com, November 29, 2017 (quote). For results see Michael Smolyansky, Gustavo Suárez, and Alexandra Tabova, "U.S. Corporations' Repatriation of Offshore Profits," FEDS Notes (Board of Governors of the Federal Reserve System), September 4, 2018; "You Know Who the Tax Cuts Helped? Rich People" (editorial), NYT online, August 12, 2018; Peter Coy, "Trump's Tax Cuts at Year 1: More Growth, More Red Ink," BW, December 17, 2018: 32–3; Tim Mahedy, "A Lot of Huff for a Little

Third, the process also highlights the necessity of trust in the negotiations around capital strikes, since capital investment and government policy can never be fully implemented at the same time. Obama's actions were intended to "boost and encourage" business confidence in the government as an ally across a range of issues. But someone had to go first. Either corporations would first invest in new hiring and trust that the Obama administration would negotiate favorable policy reforms, or the administration would first secure pro-business reforms and then trust that the corporate beneficiaries would invest in new US jobs. Congressional actions obeyed the same logic, as the Export-Import Bank renewal suggests. This "who goes first" dilemma is common to most policy negotiations between business and government.

Fourth, negotiating relationships were asymmetrical. The Obama administration was constantly trying to persuade business to trust the government, not the other way around. Government overtures to business were a gamble, since pro-business policy changes would not necessarily result in business being *confident enough* to end disinvestment. As the *Wall Street Journal* noted in late 2010, "It isn't clear how far any moves by Mr. Obama or the new Congress would go in encouraging U.S. businesses to unleash the $2 trillion in capital they are holding."[26] The renewal of corporate investment remained agonizingly slow, and hoarded profits remained at gargantuan levels at the end of Obama's time in office. The structural power of business meant that it was not obliged to negotiate in good faith. Executives could take their tax cuts and then decide to give the money to shareholders instead of investing it. Capital strikes tend to be open-ended, capable of generating a series of pro-business policy initiatives—unless government officials are willing and able to punish business for reneging, which the Obama administration was very reluctant to do.

In the end, Obama was only partly successful in restoring business confidence. While the unemployment rate had significantly declined by 2016, US companies were still hoarding some $2.5 trillion in profits in overseas tax havens. Prominent CEOs were still rehearsing the standard line: threats of continued disinvestment coupled with promises of new investments should government comply with their demands for lower taxes. The CEO of Apple, which held $181 billion overseas, said frankly that "we're not going to bring it back until there's a fair rate. There's no debate about it." General Electric's CEO said in early 2017 that the economy "is in what I would call an investment recession. Companies aren't reinvesting in capital expenditures in the U.S." Only drastic corporate tax cuts would give business "the ability to repatriate capital from around the world." The Democratic and Republican nominees to replace Obama agreed that slashing corporate tax rates was the way to "bring private sector dollars off the sidelines and put them to work here."[27] Again, the strategy was to *cajole*, not *coerce*. Outlawing tax havens or taking punitive measures were off the table.

The Trump transition in 2017 has not altered any of these basic patterns. There *was* a gradual recovery in business investment levels starting at the end of the Obama era and continuing in Trump's first years, owing to a recovery in energy prices and a modest growth in consumer demand (partly fueled by rising consumer debt, it seems). Surveys in 2018 found a significant increase in business "optimism" and plans to hire, and the official unemployment rate dropped to under 4 percent.[28] However, corporations continued to keep trillions of dollars out of the real economy, including $2.5 trillion in domestic reserves alone.[29] Moreover, they continued to make strategic use of their cash hoards to win policy changes from government. The demands had not changed: more tax cuts, more deregulation, more public subsidies, and more privileges overseas. In return, they promised to invest in the United States.

A preview of the Trump administration's approach to business came in November 2016, when Trump negotiated an agreement with the Carrier manufacturing company. Carrier and its parent company, United Technologies, had declared that they would transfer over two thousand jobs from Indiana to Mexico. Three weeks after the election, Trump gloated that he had saved over half of those jobs. Carrier's executives

27   Tim Cook, Jeffrey Immelt, and Hillary Clinton quoted in, respectively, Jena McGregor, "Tim Cook, the Interview: Running Apple 'Is Sort of a Lonely Job,'" *WP* online, August 13, 2016; "Interview: GE's Jeff Immelt," *BW*, February 13–19, 2017: 23; Jon Schwarz, "Hillary Clinton Hints at Giant, Trump-Like Giveaway to Corporate America," *Intercept*, June 27, 2016.
28   US Commerce Department, Bureau of Economic Analysis, "National Data: National Income and Product Accounts," Table 5.1, revised August 29, 2018; William C. Dunkelberg and Holly Wade, *NFIB Small Business Economic Trends* (National Federation of Independent Business, August 2018). The more realistic (U6) unemployment rate was 7.2 percent in August 2019.
29   Jeff Cox, "Cash-Rich Companies Are Set to Pour $2.5 Trillion into Buybacks, Dividends and M&A this Year," CNBC.com, June 4, 2018.

offered a clearer account of the deal, however, explaining that Trump had offered them preferential input in policymaking: "the incoming Trump-Pence administration has emphasized to us its commitment to support the business community and create an improved, more competitive US business climate," meaning tax cuts and deregulation. Economist Michael Hicks called the negotiation "damned fine deal-making" on Carrier's part: "The chance for Carrier (and their lawyers) to help craft a huge regulatory relief bill is worth every penny they might save [in exchange for] delaying the closure of this plant for a few years." The self-styled master of "the deal" had just surrendered to a classic capital strike. He had negotiated a partial postponement of Carrier's disinvestment and gained a public-relations victory, but only by promising the company future leverage over regulatory policy. Tellingly, the company stressed that the deal had not altered its policy of moving investment overseas: "This agreement in no way diminishes our belief in the benefits of free trade and that the forces of globalization will continue to require solutions for the long-term competitiveness of the US and of American workers moving forward."[30] Its control over its investment capital made it the more powerful partner in the deal.

Other companies quickly followed suit, promising investment in exchange for pro-business reforms from government. Corporate tax cuts remained a central demand. In January 2017 the CEO of AT&T vowed to "step up our investment levels" in exchange for a reduced corporate tax rate. AT&T was not holding back on US investments for lack of capital: it was posting over $1 billion a month in profits. It had also received $38.1 billion in special tax breaks from the government since 2008, more than any other company. But it still was not confident enough.[31] Even after Congress slashed the top corporate tax rate from 35 percent to 21 percent in December 2017, the fate of the hoarded cash remained far from certain. Corporations did start to repatriate their overseas money, but spent most of it on stock buybacks and dividends

30   Sources cited in Kevin Young, Tarun Banerjee, and Michael Schwartz, "Who's Calling the Shots?," *Jacobin* online, February 6, 2017. See also Bryan Gruley and Rick Clough, "Remember That Time Trump Said He Saved 1,100 Jobs in a Carrier Plant in Indiana? Globalization Doesn't Give a Damn," *BW*, April 3–9, 2017: 54–9; Jim Tankersley, "Trump's Boasts vs. Reality In Luring Jobs Back to U.S.," *NYT*, August 14, 2019: B1; Natasha Bach, "Carrier Factory 'Saved' by Donald Trump to Lay Off 200 More Workers," fortune.com, January 11, 2018.

31   Edward C. Baig, "AT&T: We'd Invest More with Tax Cut," *USA Today*, January 26, 2017: 5B; Patricia Cohen, "Profitable Companies That Paid No Taxes: Here's How They Did It," *NYT*, March 10, 2017: B6.

rather than productive investments or wage increases for workers. Business investment levels in 2018 were still much weaker than during the second half of the twentieth century.[32]

The Trump presidency has thus exhibited the same basic patterns as its predecessors. Corporate representatives have been directly involved in making policy, even more blatantly than in the past.[33] Quid-pro-quo deals have traded government handouts to corporations for new investment in the economy, asking government to trust that business leaders will follow through. And the negotiating relationship in those deals has remained asymmetrical, with capitalists free to renege on their pledges. Trump's own billionaire status and unabashedly pro-business rhetoric mark a partial difference from Obama, but he has remained subject to the same basic parameters and constraints.

Capital and the Origins of Progressive Legislation

Major legislation that challenges corporate profits or power might seem to be a different story, initiated despite business wishes rather than because of them. Many observers regard the signature legislative achievements of the Obama presidency as a reflection of Obama's electoral mandate and, by extension, the tide of public opinion. And, indeed, insofar as they sought to protect the public from business, the ACA, Dodd-Frank, and climate reform all coincided with majority opinion. However, while Obama's 2008 election victory and strong public backing played some role, it's unlikely that any of these bills would have been introduced without at least some support among business leaders.

Healthcare Reform: Setting the Table, Limiting the Menu

The healthcare reform process began in that way. In human terms, the existing system was a catastrophe: 47 million people lacked health

---

32 See note 25 and Rex Nutting, "Businesses Are Investing More, But It's Not the Tax Cut," marketwatch.com, May 7, 2018.

33 Landon Thomas Jr. and Alexandra Stevenson, "Cabinet Choices Signal Embrace of Wall St. Elite," *NYT*, December 1, 2016: A1; Derek Kravitz, Isaac Arnsdorf, and Marina Affo, "Lifting the Veil on Another Batch of Shadowy Trump Appointees," *ProPublica*, August 31, 2017; Rebecca Harrington and Skye Gould, "Meet the Cabinet: Here's Who Trump Has Appointed to Senior Leadership Positions," *Business Insider*, October 12, 2017; Jennifer A. Dlouhy and Jesse Hamilton, "In Trump's Washington, Foxes Guard the Henhouse," *BW*, December 25, 2017: 41–3.

insurance and 45,000 died each year as a result. Per-capita healthcare costs were about twice as high as in other industrialized countries yet health outcomes were much worse. A large majority of the public thought the government should ensure universal coverage.[34] However, the key impetus for national reform was not mortality rates or public opinion, but business costs. Top corporate leaders outside the healthcare sector had long sought a way to contain the cost of healthcare provision and insurance. They had tried various ways of offloading the rising costs onto their workers: capping benefits, hiring part-timers and subcontractors, or simply slashing coverage.[35] But these strategies were insufficient. In the 2000s, health costs galloped far ahead of the overall inflation rate, meaning higher and higher costs for employers. Between 2000 and 2007, employer spending on healthcare rose 87 percent, leading the majority of executives in the Business Roundtable to cite healthcare costs as "the biggest economic challenge they face."[36]

As a result, long before the Obama election or even the Democratic victories in the 2006 midterms, the business press was already noting "an ever-louder complaint from U.S. businesses that they can't compete in a global economy when companies from other countries don't have to pay for health care," leading to "the business community's heightened interest in sweeping change" at the level of government policy.[37] Several prominent business-led coalitions centered on health reform were either formed or stepped up their work. The National Business Coalition on Health (NBCH) and the business-dominated National Coalition on Health Care (NCHC) became more visible.[38] The business press from the mid-2000s was full of corporate complaints about health costs. Figure 1 shows the number of articles mentioning "health care" in three

34   Andrew P. Wilper, Steffie Woolhandler, Karen E. Lasser, Danny McCormick, David H. Bohr, and David U. Himmelstein, "Health Insurance and Mortality in US Adults," *American Journal of Public Health* 99, no. 12 (2009): 2289–95. On polling see the introduction.

35   Colin Gordon, *Dead on Arrival: The Politics of Health Care in Twentieth-Century America* (Princeton, NJ: Princeton University Press, 2003), 41, 86, 243–44.

36   Richard S. Dunham and Keith Epstein, "One CEO's Health-Care Crusade," bloomberg.com, July 3, 2007.

37   Deborah Solomon and David Wessel, "Health-Insurance Gap Surges As Political Issue," *WSJ*, January 19, 2007: A1; Dunham and Epstein, "One CEO's Health-Care Crusade." See also "GM Chief to Address Senate on Health Care," *WSJ*, July 13, 2006: A7.

38   See for instance David Stires, "By the Numbers," *Fortune*, August 9, 2004: 34; David Stires, "Half of Employers Responding to Survey on Health Care Believe Employee Involvement Has Greatest Impact on Cost," *Insurance Advocate*, November 3, 2001: 48.

of the top business magazines in the years 1995 through 2008. The annual average rose from 58 articles in 1995–1999, to 102 in 2000–2004, to 123 in 2005–2008. As with the 2009 stimulus, many business voices called for more aggressive action than what policymakers were proposing. "We don't see anything in the national debate now that's big enough or ambitious enough to address the problem," said the NCHC president in 2004.[39]

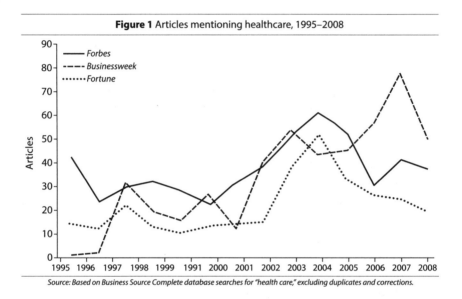

Figure 1 Articles mentioning healthcare, 1995–2008

Source: Based on Business Source Complete database searches for "health care," excluding duplicates and corrections.

By the mid-2000s the mounting concern over healthcare costs had become a steady complaint among manufacturing and commercial corporations. With increasing frequency, companies threatened to drop workers' coverage or move jobs to other labor markets. The number of US businesses offering health insurance to their workers was already declining, from 69 percent in 2000 to 60 percent in 2007. Initial government responses came primarily at the state level, with roughly a dozen state legislatures debating major reforms around this time. Business confidence was the major justification. Pennsylvania governor Ed Rendell, for instance, argued for reform by stressing the costs indirectly imposed on business by the large number of uninsured people in the state: "It is a tremendous deterrent for businesses that are considering locating in Pennsylvania to know that in addition to paying for their

---

39   Henry Simmons quoted in Sarah Lueck, "Coalition Floats Ideas to Tame Rocketing Costs of Health Care," *WSJ*, July 21, 2004: D2.

own employees' health coverage, they will be subsidizing the costs of the uninsured," whom emergency rooms could not legally turn away.[40]

By George W. Bush's second term, these threats had developed into formal demands for government action. Deere & Company CEO Robert Lane conveyed the demand when he warned Congress that rising costs could lead to the "limiting of covered services, loss of employer-provided health care . . . and even a loss of American jobs, both in the manufacturing and service sectors." Bush's January 2006 State of the Union address emphasized healthcare, which, as the *Wall Street Journal* noted, was "rare for a Republican." The reason was not public opinion but business opinion. Providers were being pushed to find "more efficient ways of delivering services," not by consumers but by other business sectors: the providers were "under pressure from health-insurance providers, who are themselves under pressure from large corporations."[41]

The presidential campaigning of 2007–08 led to increased talk of reform in Washington, but not merely to appeal to voters. In early 2008, Senate Finance Committee chair Max Baucus, whose staff would play the central role in crafting what became the ACA, committed to advancing a healthcare reform in 2009 regardless of the election's outcome. At that moment, he rehired former staffer Liz Fowler, fresh from a stint at the nation's top health insurer, who would write much of the bill herself. In June he and other members of Congress hosted a healthcare summit featuring top business executives.[42]

The industrial and commercial corporations with the largest and most expensive health plans were the foremost proponents of reform. But many health industry sectors also had grievances with the status quo. Health insurers in California, for instance, had "been falling short of their enrollment targets because the overall market [wasn't] growing." For this reason, they liked Republican governor Arnold Schwarzenegger's proposal to make the purchase of insurance mandatory. They saw it as representing "real opportunities for our business," given that it would "expand the industry's market by four million to five million currently uninsured Californians—something health plans

---

40 Rendell quoted in Solomon and Wessel, "Health-Insurance Gap Surges"; Chad Terhune and Laura Meckler, "A Turning Point for Health Care," *WSJ*, September 27, 2007: A1; "Others Join Maine in Push for Health-Care Change," *WSJ*, December 26, 2006: D4.

41 Lane quoted in Solomon and Wessel, "Health-Insurance Gap Surges"; "The Health Care Opportunity" (editorial), *WSJ*, February 1, 2006: A14; George Melloan, "The Health of the Union," *WSJ*, January 31, 2006: A15.

42 Brill, *America's Bitter Pill*, 42, 54–9, 74.

have been unable to do despite heavily marketing new products."[43] In contrast to 1993–94, when health industry resistance had sunk the Clinton health reform initiative, by 2009 healthcare providers and insurers were open to major reforms, as long as they addressed their specific complaints. Policymakers, for their part, were keenly attuned to health industry wishes, just as they were attuned to those of other business sectors. John McDonough, the top adviser on health reform for the Senate's Health, Education, Labor, and Pensions (HELP) Committee, recalls that prior to 2009, "business, insurers, manufacturers, [and] medical organizations were all calling for comprehensive reform."[44]

Support for reform by healthcare insurers and providers stemmed partly from the desire to preempt an independent overhaul of the healthcare system—which might lead to a single-payer insurance system, strict regulations on price-gouging providers, and other policies favored by the public and long present in other high-income nations. A staggering 82 percent of the public thought the US healthcare system either needed "fundamental changes" or should be "completely" rebuilt. Very few wanted the healthcare sector to be *less* regulated.[45] If business was "on the menu," rather than "at the table," the reforms might prove inimical to their interests. Industry thus took preemptive action to shape the debate over reform. In December 2008, America's Health Insurance Plans (AHIP), the top insurers' lobby, released a comprehensive reform proposal that specifically excluded a single-payer system and government control of healthcare prices.[46]

This same preemptive logic guided much of the broader corporate world, even those companies without a direct stake in the healthcare sector. Many business leaders feared that an efficient publicly-run program would increase the appeal of government-run alternatives to private capital. The *Wall Street Journal* reported that corporate leaders were willing to incur some added costs as a result of reform as long as it preserved "a market-oriented health-care system." But if the reform

43   Vanessa Fuhrmans, "Insurers See a Potential Cure," *WSJ*, January 19, 2007: A10 (second quote from UnitedHealth CEO Stephen Helmsley). See also Brill, *America's Bitter Pill*, 51–2.

44   John E. McDonough, *Inside National Health Reform* (Berkeley: University of California Press, 2011), 55.

45   Cathy Schoen, Robin Osborn, Michelle M. Doty, Meghan Bishop, Jordon Peugh, and Nandita Murukutla, "Toward Higher-Performance Health Systems: Adults' Health Care Experiences in Seven Countries, 2007," *Health Affairs* 26, no. 6 (2007): w721.

46   AHIP Board of Directors, *Now Is the Time for Health Care Reform: A Proposal to Achieve Universal Coverage, Affordability, Quality Improvement and Market Reform* (December 2008).

included an expanded Medicare system and/or government price controls, then the US might reach "a tipping point where the reforms needed to preserve an innovative, market-based health system may become politically impossible."[47] Thus, the rising pressure of healthcare costs on employers, coupled with healthcare executives' fear of something worse if they stayed on the sidelines, lay behind the diverse corporate support for reform. By 2008 business leaders across the corporate world had decided that reform was necessary, while health industry leaders had decided that reform was inevitable. Shaping that reform then became the name of the game.

And shape it they did. Since they were the "commercial interests who [would be] most affected by the proposed change," and since their "permission" was thus necessary, Democratic leaders in Congress invited them to help design the reform. John McDonough of the Senate HELP Committee reported that Senator Ted Kennedy "directed us to bring together key system 'stakeholders' to see whether they could find consensus on a path to reform." Those stakeholders included "consumers, disease advocacy, business, insurance, physician, hospital, labor, pharmaceutical, and other organizations." Although patients constituted the vast majority of the real stakeholders, they were a clear minority among the stakeholders invited to the table; in contrast, each industry sector was invited to send its own representatives. Three decades earlier, the Carter administration had taken the same approach, which, as one critic noted, may seem like "sound democratic practice, but it is also a formula for building fortifications around the status quo."[48]

The resulting "consensus" was clear before Obama entered the White House. By inauguration time, business and its representatives on the key congressional committees (Table 1) had already determined the basic framework of whatever legislation would emerge. Certain options were entirely off the table. Single-payer insurance, or "Medicare for All," was immediately ruled out by Democratic leaders. Of the presidential candidates in the 2008 Democratic primary, all except Dennis Kucinich had committed by early 2007 to keeping private insurance intact. In 2008, the two key Senate committees involved in early drafts, Max

---

47 *WSJ*, "The Health Care Opportunity"; Alan Murray, "Bush Health-Care Plan Finds Business Backers," *WSJ*, January 24, 2007: A6.

48 McDonough, *Inside National Health Reform*, 35; Daniel S. Greenberg, "Cost Containment: Another Crusade Begins," *New England Journal of Medicine* 296, no. 12 (1977): 699 (final quote).

Baucus's Finance committee and Kennedy's HELP committee, unequiv-
ocally rejected single payer. The Baucus-Fowler team's white paper of
November 2008 was vague on details, but its "one clear position" was its
opposition to single payer. Advocates of single payer, let alone socialized medicine, were entirely excluded from even testifying before
Baucus's people.[49]

Table 1: The Senate Finance Committee's ties to the healthcare sector (partial list)

Name	Position	Ties to Health Industry	Notes
Max Baucus (D-MT)	Chair of Senate Finance Committee (SFC)	Received $253k in industry donations in 2007–10, plus $201k in donations from industry lobbyists in 2007–09	3 of 5 top donors in 2007–12 were healthcare or health insurance firms
Elizabeth Fowler	Top aide to Baucus, Senior Counsel to SFC, 2008–10; previously Chief Health and Entitlements Counsel for SFC, 2001–05	VP for Public Policy and External Affairs, WellPoint insurance co., 2006–08	Helped write health-care reform bill passed by Senate in March 2010; later hired by Johnson & Johnson
Michelle Easton	Chief Health and Entitlements Counsel for SFC, 2005–08	Former VP at PhRMA; since 2008, lobbyist representing over a dozen health firms	
Jeff Forbes	Chief of Staff for Baucus, 1999–2002; Staff Director for SFC, 2002–03	Lobbyist for HCR Manor Care PAC and for lobbying firms hired by PhRMA, Merck, HCR Manor Care, and other health industry firms, 2004–present	
Scott Parven	Chief International Trade Counsel for Baucus, 2003–06	Director of Int'l Public Policy for Aetna insurance, 1998–2006; lobbyist for Pfizer, PhRMA, eHealth Inc., and other health firms	

Sources: Center for Responsive Politics (opensecrets.org); Glenn Greenwald, "The Revolving Door Spins Faster on Healthcare Reform," salon.com, July 15, 2010; Max Fraser, "The Affordable Care Attack," *NLF* 23, no. 1 (2014): 98.

Baucus and company also ruled out a robust "public option," that is, a public insurance plan open to everyone that would compete with

---

49   Brill, *America's Bitter Pill*, 18, 75 (quote); McDonough, *Inside National Health Reform*, 47. The Clinton health reform team did the same in the early 1990s, even though it found "nearly 80 percent support for 'some system of national health insur-ance'" among the public. (Survey quoted in Gordon, *Dead on Arrival*, 268.)

private insurers.[50] Insurers saw a strong public option as "disturbing, as it [would create] new government-run insurance to compete with their products" and could become a wedge for a single-payer system. In addition, "hospitals, physicians, a host of other provider groups, and most business organizations adamantly opposed" it. As so often happens, those who touted the superior efficiency of private enterprise and the market opposed a public institution that could put their argument to the test. Thanks to the concerted effort by the healthcare industry and its congressional allies, popular ideas like single-payer and a strong public option were "never envisioned in congressional reform plans," as McDonough notes.[51]

Corporations were mostly unified in rejecting these progressive proposals, but they did not necessarily agree on what reforms they wanted. Their interests varied by industry. For example, most industrial and commercial employers stood to gain from cost containment, but the health industry opposed limits on its ability to set prices. Conversely, the health industry wanted a mandate requiring employers to cover their employees, but the employers were wary. Within the health industry itself, insurers did not like being forced to insure sick patients, but healthcare providers liked the idea since it would bring them more paying customers. Given the complex web of interests at stake, pro-reform voices in government and business strove to negotiate a "corporate compromise" that would reconcile, to the greatest extent possible, all these differences.[52] If an industry was hurt by a particular element in the reform package, it would have to be compensated in some way.

The solution was the "three-legged stool": three inseparable elements that would form the framework for reform. In exchange for accepting customers with preexisting conditions—the first leg—insurers would

50   A robust version would be open to everyone, would allow the government to negotiate prices, and would force providers to accept it. During the subsequent debate, a number of "public options" were briefly considered, but all of them were targeted to a tiny fraction of the population, and therefore would neither compete with the private insurers nor allow government negotiation of prices.

51   Laura Meckler, "Health-Care Plans Aid Industry," *WSJ*, November 19, 2007: A8 (first quote); McDonough, *Inside National Health Reform*, 135 (second and third quotes). Elites with vested interests have often feared public health programs as potential "entering wedges, feet in the door, camel's noses, and Trojan horses" that could demonstrate the comparative benefits of public healthcare, leading to reduced privileges or ruin in the long run. (Gordon, *Dead on Arrival*, 127.)

52   On this concept see David U. Himmelstein and Steffie Woolhandler, "The Corporate Compromise: A Marxist View of Health Maintenance Organizations and Prospective Payment," *Annals of Internal Medicine* 109, no. 6 (1988): 494–501. We return to it in Chapter 2.

get the second leg, the individual mandate that required everyone to buy insurance. The mandate was their main demand, since it guaranteed an immense expansion of their declining customer base. Obama had vocally opposed the mandate during his campaign, but reversed his position in office to accommodate healthcare interests. The third leg of the stool involved government subsidies to the poor, which would ensure that insurers and providers could collect from their new low-income patients. The mandate, combined with government subsidies, would deliver a huge infusion of profits into the insurance industry, especially since consumers were not given the option of a strong public insurance program. This framework had long circulated in right-wing and business circles, where its regressive nature won many adherents. It resembled a Heritage Foundation proposal from 1989 and an earlier Nixon administration plan. In 2006, Governor Mitt Romney of Massachusetts had signed something very similar, with much business support. It was also the essence of the health insurers' own December 2008 proposal.[53]

The embrace of the three-legged stool and the simultaneous rejection of serious cost containment measures meant that rising healthcare costs would continue to be borne mostly by workers and patients, in the form of rising premiums, copays, and deductibles. Although the final ACA legislation included some small tax increases on the wealthy, many of its funding provisions were regressive, in that they targeted the working class. The healthy would subsidize the sick via the individual mandate, rather than the rich or corporations subsidizing the sick. Employer-based insurance would also be taxed, a measure that targeted unionized workforces with decent health plans.[54] The offloading of costs in this way helped to minimize the tensions over healthcare within the corporate elite. Disruptive mass movements might have reduced elites' power to offload costs onto those below, but mass protest was minimal.

At no time did the administration or Congress challenge the underlying premise of corporate control over healthcare. The ironclad commitment to this pro-corporate framework derived not only from health industry donations and lobbying, but also from the structural

---

53   Brill, *America's Bitter Pill*, 29–34; AHIP, *Now Is the Time for Health Care Reform*.

54   New taxes on employer-based plans were envisioned in the Senate Finance Committee's original draft legislation, though not in the House. (Brill, *America's Bitter Pill*, 115.)

position of health firms within the economy. The sector accounted for 18 percent of GDP and was the nation's leading employer.

This concentration of capital and technology within the sector further enhanced the structural power of the leading firms. That power could be exercised in several ways, including through disinvestment from key markets and through price hikes, which would become visible weapons of the insurers following the ACA's implementation. In early 2010, the Democratic Speaker of the House, Nancy Pelosi, implicitly acknowledged this power. She stressed the need to compensate insurers for accepting people with preexisting conditions by offering them the individual mandate and government subsidies to the poor. "'Otherwise, you have no leverage with the insurance companies' and they would likely increase rates," she told the press.[55] Few in Washington questioned this premise. Ensuring the high profits of the private health industries was imperative, given that policymakers had ruled out public alternatives. The system would thus be reformed, but its central premises of private control and private profit would remain intact.

All of these crucial decisions were made prior to the introduction of the legislation in Congress, during the *pre-legislative* stage of backroom discussions among "stakeholders." By the time formal debate on the healthcare bills began, the Obama administration and Congress had already adopted a framework that excluded progressive options from consideration and accommodated most of the divergent interests among businesses. As a result, costs would continue rising, and tens of thousands would still die each year for lack of coverage.

Financial Reform: Keeping Profits Strong

What of the next major legislative triumph of the Obama era, financial reform? The 2008 Wall Street crash left no doubt about the need for greater regulation. Public opinion was both united and intense in its condemnation of Wall Street's reckless and often illegal behavior. Obama's electoral victory just after the crash was due in part to his call for stricter regulation. At first glance, then, the reform process that began in early 2009 might seem to have been driven by an overwhelming surge of public sentiment.

---

55   "House, Senate Leaders Say Push for Health Care Reform Continues," CNN. com, January 28, 2010.

However, the story is again not so simple. The 2008 crisis, and the destruction of capital that it involved, set off alarm bells within the corporate world that had not been heard in decades. Beginning soon after the 2008 crash, the business press, and especially the financial press, began calling for government action to protect the system from future crises. These voices advocated significant new regulations on the financial sector. Columns in the business press condemned "Wall Street's economic crimes against humanity" and the "mass financial destruction" wrought by the derivatives industry.[56] Editors called variously for specific reforms and for a total "overhaul" of Wall Street.[57] Leading investors and hedge-fund managers called for more regulation. Even the billionaire and deregulatory crusader Carl Icahn (later hired by the Trump administration) advocated reforms that would "make corporate boards and managers more accountable to shareholders."[58] While some of these statements were surely motivated by PR concerns and a desire to "fend off" undesirable reforms,[59] they were also self-serving in a more straightforward sense: they highlighted the widespread business interest in checking the most parasitic behaviors of high finance—parasitism that victimized other businesses and wealthy investors as well as the public. The main thrust of these calls for reform focused on increased oversight of large financial institutions and stricter rules on how much capital banks needed to retain as a cushion against crisis (the "capital ratio"). Both aspects would be central to the White House's June 2009 white paper and the bills that became the Dodd-Frank Act signed in July 2010.

This general business desire for better regulation was transmitted to both Democratic and Republican Party leaders in 2008. Candidates Obama and McCain both assumed that more regulation would be forthcoming, though Obama's tone was more critical. Even much of the

---

56   Shoshana Zuboff, "Wall Street's Economic Crimes Against Humanity," *BW* online, March 20, 2009; Darrell Duffie, "Derivatives and Mass Financial Destruction," *WSJ*, October 22, 2008: A17; Charles W. Calomiris, "Financial Reforms We Can All Agree On," *WSJ*, April 29, 2009: A17.

57   "Empire State Implosion," *WSJ*, November 13, 2008: A18; David Reilly, "Banks Need More Than Just a Tuneup," *WSJ*, December 1, 2008: C8 (quote).

58   Carl C. Icahn, "The Economy Needs Corporate Governance Reform," *WSJ*, January 23, 2009: A13. See also Brad Johnson, "Maybe We Need Regulation, After All," *AB*, November 19, 2008; Paul Singer, "Free-Marketeers Should Welcome Some Regulation," *WSJ*, April 3, 2009: A15.

59   Serena Ng, "Banks Seek Role in Bid to Overhaul Derivatives," *WSJ*, May 29, 2009: C1.

Republican Party was calling for more regulation. Economist Mark Zandi, who published a scathing book-length indictment of Wall Street practices in 2008, was an adviser to the McCain campaign.[60] One of the reforms most fiercely resisted by business after Obama's inauguration, the creation of a consumer financial protection agency, had actually been proposed by George W. Bush's treasury secretary, Henry Paulson, before candidate Obama endorsed the idea. In September, the industry publication *American Banker* even commented that Obama and McCain "appear in harmony on regulation." It was only a modest exaggeration.[61]

On the other hand, business support for reform was not particularly aggressive. Corporations were not taking the lead in demanding specific regulations, and certain reform proposals like the consumer protection agency incurred strong business resistance. Sheila Bair of the Federal Deposit Insurance Corporation (FDIC) lamented that the "responsible banks" generally stayed silent while the most egregious offenders aggressively opposed new regulations.[62] Nor did most nonfinancial businesses, which had the most to gain from more regulations on their lenders, begin lobbying for specific reforms that might address their concerns. The initial reform framework thus was not a straightforward reflection of business demands.

Unlike with the ACA, where diverse corporate representatives participated directly in the early shaping, the administration and Congress were the immediate architects of the framework for financial reform. They inserted many elements that business had not specifically demanded. Obama later recalled his logic:

> My job as president of the United States is to make sure that the overall system is stable and that the economy as a whole is well-served by a healthy, functioning system that allocates capital in efficient ways. And that means the interests of any individual bank or banker are not always going to be congruent with the interests of the economy as a whole.[63]

---

60   Mark Zandi, *Financial Shock: A 360° Look at the Subprime Mortgage Implosion, and How to Avoid the Next Financial Crisis* (Upper Saddle River, NJ: FT Press, 2008); Robert G. Kaiser, *Act of Congress: How America's Essential Institution Works, and How It Doesn't* (New York: Knopf, 2013), 98.

61   Stacy Kaper, "Rivals Appear in Harmony on Regulation," *AB*, September 16, 2008; Kaiser, *Act of Congress*, 32.

62   Sheila Bair, *Bull by the Horns: Fighting to Save Main Street from Wall Street and Wall Street from Itself* (New York: Free Press, 2012), 357.

63   Interviewed in John Micklethwait, Megan Murphy, and Ellen Pollock, "'Don't

Speaking in 2009, Obama advocated new regulations to establish "clear rules of the road, not to hinder financial institutions, but to protect consumers and investors and ultimately to keep those financial institutions strong." The new rules would ensure that market players are informed and thus capable of "making decisions based on the pursuit of profits." Obama was being honest when he told top bankers in March 2009 that he was "the only thing between you and the pitchforks," and that "I want to help . . . I'm not out there to go after you. I'm protecting you." Obama, Geithner, and company were thus genuinely puzzled when Wall Street failed to appreciate their effort to "rescue the economy and their bottom lines." Likewise, the explicit goal of House Financial Services Committee chair Barney Frank was "to allow capitalism to thrive," not to punish greed or wrongdoing.[64]

In other words, Obama and the congressional champions of reform were not acting on behalf of specific corporate interests, at least not usually. Instead, they saw their duty as protecting the long-term interests of the capitalist class as a whole, including but not limited to Wall Street banks. The key point in Obama's comments was that "*the interests of any individual bank or banker are not always going to be congruent with the interests of the economy as a whole.*" Obama's commitment to "the economy as a whole" meant defending financial institutions from their own risky practices, which might deliver vast short-term profits for some firms and big bonuses for their executives, but in the long run create huge crises that would imperil both the financial and nonfinancial sectors. For capitalism to thrive, the Obama administration and its congressional allies had to save capitalists from themselves.[65]

Gamble, Invest,' " *BW*, June 27–July 3, 2016: 46.

64   Obama quoted in Greg Hitt, "Next Front: Bank Regulation," *WSJ*, February 26, 2009: A2; Gerald F. Seib, "Obama Aspires to a 'Light Touch,' Not a Heavy Hand," *WSJ*, June 17, 2009: A2; Ron Suskind, *Confidence Men: Wall Street, Washington, and the Education of a President* (New York: HarperCollins, 2011), 234–5. Last two quotes from Geithner, *Stress Test*, 404, and Kaiser, *Act of Congress*, 119 (Frank quoted).

65   Many reformers said so explicitly. The subtitle of Bair's book *Bull by the Horns* speaks of saving "Wall Street from itself," and a 2015 book by liberal economist Robert Reich, who represents the far left on the spectrum of permissible opinion, is titled *Saving Capitalism*. Our analysis here supports arguments about the "relative autonomy" of state policymakers from capitalist interests: that is, policymakers act to advance the general interests of the capitalist class as a whole rather than simply catering to individual sectors; they also have some discretion as to how they do so, rather than mechanically responding to business demands. See Nicos Poulantzas, *Political Power and Social Classes*, trans. Timothy O'Hagen (London: Verso, 1973); Fred Block, "The Ruling Class Does Not Rule: Notes on the Marxist Theory of the State," *Socialist Revolution* 33 (1977): 6–28.

However, their ability to do so was constrained by Wall Street's control over investment. If Washington wanted banks to unleash their hoards of cash, it could not be too rough on them. There *were*, in fact, some options that could have reduced the banks' power over investments. The government could have nationalized part or all of the financial sector, or at least forced banks to restructure or reduce their size so as to avoid the "too-big-to-fail" predicament in the future. The problem was that such options would have reduced corporate control over capital flows, and even a hint of infringing on this sacred right of capital would have undermined Wall Street confidence—and probably the confidence of other business sectors—in a dramatic way. Administration officials and the key congressional reformers thus opposed measures to restructure banks or to prohibit "too-big-to-fail" financial institutions. As economist Joseph Stiglitz observed, "The Obama administration has argued that the big banks are not only too big to fail but also too big to be financially restructured."[66] In taking government intrusion into investment policy off the table, the administration and Congress were abandoning reforms that could have forced renewed investment in Main Street. The preservation of the decision-making prerogative of Wall Street had a kind of closed-circuit logic: since the leverage wielded by the banks derived from their control of capital flows, the rejection of policies that would limit their discretion over investments helped ensure their continuing power.

As a result, the reform agenda was confined to relatively modest proposals to regulate the most destructive behaviors of Wall Street. The administration's June 2009 white paper, which set the framework that would become Dodd-Frank, was "far less revolutionary than some either feared or hoped for," noted the financial law firm Davis Polk & Wardwell.[67] We see, in this process, another facet of the pre-legislative phase: even when left alone to shape the initial legislative proposals, executive and congressional leadership remove from consideration most of the policies that might generate elite opposition.[68]

---

66 Joseph Stiglitz, *Freefall: America, Free Markets, and the Sinking of the World Economy* (New York: Norton, 2010), 118. See also Michael Hirsh, "Obama's Old Deal," *Newsweek*, September 6, 2010: 26–9; Kaiser, *Act of Congress*, 129.

67 Quoted in Kaiser, *Act of Congress*, 90. Key elements in the white paper included new systemic oversight power for the Federal Reserve and stricter capital requirements for banks.

68 This routine pre-censorship does not assure a smooth road in later stages, however. Even the bland regulatory proposals crafted during the pre-legislative process

Derivatives regulations were a prime example of this process of government bending to the demands of Wall Street. Derivatives are financial contracts whose value is based on that of other assets. One type of derivatives, mortgage-backed securities, had been central to the financial crisis. Banks had made millions of risky and manipulative home loans, then repackaged those loans into bonds that they sold on the derivatives market. The derivatives had obscured the risk tied to the loans, which caused havoc when lenders raised interest rates and borrowers defaulted. Reform proposals in 2009 stressed the need for two modest changes: new reporting requirements and centralized clearinghouses for derivatives trades, both designed to introduce greater transparency in the market. Yet, even here, the administration's August 2009 draft legislation included major loopholes. For example, derivatives trades between banks and other businesses were exempted from the clearinghouse requirement. One Congress member who was closely involved in the derivatives fight complained that the bill "has so many loopholes that the loophole eats the rule."[69] Barney Frank's House Financial Services Committee then expanded the loopholes still further in its October draft of a derivatives bill—not surprising given that "well-placed sources" reported that "major sections were literally drafted by lawyers for the banking industry."[70]

Banks' influence over the derivatives provisions and other aspects of Dodd-Frank resulted from their use of two main weapons. One, clearly, was campaign cash. Obama was the leading recipient of Wall Street cash in 2008, and his economic team showed it. Timothy Geithner and Lawrence Summers, Obama's top two decision-makers on financial reform, were both members of the Robert Rubin school of Wall Street–friendly economics. The congressional captains of the process, Barney Frank and Chris Dodd, were both major recipients of bank cash. Frank drew over $1 million from the financial sector for the 2008 election, 45 percent of his total. Dodd got $6 million.[71] Banks were not as directly involved in the drafting of Dodd-Frank as industry had been in the case of the Obama trade negotiations and the ACA. But campaign donations helped ensure that they would have strong allies in the drafters. The autonomy of Congress and the administration from Wall Street was thus illusory.

---

would later face fierce resistance from banks, as we will show.

69 Maria Cantwell quoted in Kuttner, *A Presidency in Peril*, 191.

70 Kuttner, *A Presidency in Peril*, 106. The draft sent to Frank in August was a revised version of the June white paper.

71 Kaiser, *Act of Congress*, 89, 129.

A second vital source of Wall Street power was the capital strike: the ongoing disinvestment from the US economy and the threat of continued or even intensified disinvestment if the government imposed new regulations that it found distasteful. Wall Street held the purse strings for the real economy, and it used them. For financial firms, the capital strike typically takes the form of withholding credit and/or raising the prices of their services. Threats were explicitly and frequently communicated to policymakers. When the June 2009 white paper proposed to regulate derivatives, the industry immediately threatened that regulations "could drive up costs for a variety of financial and industrial companies."[72] The testimony of Sheila Bair, the FDIC chair during this period, suggests the frequency with which banks wielded the threat of capital strikes in response to regulatory proposals. Bair recalls that industry representatives constantly warned that "our regulatory initiatives would hurt lending. Throughout my tenure at the FDIC, that was the standard refrain from industry lobbyists virtually anytime we tried to rein in risky practices or ask the industry to pay for the costs of bank failures."[73] Within policymaker circles, Geithner, Summers, and other representatives of Wall Street were especially sensitive to this threat. New York senator Chuck Schumer, a longtime champion of Wall Street, warned Dodd in January 2009 that new regulation "could put New York at a competitive disadvantage to London and other global financial centers."[74]

In response to these threats of disinvestment, policymakers repeatedly sought to assure Wall Street about their determination not to "hurt lending" by harming business confidence. White House language was carefully calibrated. When Obama later made an extemporaneous remark in a 2014 interview about potentially "restructuring the banks themselves," White House spokespersons moved quickly to dispel bankers' fear of such initiatives,[75] since even a vague hint of such restructuring would reduce confidence and further reduce investment in the capital-starved economy.

It is worth noting that the economic crisis had nothing to do with onerous government regulations. Indeed, the lack of regulation had caused the crisis. And there was no "natural," market-driven reason

---

72 Theo Francis, "Financial Regulation: Industry Objections Increasing," bloomberg.com, June 26, 2009.

73 Bair, *Bull by the Horns*, 24.

74 Kaiser, *Act of Congress*, 73.

75 Damian Paletta, "Obama: Further Bank Curbs Are Needed," *WSJ*, July 3, 2014: C2.

why granting Wall Street's demands for light regulation would get credit flowing again. But there was a political reason: granting those demands might convince bankers to trust that the government was on its side, enough to release the capital needed to ease the economic disruption. This deference to banks was necessary because Obama, Dodd, Frank, and the rest of the reformers had committed to safeguarding private control over investment decisions. Once they made that decision, they deprived themselves of the power to defy Wall Street threats. Ultimately, they also jeopardized their own quest to "save Wall Street from itself."[76]

Climate Reform: Making Sure It Works for You

Nowhere, however, was the accommodation to capitalists more catastrophic than in the failed climate legislation of 2009–10. In 2008, Obama had promised that his presidency would be "the moment when the rise of the oceans began to slow and our planet began to heal."[77] At the time, a number of congressional leaders were pursuing climate legislation to curb greenhouse gas emissions. The impetus for Obama's rhetoric and the congressional bills came partly from electoral considerations. Government action to regulate polluters had strong public support, including large majorities favoring a global treaty to reduce carbon emissions and domestic regulations that would force utilities to use more clean energy sources.[78] Moreover, Obama and the key congressional advocates of climate reform were not big recipients of donations from fossil fuel companies, in theory giving them relative freedom to pursue reform.

But there was a key difference between climate reform and the other reforms we have analyzed. Climate chaos did not pose the immediate threat to most corporate bottom lines that a major recession, rising healthcare costs, or reckless financiers did. For this reason, the demand for climate legislation was less widespread in the business world. Some corporate support for a cap on greenhouse gas emissions did materialize, including from ten Fortune 500 companies that joined with four environmental organizations to form the US Climate Action Partnership (USCAP) in January 2007. But it was probably driven more by those

76 See note 65.
77 "Obama's Nomination Victory Speech in St. Paul," huffingtonpost.com, June 3, 2008.
78 "Obama, McCain Supporters Largely Agree on Approaches to Energy, Climate Change," worldpublicopinion.org, September 23, 2008.

corporations' desire to preempt EPA regulations or other unfavorable policy changes than by any economic forecast about the threat of global warming to profits.[79] Even the USCAP members' commitment to legislation was highly tenuous. The limited breadth and intensity of corporate support, alongside furious resistance from most of the top polluters, would ultimately scuttle all the major climate bills introduced in 2009–10.

The pre-legislative phase closely paralleled that of the other progressive bills, in that robust progressive options were taken off the table even before congressional deliberation got underway. Congressional leaders, the administration, and mainstream environmental groups all realized that "any bill needed to get the power barons to sign on."[80] Senator Joseph Lieberman, who cosponsored the Senate's major climate bill in 2010, would later recount that his team "worked very hard to get everybody on common ground—that is to say, particularly industry, particularly the utility industry and environmentalists."[81] Obama did not make climate a priority in his first term, but he did promise business leaders in March 2009 that in the event of any new climate legislation, "we're going to make sure that it works for you."[82]

The imperative of securing business support was a lesson of past legislative battles on climate. In 1993, the National Association of Manufacturers, American Petroleum Institute, and other corporate lobbies had killed a carbon tax proposal. In 2008, business opposition, including from high-profile USCAP member Jim Rogers of Duke Energy, had led the Senate to defeat a bill sponsored by Lieberman and Mark Warner.[83]

Now, in the early negotiations between policymakers and polluters,

---

79   In April 2007, the Supreme Court confirmed that the EPA had the authority and duty to regulate greenhouse gas emissions under the Clean Air Act (*Massachusetts et al. v. Environmental Protection Agency et al.*, 549 U.S. 497 [2007]). In 2012, the DC Court of Appeals upheld the EPA's "endangerment" finding (*Coalition for Responsible Regulation, Inc. v. EPA*, 684 F.3d 102 [D.C. Cir. 2012]). In 2016, however, the Supreme Court placed a stay on the EPA's rule to cut emissions from coal-fired power plants. The Trump ascension appeared to signal the rule's demise; see Lisa Friedman, "U.S. to Propose Coal-Plant Rules Be Up to States," *NYT*, August 18, 2018: A1.

80   Eric Pooley, *The Climate War: True Believers, Power Brokers, and the Fight to Save the Earth* (New York: Hyperion, 2010), 193.

81   Quoted in Josh Voorhees and Robin Bravender, "Clock Winding Down on Carbon Cap Efforts," *E&E Daily*, July 16, 2010.

82   Quoted in Pooley, *Climate War*, 345. Obama made his promise to the Business Roundtable, one of the major corporate coalitions. On the White House's refusal to prioritize climate legislation see ibid., 279–80, 326, 348–9, 392, 417–18, 431–2.

83   Pooley, *Climate War*, 86–7, 220, 226.

the mutually understood business condition for any new legislation was that "it work for," and not "punish," business. Policymakers would seek "to arrive at a grand bargain that could reduce greenhouse gas emissions without punishing consumers *or corporations*," as journalist Eric Pooley describes.[84] Any new regulations would need to abide by the standard compensatory principle: infringements on corporate profits or control must be balanced out by inducements that bolster corporate profits or control. Encouragement of renewable energy was permissible as long as it conformed to the "all-of-the-above" maxim on energy— that is, as long as its scale remained modest and it did not target the fossil fuel industry. The major Senate legislation could aim to cut emissions, but it also aimed to expand offshore oil drilling, to "jettison cumbersome regulations" on nuclear power, and to promote the mythical "clean coal."[85]

Enormous efforts were made to win industry support. The major House legislation, sponsored by Henry Waxman and Edward Markey and narrowly passed in June 2009, was largely based on the joint proposal of USCAP and the Environmental Defense Fund.[86] Waxman-Markey (and all of the other climate bills in 2009–2010) eschewed a carbon tax, which would impose a fee on carbon emissions and thus give business an incentive to use more renewable energy. Instead, the bills opted for a cap-and-trade approach that would establish a ceiling on total carbon emissions while allowing individual businesses to purchase the right to maintain or even expand their own level of emissions.

While either a tax or cap-and-trade had the potential to achieve major emissions reductions, the details of the design matter tremendously, since they determine the incentives and disincentives that are central to regulating business behavior. For instance, how low would the cap be set? If it were set too high, the price of emissions permits would be too low to influence business decisions. Would emissions permits be auctioned off to businesses, with the proceeds going into public coffers to fund renewable energy investments, or would they be given away to polluters for free? If the latter, polluters would effectively be rewarded, and there would be no new public revenue to fund

---

84   Ibid., 402. Emphasis added.
85   John Kerry and Lindsey Graham, "Yes We Can (Pass Climate Change Legislation)," *NYT*, October 11, 2009: WK11. On the myth of clean coal see David Biello, "The Carbon Capture Fallacy," *Scientific American*, January 2016: 59–65.
86   Pooley, *Climate War*, 375.

renewables. Would consumers receive rebates to shield them from polluters' attempts to pass along the costs? If not, the price hikes at the gas pump would punish and enrage the public.[87] We will address some of these details in the next chapter, since they were determined by congressional deliberations.

One starting premise of Waxman-Markey's pre-legislative phase was especially notable, though: the need to give away the vast majority of emissions permits for free, rather than through auction. The two major Senate bills introduced after Waxman-Markey's passage, the Kerry-Boxer (September 2009) and Kerry-Lieberman (May 2010) bills, followed suit.[88] Unlike these other bills, a December 2009 Senate bill that proposed to auction off all emissions permits (while refunding 75 percent of proceeds directly to consumers) failed even to achieve serious consideration, and went nowhere.[89] Pooley writes that although all the leading Democratic presidential candidates in 2008 had promised to support auctions for all permits, they "knew it would never make it into law, because [free] allowances were the sweetener any bill needed to get the power barons to sign on. Call them transitional assistance or call them bribes—if you didn't have free allowances, you didn't have industry."[90] Polluters were demanding the freedom to continue polluting for free. Without it, there would be no legislation.

The explanation for this pattern, as in the other cases we have examined, lies largely in the structural power exercised by business. The constant war cry of polluters was that the climate bills would impose exorbitant costs that would either limit energy resources or increase energy prices for household consumers and energy-dependent businesses. The threat to move manufacturing operations offshore in response to the predicted rise in energy prices was often made explicitly. The president of the American Chemistry Council, for example,

---

87   For general discussion of cap-and-trade and other climate policy options see Robin Hahnel, *Green Economics: Confronting the Ecological Crisis* (Armonk, NY: M. E. Sharpe, 2011), 127ff.

88   Waxman-Markey would have initially given away 85 percent of permits for free, Kerry-Boxer 90 percent, and Kerry-Lieberman 75 percent. In the future these figures would gradually be reduced. See Pooley, *Climate War*, 397; Pew Center on Global Climate Change, "At a Glance: Clean Energy Jobs and American Power Act," October 2009; Darren Samuelsohn, "Kerry-Lieberman Bill Uses 'Fewer Buckets' in Giving Out Highly Prized Allowances," *E&E Daily*, May 14, 2010.

89   On the CLEAR Act sponsored by Maria Cantwell and Susan Collins see Mike Sandler, "The Cantwell-Collins CLEAR Act Helps Consumers, the Climate, and the Economy," huffingtonpost.com, December 14, 2009.

90   Pooley, *Climate War*, 193.

warned that a cap on utilities' emissions "would harm the global competitiveness of the U.S. chemical industry and stall economic recovery." The leader of the American Iron and Steel Institute warned about regulations "causing the leakage of jobs and emissions to unregulated jurisdictions."[91] The message was reinforced by congressional politicians with close ties to polluters. Democrats like steel industry champion Mike Doyle of the House Energy and Commerce Committee warned of capital flight if a price were placed on carbon. The crafters of the main 2010 Senate bill, John Kerry and Lindsey Graham, took pains to assure business that their legislation would cut emissions "without hindering global competitiveness or driving more jobs overseas."[92]

In another parallel with healthcare and financial reform, the need to maintain the profitability of polluters generally went unquestioned. For most politicians, regulators, and commentators, the threat of capital flight and price hikes was not a political strategy but an objective law of nature: *of course* polluters would pass along their costs, and we would be powerless to stop them. This assumption is evident in journalist Eric Pooley's own rebuttal to those who insisted that polluters should pay for their emissions permits:

> The punitive fantasy missed an important detail. The polluter wouldn't really pay; the polluter's *customers* would, because regulated utilities pass their costs to the rate payers ... Heavy industries that released a great deal of carbon dioxide—paper-, cement-, and steel-makers, for instance—were already fighting for their lives against foreign competitors with lower labor costs. If cap and trade raised their energy costs, it could put them out of business or drive their manufacturing facilities overseas to non-cap-and-trade countries. You'd have to be crazy not to give them free allowances. It could be the difference between keeping them in business and letting them die.[93]

This logic is misleading on two counts. First, it takes the polluters at their word when they complained about cost increases imposed on their businesses. As with most progressive reforms, business habitually exaggerated the potential hit to their profit margins; a modest reduction in their high profits would not put them out of business, it would simply

---

91   Voorhees and Bravender, "Clock Winding Down." The latter is a direct quote.
92   Pooley, *Climate War*, 344; Kerry and Graham, "Yes We Can."
93   Pooley, *Climate War*, 192.

force them to absorb part of the cost of pollution reduction. Second, whether the costs were real or invented, the argument ignores the ways that government action can neutralize business attempts to offload those costs. A climate bill could include a rebate mechanism that reimbursed consumers for rising utility and gasoline prices. And "regulated utilities" are, of course, regulated. By law, government agencies like the Federal Energy Regulatory Commission must typically approve proposals by utilities "to pass their costs to the rate payers."

But while the laws of economics did not require policymakers to avoid punishing polluters, the polluters' centrality to the US economy lent them awesome disruptive power. Continued high unemployment gave business threats even more salience. As business leaders warned, they had the power to "stall economic recovery" by raising prices or laying off workers. Fossil fuel and especially manufacturing companies could plausibly threaten to relocate to "unregulated jurisdictions," wreaking havoc on local and state economies. These threats were reinforced by politicians on key congressional committees like Mike Doyle and Rick Boucher, who depended on polluters (steel and coal, respectively) both for campaign cash and for employment in their districts.[94] Whether or not the polluters would *actually* move or lay off workers is not clear, since environmental regulations typically account for only a very small portion of total business costs.[95] But the threat was still credible. Most climate reformers in government thus agreed to respect polluter profitability and control over investment decisions—they *would have to be crazy not to.* As in the cases of healthcare and financial reform, it was a closed-circuit logic: polluters wielded power based on their control over investments, and the government's failure to challenge that control undermined attempts at reform.

Disruptive Movements and the Birth of Progressive Legislation

In none of the cases we have just discussed was social movement disruption essential to the initiation of the reform bills. However, movements do sometimes influence the legislative agenda by impelling policymakers to introduce progressive reform bills.[96] Consider two examples. First, the

94 Ibid., 329.
95 Eban Goodstein, *The Trade-Off Myth: Fact and Fictions about Jobs and the Environment* (Washington, DC: Island, 1999), esp. 41–69.
96 Many scholars acknowledge this point, but say little about the role of

December 2010 repeal of "Don't Ask, Don't Tell" was the result of internal disruption and activists' targeting of the military with legal action, which led top commanders to change their position on DADT. While the "most affected" institution in this case was the military, not business, the DADT repeal illustrates how movements can sometimes force elite institutions to support new legislation.

A second and better-known historical example is the labor legislation of the 1930s. In this case, disruption caused a split between state and corporate elites. Incessant strikes and other working-class protests drove Congress to pass a bill guaranteeing workers' right to collective bargaining, over the opposition of business leaders. As in the Dodd-Frank Act of 2010, state officials took it upon themselves to protect the long-term interests of business through system-stabilizing reform. Unlike with financial reform, there was no substantial business support for unionization rights. But there was a mass movement disruptive enough to neutralize the ferocious opposition of employers.

A Threatened Military Consents to DADT Repeal

The DADT policy had originated in 1993 when President Clinton sought to legalize military service by gays and lesbians. When the Joint Chiefs of Staff concluded that the threat of disruption outweighed the benefits of an open policy, DADT was enacted as a compromise: gays and lesbians could stay in the military, as long as they abstained from any homosexual activity and didn't talk about it.[97] Although Clinton was nominally commander-in-chief of the military, and although Congress nominally had the power to make laws, in practice the permission of the top military brass was necessary for any major change in the institution's policy. The same relationship continued after Barack Obama took office, requiring Obama and congressional Democrats to seek the support of the Joint Chiefs of Staff if they wanted to end DADT. Just as the "permission" of the "most affected" corporations is typically

---

disruption in generating pressure; e.g., Frank R. Baumgartner and Christine Mahoney, "Social Movements, the Rise of New Issues, and the Public Agenda," in *Routing the Opposition: Social Movements, Public Policy, and Democracy*, ed. David Meyer, Valerie Jenness, and Helen Ingram (Minneapolis: University of Minnesota Press, 2005), 65–86. In our view large non-disruptive movements may exert some impact, but less than large disruptive movements.

97   Steve Kornacki, " 'Don't Ask, Don't Tell': 1993–2010," *Salon*, December 18, 2010; Carl Hulse, "Senate Ends Military Ban on Gays Serving Openly," *NYT*, December 19, 2010: A1.

necessary for reforms affecting their interests, the permission of the military leadership was necessary for reforms affecting the military.

The Obama White House followed this protocol carefully. When it took up the issue in early 2010, it "took pains to get Pentagon and military leaders aboard," promising to avoid "an executive order or legal fight."[98] While an executive order was technically within the president's power, the Pentagon "wouldn't let it happen in a million years," according to one of the lead organizers of the repeal campaign, Alexander Nicholson.[99] The administration avoided advocating repeal in its 2010 "defense policy transmittals," which typically accompany annual military spending bills, and its Department of Justice quietly sought to prevent any legal challenges to DADT.[100]

A major step toward the necessary consensus came in February 2010, when the Chairman of the Joint Chiefs of Staff, Mike Mullen, and Defense Secretary Robert Gates publicly voiced support for repeal in testimony before the Senate Armed Services Committee. Nonetheless, there were still divisions among military commanders, some of whom "warned that changing the practice would prove disruptive."[101] This dissension led the Pentagon to undertake a nine-month comprehensive review of the likely impact on soldiers' morale. The results of the review, announced on November 30, predicted "few risks" from repeal. Additional high-level military voices endorsed repeal.[102] Though the Joint Chiefs still lacked internal consensus, there was strong support for repeal among some, including the chairman, and the opposition of the holdouts had been weakened.

During the nine months preceding the completion of the Pentagon study, congressional advocates of repeal began quietly drafting repeal

98   Kornacki, "'Don't Ask, Don't Tell.'" See also Craig Whitlock and Greg Jaffe, "Pentagon Now Backs Gays Serving Openly in the Military," *WP*, February 3, 2010: A1.

99   Alexander Nicholson, *Fighting to Serve: Behind the Scenes in the War to Repeal "Don't Ask, Don't Tell"* (Chicago, IL: Chicago Review Press, 2012), 78.

100   Nicholson, *Fighting to Serve*, 122, 201–2. Regarding the DoJ's defense of DADT, the administration claimed that it was obliged to uphold all current laws. But it went above and beyond in its aggressive efforts to block lawsuits from even getting a hearing. Its later decision not to defend the Clinton-era Defense of Marriage Act in court demonstrates the flexibility of the executive branch's enforcement obligations (ibid., 215). The difference between the administration's behavior in the two cases may reflect its greater need to maintain military leaders' "confidence," versus the confidence of religious-right institutions, to which it was not particularly beholden.

101   Hulse, "Senate Ends Military Ban."

102   Lisa Daniel, "Repeal of 'Don't Ask, Don't Tell' Offers Few Risks, Report Finds," *DoD News*, November 30, 2010; Karen Parrish, "Joints Chiefs Vice Chairman Recommends 'Don't Ask' Repeal," *DoD News*, December 3, 2010.

legislation in the House and Senate.[103] Participants in the formulation process understood that "Pentagon support would be a must to gain the support of a critical mass of senators." To secure that Pentagon support, sponsors added a provision that "gave the Pentagon the power to dictate how long it would take to put the new policy into effect, and it actually gave them veto power over doing so if they decided they just didn't want to."[104] The amendment was a telling reminder of where the real power resided.

But the fact was that top military leaders, starting with Mullen, were slowly coming around to the idea. Why? The key difference between 1993 and 2010, when Congress finally repealed DADT, was that, by 2010, a sizeable movement of LGBT soldiers had put increasing pressure on military leaders. [105] The pressure took two main forms. One was the disruption within the military caused by the discharge of over 13,000 soldiers since 1993. That figure included scores of Arabic and Farsi linguists who were essential to the prosecution of US wars in the Middle East and Afghanistan.[106] The discharges occurred in a variety of circumstances. Some came when LGBT soldiers openly refused to hide their identities, some came when they were accidentally discovered, and some came after commanders or other soldiers targeted individuals as a form of retaliation. Whatever the immediate cause, the loss of soldiers was disruptive, especially in the case of high-skill personnel. And, as the number of openly LGBT soldiers continued to increase, the military faced two unsavory choices: either invest resources in expelling and repelling LGBT soldiers, losing more and more valuable personnel, or tolerate an ever-growing number of openly LGBT soldiers. Either course of action might be highly disruptive.

The second source of disruption was the multiple lawsuits that LGBT soldiers and their supporters launched against DADT in the first decade

---

103   The content of these bills was based largely on the preexisting Military Readiness Enhancement Act, first introduced in 2005.

104   Nicholson, *Fighting to Serve*, 165–7.

105   The shorthand "LGBT" is somewhat misleading here, in that the terms of the public debate focused mostly on "gay and lesbian" soldiers (with some LGB soldiers distancing themselves from their transgender counterparts), and the 2010 DADT repeal did not legalize military service by openly transgender soldiers. Repeal of the prohibition against transgender soldiers came in 2016, though Trump has sought their re-prohibition.

106   DoD, Jeh Charles Johnson, Carter F. Ham, Gerald F. Goodwin, and Benjamin Bryant, *Report of the Comprehensive Review of the Issues Associated with a Repeal of "Don't Ask, Don't Tell,"* November 30, 2010: 23; Stephen Benjamin, "Don't Ask, Don't Translate," *NYT*, June 8, 2007: A29.

of the millennium. At first, the government had been able to rely on the federal courts to quickly quash legal challenges to DADT. But over the years, the legal challenges had become more frequent and robust. In September 2010, a federal district court judge in California ruled the policy unconstitutional and followed with an injunction prohibiting the discharge of gay and lesbian service members.[107] Though the decision came from a lower court, it was treated by LGBT activists as parallel to the Supreme Court's 1954 *Brown v. Board of Education* ruling against school segregation. Although a federal appeals court soon suspended the judge's order, there was a tangible possibility that either the ruling or a subsequent lawsuit would be endorsed by the Supreme Court in the midst of a rising tide of gay soldiers violating DADT. The disruption was not going to go away.

When announcing the results of the Pentagon review in late November 2010, Defense Secretary Gates invoked the threat of further legal challenges and the potential for personnel disruption as key factors in the decision to abandon DADT:

> [It is] only a matter of time before the federal courts are drawn once more into the fray, with the very real possibility that this change would be imposed immediately by judicial fiat—by far the most disruptive and damaging scenario I can imagine, and the one most hazardous to military morale, readiness and battlefield performance.[108]

The threat of a losing legal fight tipped the scales among military commanders. According to the *New York Times,* the decisive factor in the repeal decision was that voluntarily "ending the ban" was deemed "a better alternative to a court-ordered end."[109] The threat of judicial action may also have influenced commanders' interpretation of the review released in November, which included extensive polling of service members. While most publicity stressed soldiers' support for repeal, the review in fact found that "around 30 percent overall (and 40–60 percent in the Marine Corps and in various combat arms specialties)" expressed "negative views

---

107   Jim Garamone, "Department Abides by 'Don't Ask, Don't Tell' Injunction," *DoD News,* October 14, 2010.

108   Robert M. Gates, "Statement on 'Don't Ask, Don't Tell' Report," DoD, November 30, 2010.

109   Hulse, "Senate Ends Military Ban"; Nicholson, *Fighting to Serve,* 201, 209–10. Nicholson's insider account stresses the importance of this factor in boosting support for repeal within the Pentagon, the White House, and Congress.

or concerns" about repeal.[110] The Pentagon might just as well have empha-sized those high numbers in choosing to oppose repeal. But most Pentagon leaders came to deem the potential disruption of maintaining the policy to be greater than the potential disruption of ending it on their own terms.[111]

The movement was responsible for this shift in thinking. Soldier resistance had put direct pressure on military leaders and on the judici-ary. By threatening the military and enlisting another powerful segment of the state against the DADT policy, the movement convinced military leaders that ending DADT was the lesser-evil option. Then, and only then, did the repeal bill pass through Congress to the president's desk.

Trying to Close the Gates of Hell

A much more overt form of disruption led to the progressive labor legislation of the 1930s. In contrast to the Obama era, that decade saw a number of major social-democratic reforms that significantly altered the balance of forces in society. Several of those reforms reshaped the relationship between bosses and workers. The 1935 National Labor Relations Act (NLRA), often called the "Wagner Act" after key sponsor Senator Robert Wagner of New York, sought to guarantee workers' right to unionize and engage in collective bargaining with their employers. This and other New Deal reforms were deeply flawed, most notably in their racist exclusion of agricultural and domestic workers (who were disproportionately black) at the behest of Southern capitalists. But the Wagner Act nonetheless imposed substantial and unwanted constraints on major corporations.

The Wagner Act, and the similar laws that preceded it, were mainly a response to the explosive worker unrest affecting key industries. Strikes and other disruptive actions plagued business owners in

---

110   DoD et al., *Report of the Comprehensive Review*, 4.

111   Apparently, the Pentagon knew that repeal might endanger recruitment, but apparently considered a decline in enlistment rates to be less disruptive than maintain-ing the policy. Over a quarter of military personnel said they would be less likely to recommend enlistment to friends or family as a result of repeal, versus just 6 percent who said repeal would make them more likely to do so (ibid., 68). On the other hand, there is evidence that leaders considered that repeal might boost recruitment by making gays and lesbians (and perhaps other liberal young people) more likely to enlist, as when Gates spoke of the need for a military that "welcomes all who are qual-ified and capable" ("Statement on 'Don't Ask, Don't Tell' Report"). Joseph Lieberman was motivated to sponsor Senate repeal legislation in part out of a desire to expand military recruitment programs on college campuses that had banned them due to the military's antigay discrimination (Nicholson, *Fighting to Serve*, 59–60, 129–30).

1933–34, and even conjured fears of revolutionary change if elites did not act prudently to stem the tide. Wagner cited the "rising tide of industrial discontent" to justify the need for reform. His counterpart in the House, William Connery, urged his colleagues to support the House version by cautioning that "you have not yet seen the gates of hell opened."[112] These dire warnings were not mere hyperbole designed to sway their opponents in Congress. Wagner and his allies had both principled and pragmatic motives: they did believe in workers' right to unionize, but they were driven just as much by the desire to end economic disruption.[113] The strikes were the most immediate reflection of that disruption, though for Wagner the problem went deeper. In his view the structural root of the disruption in the post-1929 economy was workers' low purchasing power, a problem that he thought could be ameliorated through collective bargaining. Wagner was no radical. He in fact denounced many strikes and opposed a bill to limit the workweek to thirty hours. His pragmatic goal was, in the words of one scholar, to "complement the existing organization of American capitalism and allow it to continue fulfilling its endless potential."[114]

At first, Wagner was very lonely. His 1934 bill found scant support in Congress and President Roosevelt refused to endorse it. The Senate Labor Committee substituted a much weaker version that, when passed, was simply disregarded by industry.[115] A year later, however, Wagner's 1935 bill was overwhelmingly approved by both the House and Senate, and signed by Roosevelt. Why did Roosevelt and most members of Congress suddenly change their minds? Answering this question requires a closer examination of events between the time of Roosevelt's 1933 inauguration and the July 1935 signing of the new law.

Roosevelt did not take office in 1933 with the intention of overhauling labor laws. He had campaigned on a platform of fiscal austerity and

---

112   Both quoted in Michael Goldfield, "Worker Insurgency, Radical Organization, and New Deal Labor Legislation," *APSR* 83, no. 4 (1989): 1273.

113   See the interviews with Wagner's assistant Leon Keyserling and other key players in Kenneth M. Casebeer, "Holder of the Pen: An Interview with Leon Keyserling on Drafting the Wagner Act," *University of Miami Law Review* 42, no. 2 (1987): 300, 309; Theodore J. St. Antoine, "How the Wagner Act Came to Be: A Prospectus," *Michigan Law Review* 96, no. 8 (1998): 2205–7.

114   Christopher L. Tomlins, *The State and the Unions: Labor Relations, Law, and the Organized Labor Movement in America, 1880–1960* (Cambridge: Cambridge University Press, 1985), 104 (quote), 109–10, 132.

115   Irving Bernstein, *Turbulent Years: A History of the American Worker, 1933–1941* (Boston, MA: Houghton Mifflin, 1969), 192, 195–7, 205.

had made no mention of government protecting workers' right to collective bargaining. Even upon signing the 1933 National Industrial Recovery Act (NIRA), Roosevelt called for "mutual confidence and help" between workers and owners.[116] The new law's provision on collective bargaining went entirely unenforced, as employers and the federal government simply ignored it. In March 1934, Roosevelt sealed its death when he supported an auto industry proposal that effectively permitted company unions and rejected the principle of exclusive representation sought by labor unions.[117]

The administration's approach began to change only after a surge of strikes over the right to organize in 1933–34. The number of workdays lost to strikes more than quadrupled between the first and second halves of 1933. In 1934, an estimated 1.5 million workers took part in 1,856 work stoppages.[118] By summer 1933, this disruption had started to compel a positive response from government officials and some corporate titans.

The Standard Oil and General Electric executives who were advising the National Recovery Administration joined labor representatives in urging the creation of a National Labor Board that would handle labor disputes. Historian Irving Bernstein notes that their concern, and that of Democrats in government, was "that these stoppages would impede the recovery of business." In August 1933 Roosevelt agreed to create the board at their suggestion, announcing its establishment by simply releasing the statement of the business and labor advisers.[119] This manner of establishing a new state agency was revealing: the leaders of top corporations changed their minds, leading the president to change his.

Roosevelt nonetheless opposed Wagner's 1934 bill, contributing to

---

116   Bernstein, *Turbulent Years*, 3, 172 (quote).

117   Ibid., 172–85. Section 7(a) of NIRA technically prohibited employers from forcing workers to join company unions or to sign "yellow-dog" contracts promising not to join independent unions.

118   Ibid., 172–3, 185, 217. NIRA's section on collective bargaining unwittingly helped unleash the strikes, much to Roosevelt's chagrin.

119   Ibid., 173. The NLB was a predecessor of the NLRB. It was headed by Wagner and included three representatives from labor and three from business (Walter Teagle of Standard Oil, Gerard Swope of GE, and Louis Kirstein of Filene's). For Teagle and Swope's other roles in advising the administration see Thomas Ferguson, *Golden Rule: The Investment Theory of Party Competition and the Logic of Money-Driven Political Systems* (Chicago, IL: University of Chicago Press, 1995), 152–3. Ferguson argues that capital-intensive industries like oil and high-tech manufacturing (and politicians from regions where those industries were concentrated, like Robert Wagner of New York) were the most likely to support New Deal reforms.

its demise in spring of that year. In June came a surprise, though. As Christopher Tomlins observes, "the administration found itself suddenly confronted with a massive strike wave in mass production industries without any policy to deal with it." Roosevelt had undercut his own National Labor Board through his settlement with the auto companies. Thus "the only option appeared to be a hasty resort to a stopgap." On June 13, he requested that Congress pass an "emergency enabling resolution," which became known as Public Resolution 44.[120] The resolution provided for the creation of a National Labor Relations Board designed to promote conciliation and avert strikes. Roosevelt was not yet supporting unionization rights. But he was shifting, in response to the disruption, toward activating the government as the mediating force that could end the chronic work stoppages that threatened to deepen the Depression.

The Democratic position in Congress also underwent a marked change as labor disruption exploded between 1933 and 1935. The continued disruption of the strikes, and the new agencies' inability to overcome employer intransigence, helped convince Democrats that the only way to close "the gates of hell" was through Wagner's legislation. Wagner's 1935 bill won newfound support from the Senate Labor Committee chair and other powerful figures, including Roosevelt himself, who finally offered his tepid endorsement at the last minute. It passed the Senate and House by large majorities and was signed by Roosevelt in July.[121] Implementing the law would be a very different story: it would go mostly unenforced until the end of the 1930s, as we will see in Chapter 4. But labor disruption had formed the key impetus for congressional passage, compelling government to enact a law that most in Congress and the Roosevelt administration had opposed only months before. The role of mass disruption in producing government reforms marks a major difference between the Wagner Act and most progressive legislation of the Obama era.

---

120 Tomlins, *State and the Unions*, 127.
121 Bernstein, *Turbulent Years*, 185, 340–2. Theda Skocpol points to the decline in strikes in early 1935 to argue that the 1934 midterm elections and Wagner himself were more important in producing the Democrats' shift. But as Goldfield notes, Congress's *perception* in early 1935 was one of continued labor unrest. Conservative union officials in the American Federation of Labor (AFL) and their sympathizers in government also feared that the business-friendly AFL officialdom would be displaced by more radical activists. See Theda Skocpol, "Political Response to Capitalist Crisis: Neo-Marxist Theories of the State and the Case of the New Deal," *PAS* 10, no. 2 (1980): 187–9; Goldfield, "Worker Insurgency," 1273, 1276.

There is one other big difference. Unlike Obama-era reforms affecting business, the Wagner Act did not have the support of many capitalists when it was passed. Congress and the Roosevelt administration acted without the consent of corporate elites, who were almost unanimously opposed to the law at the time of its passage. Obama's reforms met with capitalist opposition, but they also had support from counter-coalitions of capitalists. The Wagner Act is thus an example of how mass disruption can expand the limits of what is possible. It drove state elites to enact reforms over the fierce and unified opposition of business. Notably, however, the movement's disruptive pressures were directed mainly at employers, not politicians. It was the latter who had the foresight to understand that continued unrest imperiled business profits and potentially capitalism itself. The politicians then acted, independently of business, but with the goal of protecting business's long-term interests. In this case, it was the far-sighted captains of state, rather than business, who initiated progressive reforms meant to stabilize the system.[122]

Conclusion

In this chapter, we have analyzed some of the pathways through which congressional legislation is initiated. In one pathway, politicians introduce bills that advance elite interests while hurting most of the public. Corporate tax cuts and foreign trade and investment treaties are two of the clearest examples of the Obama and Trump eras. These bills originated only partly from politicians' desire to reward campaign donors or advance their own class interests. They were mainly aimed at bolstering business confidence and investment in the economy in the context of a historic disinvestment crisis.

The second category of bills we analyzed are those containing a major progressive thrust, in that they potentially infringe on the profits or decision-making power of business or other elite institutions. The pressure for these bills can come from several different sources. One is elections and public opinion. Widespread public concern around an issue, particularly among an election victor's voting base, can help establish a legislative agenda, as illustrated by the healthcare, financial,

---

122   There were still real limits to what working-class disruption accomplished: the reforms excluded most black workers, for instance. In this case, where business was not "at the table," it was state officials themselves who took certain options, such as black inclusion, "off the table" (though they were in contact with Southern capitalists).

climate, and DADT repeal bills of 2009–10, which all originated in part due to the 2008 election results and public sentiment. But this electoral impetus by itself is insufficient. Active support by business or other elite institutions is necessary before a bill can be introduced.

Elite support for progressive reform can itself have various causes. Certain sectors of the business world may favor "progressive" legislation for their own purposes, as we saw in the case of the healthcare and financial reform bills.[123] The voice of those business sectors is amplified when government officials are far-sighted enough to see the need for reforms to keep the system stable and profitable. Barack Obama was one such visionary. Part of his motivation for financial reform was to "protect those financial institutions" and a system "based on the pursuit of profits"; this vision was amplified by the presence of business representatives in the legislative planning process.

Whether or not corporations initially support a reform proposal, if reform becomes a real possibility they will usually seek a seat at the table. Access to the negotiations then allows them to prevent the consideration of provisions they find offensive or defeat them after they are aired. The threat of disruptive action—usually in the form of threatened or actual disinvestment—becomes a key negotiating tool. Astute politicians internalize this logic, so that progressive options are often discarded preemptively without any visible business veto being exercised. The early framing of reform legislation in the Obama era offers many examples.

The latter part of this chapter introduced another factor into the equation, highlighting how disruptive mass pressure can alter the balance of forces and compel the introduction of progressive bills. The combination of elections, public support, and business support may generate some progressive reform, but that reform will usually be weak when mass disruption is absent. Strong reform bills require disruptive and sustained mass action that threatens the elite institutions that wield power over the policy process. This disruption can counter the disruptive power of elite institutions. It can force the leaders of business and state institutions to

---

123 Many historical analogues exist. For instance, businesses have sometimes lobbied for increased regulation of their own industries due to fears of competition. See Gary D. Libecap, "The Rise of the Chicago Packers and the Origins of Meat Inspection and Antitrust," *Economic Inquiry* 30, no. 2 (1992): 242–62; Marc T. Law and Gary D. Libecap, "The Determinants of Progressive Era Reform: The Pure Food and Drugs Act of 1906," in *Corruption and Reform: Lessons from America's Economic History*, eds. Edward L. Glaeser and Claudia Goldin (Chicago, IL: University of Chicago Press, 2006), 319–42; Kenneth Prewitt and Alan Stone, *The Ruling Elites: Elite Theory, Power, and American Democracy* (New York: Harper & Row, 1973), 31–52.

alter their cost-benefit analyses, supporting legislative reform as a lesser evil compared to continued disruption. In the DADT repeal, we caught a glimpse of how a relatively small but strategically placed group of organizers forced the passage of progressive legislation, by exerting disruptive pressure on the "most affected" elite institution and altering the calculations of its leaders. In this case, the key elite institution was the military rather than business, but similar pressures can move business to support the introduction of new legislation.

In the example of 1930s labor legislation, the sustained disruption to the corporations at the center of the US economy paved the way for a reform bill much more robust than anything even considered during the Obama era. Business leaders did not support the 1935 Wagner Act in large numbers, though they may have tempered their resistance to it behind the scenes, figuring they could just ignore it once it passed (which they did, as we'll discuss in Chapter 4). Instead, far-sighted visionaries in government understood the threat that working-class disruption posed to capitalists, better than the capitalists themselves did.

The story of 1930s labor law reform suggests why Obama-era progressive reforms were so weak. The weakness of Obama-era social movements was the result not just of their small size but of the flawed strategies of the leading movement organizations. The most visible segments of the healthcare, financial reform, and environmental movements focused on insider bargaining in Washington and strove to maintain cordial relations with corporations and politicians. Some of them did target corporations, but in the wrong way: through polite outreach rather than mass disruption.[124]

The shortage of mass disruption gave business leaders even greater freedom to shape the reform bills as they were debated in Congress, as we will see.

---

124   There were disruptive currents *within* these movements, some of which expanded in numbers and activity after 2010. But their impact on legislation is so far unclear.

2

Seeking Consensus with Industry: The Revision Process in Congress

Today, virtually no piece of legislation can get passed unless it has the OK from corporate America.

Bernie Sanders, tweet from June 20, 2013

You know, just about whatever anyone proposes, no matter what it is, the banks will come out and claim that it will restrict credit and harm the economy . . . It's all bullshit.

Former Federal Reserve chairman Paul Volcker, ca. 2009

"Laws are like sausages, it is better not to see them being made," the nineteenth-century Prussian leader Otto von Bismarck reportedly said. Commentators on US congressional politics often echo this sentiment. Dozens or hundreds of unsavory elements are slipped in as the sausage's skin expands. Those who must consume the final product are often unaware of what it actually contains.

The analogy captures the way in which entrenched interests shape legislation in their favor, usually to the detriment of the broader society. As we have seen, this metaphor could be extended backwards to the earlier stage when the principal ingredients were being selected. The cooks preparing an "all-beef" sausage might collectively decide to skimp on costs by using snouts, cartilage, and other unappetizing body parts, or by polluting the air or releasing runoff into a nearby river. Healthier and more humane protein alternatives—tofu or tempeh or lentils—are kept off the counter entirely. In like fashion, in the first stage of the legislative process policymakers decide to include certain elements and exclude others. These choices are typically made before the actual sausage-making. Well before congressional debate begins, the broad outlines of new bills are determined via class-wide discussions among capitalists and state officials.

Our focus in this chapter is the next stage, when these same players battle it out among themselves over the details. The various cooks who are allowed into the kitchen compete to determine the particular mix of ingredients, each acting in accordance with their own particular interests. Politicians mediate this battle with the goal of arriving at a final recipe that is congenial to all.

While pressures emanating from social movements and/or public opinion may help to shape this stage of the process—enabling the survival of a few high-quality ingredients in the sausage—the congressional revision process is typically more insulated from public pressures than other stages of policymaking. If capitalists exert strong influence over the initiation of reform bills, their ability to shape the sausage-making process itself is even more dramatic. The changes that Congress made to Obama-era legislation usually resulted from quiet backroom deals that escaped public scrutiny. Specific privileges were granted to specific companies and industries, even at the expense of other elites.[1] In obtaining those deals, business utilized not only the standard bribery of campaign finance and an army of lobbyists, but also the continuous threat of disinvestment should Congress enact unwanted reforms. As a result, "consensus with industry," or at least significant parts of industry, was imperative for final passage.

This pattern is evident in the major legislative reform efforts of the Obama era: the healthcare (ACA), financial regulation (Dodd-Frank), and climate legislation of 2009–10. In each case, the most substantive decisions had been made long before Congress openly debated the bills, reflected in the initial white papers and proposals drawn up by the White House or congressional committee leaders. However, congressional rehashing provided business leaders with another opportunity for watering down or deleting offensive provisions that had survived the earlier screening process. We highlight some of the key revisions and the means by which business achieved them, drawing special attention to the role of capital strikes and strike threats.

We close the chapter by addressing conflicts within the business world. All three reform initiatives sought to restrain particularly

---

1   This is part of the "special-interest process" described in G. William Domhoff, *The Powers That Be: Processes of Ruling-Class Domination in America* (New York: Random House, 1978).

parasitic industries that harmed the capitalist class as a whole. But in each case, the tweaking process vitiated this goal, bringing victories for narrow industry interests at the expense of long-term profits and stability for other corporate sectors. In the final ACA legislation, the health industries were subjected to some new constraints, but they gained more than they lost. Crucially, they preserved their freedom to determine prices for drugs, medical care, medical devices, and insurance. "We got a good deal," said the senior vice president of the Pharmaceutical Research and Manufacturers of America (PhRMA), the main drug industry lobby.[2] Wall Street likewise killed or watered down key aspects of Dodd-Frank during the legislative negotiations, surprising even itself with its power. By the end of 2009, the director of a financial research firm would comment that some aspects of the House bill were "irritating," yet "compared with what we thought we were going to get over the summer, it's night and day." The victories of the health and financial industries came at the expense not only of the public, but of other corporate sectors.[3]

Tellingly, though, there was little overt criticism of the health, finance, and fossil fuel industries by other capitalists during these processes. In all three cases, there was considerable class-wide solidarity with the targeted industries. We argue that this solidarity stemmed from three factors. One was the direct financial and personnel ties connecting diverse segments of US business, visible in interlocking boards of directors, portfolio investments, common membership in advisory councils and social clubs, and other relationships. This factor is sometimes cited to explain why non-healthcare businesses have been so reluctant to push for single-payer healthcare, a program that would collectively save them trillions of dollars in the future. Second, the targeted industries threatened to respond to reforms by raising prices that would affect corporate buyers of their products, thus changing the equation of interest for the capitalist class as a whole. Third, the offloading of costs onto the working and middle classes, especially in the form of price increases, served to mitigate the tensions between the parasitic industries and other corporate sectors.

---

2 Bryant Hall quoted in Peter Baker, "Obama Pushed by Drug Lobby, E-mails Suggest," *NYT*, June 9, 2012: A1.

3 Chris Whalen of Institutional Risk Analytics, quoted in Alison Vekshin and Dawn Kopecki, "Not So Radical Reform," *BW*, January 11, 2010: 28. The climate legislation was a somewhat different case, in that few capitalists would be directly hurt by the failure of reform—which helps explain why the bills were defeated.

Seeking Consensus on Healthcare Reform

As we have seen, the quest for "consensus" among "key system stake-holders"—specifically the health industries and non-health industries—shaped the initial blueprints for healthcare reform. The business stakeholders had been unanimous that reform must preserve and strengthen the position of existing healthcare sectors, and that certain ingredients—most importantly single-payer insurance—must be kept off the table. With those parameters settled, the sausage-making began. Pleasing all the key stakeholders required many additional modifications as the legislation proceeded through the various congressional committees. Most of the significant changes during this stage were industry-friendly, typically scrapping protective regulations or increasing subsidies to private healthcare interests.

A series of changes sought to solidify the insurance industry's support. In the final Affordable Care Act, even the weak public option favored by the Senate Health, Education, Labor, and Pensions (HELP) Committee was eliminated for fear that it would compete with the inefficient and expensive private insurance industry. As Senator Chuck Grassley put it, "we have to keep what we have now strong, and make it stronger." The public option "is an unfair competitor."[4] To replace it, another government subsidy was added to the legislation: the creation of government-financed exchanges that directed consumers to private insurance, without the insurers paying for the service.[5] However, the nonprofit, multiemployer insurance plans that covered 20 million union workers would be denied access to the subsidies available to nonunion employers on the new exchanges. The law would thus create an incentive for employers to withdraw from the nonprofit plans and force their workers into for-profit plans run by private insurance companies. It thus provided an extra, indirect subsidy to the for-profit insurers.[6] In other key changes, Congress discarded a Medicare buy-in option for patients aged fifty-five to sixty-four, thus assuring the continuation of a

---

4   Quoted in Steven Brill, *America's Bitter Pill: Money, Politics, Backroom Deals, and the Fight to Fix Our Broken Healthcare System* (New York: Random House, 2015), 88.

5   The exchanges were also a feature of prior Republican proposals, originally conceived as a business-friendly alternative to single-payer models. See Paul Starr, *Remedy and Reaction: The Peculiar American Struggle over Health Care Reform* (New Haven, CT: Yale University Press, 2011), 202–3.

6   Max Fraser, "The Affordable Care Attack," *NLF* 23, no. 1 (2014): 96–8; James McGee, "Union Health Plans Will Suffer under Obamacare," *LN*, March 2013: 14–15.

profitable market segment; it increased the penalties for violating the individual and employer mandates as a way of compelling healthy people to buy private coverage; and it doubled the surcharge that insurers could assess to older customers.[7]

These and other changes were engineered by congressional representatives who had long-term alliances with healthcare sectors. Within the Senate Finance Committee, for example, independent senator Joseph Lieberman and Democratic senator Ben Nelson—who had each received well over $1 million from health professionals, pharmaceuticals, and the insurance industry in 2008—were key activists in torpedoing the public insurance and Medicare buy-in options.[8] Senator John Kerry added a tax on employer-based health coverage, targeting union-won health insurance plans that were allegedly overly generous.[9]

The freedom of the corporate healthcare sectors to set prices is an essential lever of their political power. Investment capital in healthcare is less mobile than in some sectors, such as finance, meaning that disinvestment from certain countries or regions is less feasible (though not impossible, as the saga of ACA implementation in Chapter 3 will show). The freedom to raise prices is thus central not only to high profits but to health industries' power to thwart unfavorable policy changes. Preserving that freedom is essential. During the legislative process, health insurers and providers often threatened to raise prices in response to proposals that would increase taxes on the industry, expand public healthcare options like Medicare, or otherwise undermine their profits.[10] And, having preserved their control over prices during the legislative phase, the various industry sectors would use the threat of price increases as a critical weapon in further eroding the impact of the ACA.

---

7 This last element is known as the "age band." Brill, *America's Bitter Pill*, 173, 176, 192, 132, 280. In the House alone, HELP Committee members submitted 788 amendments, of which 161 were wholly or partially adopted. John E. McDonough, *Inside National Health Reform* (Berkeley: University of California Press, 2011), 83.

8 Brill, *America's Bitter Pill*, 173, 176; McDonough, *Inside National Health Reform*, 136.

9 McDonough, *Inside National Health Reform*, 61, 88; Brill, *America's Bitter Pill*, 164–5, 168–9, 192; David M. Herszenhorn, "Obama Urges Excise Tax on High-Cost Insurance," *NYT*, January 6, 2010: A21. Workers and other critics noted that the tax would encourage employers to reduce their health coverage and shift more costs to workers. Candidate Obama had vehemently opposed the tax for this reason, but in January 2010 he endorsed it.

10 See for instance Chad Terhune and Keith Epstein, "Why Health Insurers Are Winning," *BW*, August 17, 2009: 36; Alex Wayne and Drew Armstrong, "Despite a Deal, More Roadblocks Ahead for Health Bill," *CQ Weekly*, December 14, 2009: 2884.

Congress's changes to the draft ACA legislation helped preserve the industry's price-setting power, thus constraining the law's ability to achieve cost containment. The insurers were left free to set their rates, preserving a key tool that they would utilize continuously over the coming years. Even more importantly, the pharmaceutical and hospital industries—whose price-gouging is ultimately a bigger contributor to total healthcare costs—also maintained their freedom to set prices. During the spring and summer of 2009, the White House, the Senate Finance and HELP Committees, and the House Energy and Commerce Committee struck agreements with PhRMA, wherein the latter would publicly support reform legislation in exchange for three key concessions.[11] First, Medicare would continue to be prohibited from negotiating drug prices, despite the $40 billion annual estimated cost to taxpayers. Second, there would be no importation of lower-cost drugs from Canada, which could have saved patients 30 to 50 percent on drug prices. Third, the committees granted the industry's request for twelve years of patent protection for biologics, a type of drugs made from natural sources. The Senate Finance Committee estimated that the law would deliver over $200 billion in extra revenue to the drug industry over the coming decade. In exchange, it asked the industry to agree to cut costs and accept new taxes worth $80 billion, down from the $130 billion that the committee had originally requested. Yet even this $80 billion "giveback," which would have yielded a net profit increase of $120 billion over the first ten years of the ACA, was agreed to be a voluntary commitment.[12] The hospital industry's concessions totaled $155 billion, and were largely composed of "lower *increases* in Medicare payment rates" than what the hospitals wanted to charge.[13]

At the same time that they enhanced their profits, industry interests also preserved their structural power by preventing the consideration of policy options, such as price controls, that would rein it in. Public threats of price hikes or disinvestment were part of their arsenal, but at

---

11   Concretely, its support included a promise to spend $150 million on advertising, thus funding the bulk of the ad campaign's costs. See Brill, *America's Bitter Pill*, 100; Paul Blumenthal, "The Legacy of Billy Tauzin: The White House-PhRMA Deal," Sunlight Foundation, February 12, 2010.

12   Brill, *America's Bitter Pill*, 97–101, 124–9, 132–4; McDonough, *Inside National Health Reform*, 235–7; Blumenthal, "The Legacy of Billy Tauzin"; Robert Pear, "Health Care Industry Is Said to Promise to Hold Down Costs Voluntarily," *NYT*, May 11, 2009: A12; Janet Adamy, "Health Groups Detail Plans to Reduce Costs," *WSJ*, June 2, 2009: A3; Baker, "Obama Pushed by Drug Lobby": A1; Starr, *Remedy and Reaction*, 14, 187, 204–5, 218–19.

13   Brill, *America's Bitter Pill*, 130. Emphasis added.

this stage they usually relied on their lobbyists and conduits within government to convey their demands more quietly. The centrality of pro-industry voices within the executive and legislative branches helped ensure scrupulous respect for the decision-making prerogatives of industry, thus preserving the industries' structural power.

In the end, the 2010 Affordable Care Act included some new and progressive regulations on health insurance companies, resulting in a significant expansion of healthcare coverage. Yet this improvement was accompanied by new or amplified problems for the US population. The new law further strengthened private health interests' control over the healthcare market, most notably through the mandate that individuals purchase coverage. Despite the law's goal of cost containment, insurance premiums and overall healthcare costs continued to rise at rates well above the average inflation rate in the rest of the economy. The share of costs borne by patients themselves also increased, with a 2017 report finding that "patient cost-sharing rose substantially faster than payments for care by health plans as insurance coverage became a little less generous." The rate of insurance company profits (known as the "medical-loss ratio") remained steady. And, by the end of 2016, 28 million people in the United States remained uninsured.[14]

Financial Reform, Disinvestment, and Bullshit

As with the ACA, the congressional sausage-making of financial reform proceeded within previously established parameters. The essential ingredients and the contours of the slimy skin had already been collectively agreed upon, with nationalization of banks and other disagreeable options excluded from the recipe. The cooks then set about fine-tuning their greasy concoction.

---

14 Kaiser Family Foundation, "Premiums and Worker Contributions Among Workers Covered by Employer-Sponsored Coverage, 1999–2017," September 19, 2017; Gary Claxton, Larry Levitt, Michelle Long and Erik Blumenkranz, "Increases in Cost-Sharing Payments Have Far Outpaced Wage Growth," *Kaiser Family Foundation*, October 4, 2017 (quote); Michelle Long, Matthew Rae, Gary Claxton, Anne Jankiewicz, and David Rousseau, "Recent Trends in Employer-Sponsored Health Insurance Premiums," *Journal of the American Medical Association* 315, no. 1 (2016): 18; Benjamin Day, David U. Himmelstein, Michael Broder, and Steffie Woolhandler, "The Affordable Care Act and Medical Loss Ratios: No Impact in First Three Years," *International Journal of Health Services* 45, no. 1 (2015): 127–31; Kaiser Family Foundation, "Key Facts about the Uninsured Population," September 19, 2017.

Congress's input into financial policy was somewhat limited. The executive branch dominated the TARP bailout legislation (first under Bush, then Obama), and the Obama White House and Treasury played the lead role in designing the blueprint for financial reform. Executive branch agencies would also do most of the crucial shaping of financial regulatory policy after the new law was signed, during the extended rulemaking process. Nonetheless, Congress made several substantial modifications, often in conjunction with the administration.

An early and ominous change involved the new administration's housing initiative, the Making Home Affordable program announced in February 2009. Like Bush, Obama aimed to avoid any infringement on banks' property rights or decision-making power while encouraging—but not forcing—them to reinvest in the economy at a time of deep disinvestment and recession. Both administrations' policies on housing were limited almost entirely to creating incentives that would encourage voluntary action by banks.[15]

The major exception to this rule was a section in the 2009 bill empowering bankruptcy judges to reduce mortgage interest rates and monthly payments. This reform would have kept numerous struggling homeowners in their houses, while limiting banks' ability to maximize their profits, at least in the short term. Of the many dangers facing Wall Street in late 2008 and early 2009, this provision was the "big one," said a lobbyist for the Mortgage Bankers Association.[16] The Senate obliged by killing it, with the tacit blessing of the Obama administration. Treasury Secretary Tim Geithner told economist Robert Kuttner "that the industry experts he relied upon counseled against this bankruptcy authority." So Geithner and Obama "did nothing to promote it," and Congress understood "that this was not a provision that mattered to the White House."[17] It did not "matter" to the White House because Wall Street sympathizers held the key positions in the White House. Banks had exercised their power through the personnel that they had helped put in office, most notably Geithner, who was known to be in daily

---

15   Robert Kuttner, *A Presidency in Peril: The Inside Story of Obama's Promise, Wall Street's Power, and the Struggle to Control Our Economic Future* (White River Junction, VT: Chelsea Green, 2010), 49–59; Alan S. Blinder, *After the Music Stopped: The Financial Crisis, the Response, and the Work Ahead* (New York: Penguin, 2013), 320–42.

16   Francis Creighton quoted in Stacy Kaper, "Bankers Bracing for a Shake-Up on the Hill," *AB*, October 31, 2008.

17   Kuttner, *A Presidency in Peril*, 51.

contact with executives from Citigroup, JPMorgan, and Goldman Sachs.[18]

In the House and Senate bills that would become Dodd-Frank, Wall Street and other business interests also obtained a variety of important changes from Congress. In each case, they made overt threats of disinvestment, which pro-industry personnel within Congress then cited in order to either amend the legislation or defeat proposed amendments.

The fight over derivatives regulation illustrates the pattern. As we have noted, banks were able to carve out major loopholes even prior to congressional debate. After the draft legislation was introduced, they took action to eliminate or water down surviving elements that might curb their profits from derivatives. Banks claimed, as Paul Volcker predicted they would, that new regulations "would force derivatives trading overseas" to less regulated markets.[19] They conveyed that message to Congress, including the staff members who were finalizing the derivatives provisions of the legislation. They directly lobbied Julie Chon, the key staff person for the issue on the Senate Banking Committee, and who had previously worked for JPMorgan, Citigroup, and other top banks.[20] In one specific instance, an amendment to the House bill would have empowered regulators to prohibit certain types of swaps trades, but it was defeated after the chair of the House Committee on Agriculture, which plays a central role in overseeing the derivatives market, threatened "that if we ban these products, they will simply move overseas."[21] The amendment had been sponsored by a group of Democrats who were not particularly dependent on Wall Street donations, and killed by others who had closer relationships to the finance industry.[22] Here, again, banks exercised leverage by combining threats of disinvestment (in this case, moving derivatives trading overseas) with outreach to their trusted supporters on the inside, whom they had helped place in office.

The so-called New Democrat Coalition, which included sixty-eight House Democrats who were especially friendly to Wall Street, played a

---

18   AP, "Mr. Geithner, Wall Street Is on Line 1 (Again)," October 8, 2009.

19   Robert G. Kaiser, *Act of Congress: How America's Essential Institution Works, and How It Doesn't* (New York: Knopf, 2013), 305.

20   Kaiser, *Act of Congress*, 284–8.

21   Collin Peterson (D-MN) quoted in Kuttner, *A Presidency in Peril*, 114–15.

22   The securities and investment industry was not even among the top twenty contributors to the lead sponsor for the amendment, Bart Stupak (D-MI), in 2008 (nor during his career as a whole); it ranked seventh among industries contributing to Peterson's 2008 campaign.

major role in winning amendments to the House bill. According to the business press, the top banks went directly to New Democrats when faced with the prospect of derivatives regulation. New Democrats, including Melissa Bean, Mike McMahon, Joseph Crowley, and Goldman Sachs alum Jim Himes, conveyed Wall Street's concerns to Barney Frank and Tim Geithner. McMahon specifically warned Frank that the administration's proposal on derivatives "would push jobs overseas." The threat helped rein in the bill's already modest ambitions. The legislation passed by the House in December 2009 allowed the category of "standardized" derivatives to remain exempt from trading platforms overseen by regulators.[23]

Perhaps most remarkable was the banks' success in rallying nonfinancial businesses to their side. In October 2009, 171 businesses and industry lobbies calling themselves the Coalition of Derivatives End-Users issued an open letter to Senate Majority Leader Harry Reid. The letter cautioned policymakers against any action that "would increase business risk and raise costs." Regulating the derivatives market in which those businesses participated would, they warned, limit their ability to "make new investments and retain and create new jobs," thereby hindering the goal of "promoting economic recovery" in the country.[24] This not-so-subtle threat helped win an exemption from derivatives regulations for nonfinancial companies.

One of the biggest battles involved the proposal for a consumer protection agency with the power to punish abuses by the financial industry. The agency was one of the few robust regulatory changes that had survived the pre-legislative process and made its way into the sausage-making process on the floor of Congress. The banks immediately went into war mode over the proposal, spending millions on lobbying Congress against it and making all the usual threats. Here, too, they successfully mobilized nonfinancial businesses to join their fight. The original proposal included regulation of the credit operations of certain non-bank entities as well, including auto dealers and other corporations that issued loans or sold other financial services to consumers. The Chamber of Commerce spent some $2 million on ads claiming that protective regulations on these non-banks would make it

---

23   Vekshin and Kopecki, "Not So Radical Reform," 27–8. Standardized derivatives are distinct from the "over-the-counter" types that are traded directly between parties, outside of exchanges.

24   The letter, dated October 12, 2009, is available at businessroundtable.org.

harder for consumers to finance new cars and other major purchases.[25] These warnings of harm to consumers were implicit threats that lenders would respond to regulation by raising interest rates and shifting their capital elsewhere. In response, Barney Frank amended the bill to exempt all nonfinancial businesses from the agency's oversight, and deleted a provision requiring banks to offer customers "plain-vanilla" (i.e., user-friendly) mortgages and credit cards. Additional bank-friendly revisions included a House amendment by close Wall Street ally Melissa Bean to give federal authorities more power to override state-level consumer protections and, in the Senate, a requirement that the new protection agency "consider the economic impact of its regulations on small businesses before issuing them."[26]

To be sure, Wall Street did not score a total victory. The 2010 legislation included some new checks on Wall Street, such as the Consumer Financial Protection Bureau (CFPB). Although the banks weakened the bureau and constrained its purview, it nonetheless emerged in the final law as a potentially robust mechanism for regulation and enforcement. For that reason, it would remain an ongoing target of Wall Street after 2010, besieged by lawsuits, new congressional attacks, and Trump-era appointments designed to bring enforcement to a halt.[27]

Yet banks were able to defeat or at least greatly water down most of the provisions they found offensive. Perhaps most importantly, Dodd-Frank did not noticeably reduce the size or systemic importance of the largest banks, an option that policymakers had taken off the table from the start. In 2016, Neel Kashkari, the president of the Minneapolis Federal Reserve and a Goldman Sachs alum, argued that "the biggest banks are still too big to fail and continue to pose a significant, ongoing risk to our economy." One JPMorgan executive, speaking soon after Dodd-Frank's passage, offered a more positive evaluation: "We may be pissed at Obama, but when it comes down to it, he was pretty good for our business." In the years that followed, bank revenues and profits increased to record levels. The Trump administration's corporate tax

---

25   Kuttner, *A Presidency in Peril*, 99; Kaiser, *Act of Congress*, 222.

26   Vekshin and Kopecki, "Not So Radical Reform," 27–8; Kaiser, *Act of Congress*, 165, 173, 318 (quote), 323–4; 343–4.

27   See for example Renae Merle, "Senate Bars Rule That Lets Consumers Sue Their Banks," *WP*, October 25, 2017: A15; Alan Rappeport, "Mulvaney, in First Report to Congress, Urges Weakening of Consumer Bureau," *NYT*, April 3, 2018: A10. Trump's CFPB essentially halted enforcement activities; see AP, "Under Trump, a Voice for the American Consumer Goes Silent," April 10, 2018; Public Citizen, *Corporate Impunity: "Tough on Crime" Trump Is Weak on Corporate Crime and Wrongdoing* (July 2018).

cuts merely accelerated the upward trend, driving profits into the stratosphere.[28]

Wall Street's victories resulted from the simultaneous deployment of all the tools in the corporate toolkit. Campaign donations to Frank, Dodd, the New Democrats, and other members of Congress guaranteed that business complaints would be heard. The complaints themselves were communicated through lobbyists, the media, and sympathetic personnel lodged in government, some of whom, like Julie Chon and Jim Himes, had come to government from Wall Street. The voices of pro-business personnel in Congress were greatly amplified by the structural leverage – in the form of disinvestment threats – wielded by banks and nonfinancial businesses. Those individuals' commitment to serving business was further enhanced by the centrality of key industries to employment levels and tax revenue in their home districts.

This multipronged influence over the legislative process can be seen most vividly in New York, where Wall Street directly accounted for almost 20 percent of the state's total wages in 2007 and a major share of its tax revenue, leading the *Wall Street Journal* editors to note that "state spending has tracked closely with booms and busts on Wall Street."[29] New Democrat Joseph Crowley of New York stressed the dependence of ordinary workers on Wall Street's prosperity, saying "that workers in his Bronx and Queens district sweep the floors, drive the cars, and pull the beer taps for Wall Street traders." In other words, the prosperity of all New Yorkers depended on the continued prosperity and unfettered freedom of Wall Street.[30]

Even liberal Democrats with less intimate ties to the financial industry often echoed this logic. Barney Frank occupied a safe House seat and probably could have done without Wall Street's largesse, but he complied with many of its demands. Later on, Senator Jeff Merkley insisted that the so-called Volcker Rule, designed to prevent banks from speculating with their own money, include exemptions for "insurance companies and real estate investments because those industries were

28 Kashkari, "Lessons from the Crisis: Ending Too Big to Fail," speech at the Brookings Institution, February 16, 2016; executive quoted in Charles Gasparino, "Wall Street Still Doesn't Love the GOP," *WSJ*, November 1, 2010: A21. On revenues and profits see Andrew Ackerman and Lalita Clozel, "Tax Law Helps Boost Bank Profits to Record," *WSJ*, February 22, 2019: B10; FDIC, "Commercial Banks: Historical Statistics on Banking," Table CB04, fdic.gov.

29 "Empire State Implosion" (editorial), *WSJ*, November 13, 2008: A18.

30 Vekshin and Kopecki, "Not So Radical Reform," 26.

vital to his state, and to many other pro-reform senators."[31] And all of these debates took place against the backdrop of businesses' ongoing historic disinvestment from the US economy in the aftermath of the Great Recession, which enhanced the credibility of their disinvestment threats.

Many critics dismissed the banks' threats as self-interested hyperbole. As former Federal Reserve chair Paul Volcker argued, the banks' invariable claim that reform would "restrict credit and harm the economy" was "all bullshit." FDIC chair Sheila Bair called the banks' threats "self-serving nonsense." Indeed, studies before and after 2010 have shown that regulations such as higher capital ratios have little or no automatic impact on bank lending, suggesting that the ultimate cost to banks is not very high.[32] (Low capital ratios were a major source of the 2008 crash, which we'll discuss in the next chapter.)

But while the argument that regulation would distort the loan market and thus force banks to restrict credit was "bullshit," there was nevertheless a strong *political* reason why the banks might choose to restrict credit, in keeping with the quid-pro-quo logic we have already examined. Continuing to withhold investments would allow banks to extract further concessions from government. If capital hoarding had originated in market-driven processes, its continuation was driven by a mix of market-based disinvestment and a strategic capital strike. The banks' argument that regulation would automatically lead to tightened markets was false, but their willingness to continue their capital strike despite attractive investment opportunities was a political sledgehammer.

Climate Reform and the Threat of Economic Downturn

The same prioritization of corporate profit over public interest applied in the legislative sausage-making around climate change in 2009–10, with dire consequences. Polluters, of course, claimed that any new regulations on their freedom to pollute would bring higher energy

---

31   As reported by Timothy F. Geithner, *Stress Test: Reflections on Financial Crises* (New York: Crown, 2014), 420–1. Ironically Merkley had co-sponsored the Volcker Rule provision in the original legislation.

32   Volcker quoted in Jeff Connaughton, *The Payoff: Why Wall Street Always Wins* (Westport, CT: Prospecta, 2012), 200; Sheila Bair, *Bull by the Horns: Fighting to Save Main Street from Wall Street and Wall Street from Itself* (New York: Free Press, 2012), 225. See Chapter 3 for additional citations.

prices, unemployment, and disinvestment from the United States. But as with financial reform, there was no natural reason why regulations should cause higher prices or disinvestment. The argument that increased environmental regulation hinders economic prosperity was discredited long ago. Environmentally friendly investments tend to generate more employment than dirty industries, meaning that the overall economy, including workers, would be well served by a full transition to renewable energy. Increased regulations on polluters do not even necessarily lead to layoffs in those industries.[33]

However, regulations might reduce polluters' profits, and so the prospect of climate reform drew intense polluter opposition. The dirty industries directly or indirectly controlled most of the economy, and therefore possessed formidable powers of disruption. Strong regulations could have directly stopped polluters from raising prices or disinvesting. But since policymakers had abjured the regulation of prices or investment decisions, the polluters retained their power to threaten the economy. They used threats of higher energy prices and reduced investment in the United States to ensure that robust regulations did not survive the congressional revision process.

Al Gore's 2010 post-mortem of the failed Senate climate bills suggested the importance of these threats: the fossil fuel industry was "able to use the fear of the economic downturn as a way of slowing the progress toward this big transition that we have to make."[34] He might have added that a "downturn" was by no means automatic or inevitable. The industry vastly exaggerated the costs it would bear as a result of the legislation. And even if polluters chose to respond to reform by raising prices—and if their control over markets allowed them to do so without sales suffering—then a downturn was still unlikely. A rebate mechanism could have compensated consumers, effectively forcing the polluters themselves to bear the full cost of decarbonization while stimulating growth in other industries. Yet polluters' threats, however factually dubious, helped sow uncertainty about the economic fallout of climate reform.

---

33   Robin Hahnel, *Green Economics: Confronting the Ecological Crisis* (Armonk, NY: M. E. Sharpe, 2011), 96–100; Eban Goodstein, *The Trade-Off Myth: Fact and Fictions about Jobs and the Environment* (Washington, DC: Island, 1999); Robert Pollin, Heidi Garrett-Peltier, James Heintz, and Bracken Hendricks, *Green Growth: A U.S. Program for Controlling Climate Change and Expanding Job Opportunities* (Amherst, MA: Political Economy Research Institute, and Washington, DC: Center for American Progress, 2014).

34   Quoted in Ryan Lizza, "As the World Burns," *TNY*, October 11, 2010: 83.

As Congress considered the various climate bills that we have discussed, polluters worked through their congressional allies to engineer debilitating changes in the proposed legislation. The final version of the Waxman-Markey bill, which eventually passed the House but died for lack of Senate support, gave coal-fired power plants a blanket exemption from carbon-capture-and-storage performance standards. Its emissions target was decreased to an exceedingly modest 17 percent reduction over 2005 levels by 2020. And, perhaps most egregiously, the bill's authors agreed to a provision that would have stripped the EPA of its authority to regulate power plant emissions under the Clean Air Act.[35]

Many members of Henry Waxman's Energy and Commerce Committee were conduits for the demands of the polluting industries. Committee members had received at least $6.2 million from energy sector donors in the 2008 elections. The committee's Republicans were obviously never going to vote for the bill, which gave added clout to Democratic allies of the fossil fuel industries. Democratic Representative Rick Boucher of Virginia, who had just received over $400,000 from the energy sector, was by his own admission instrumental in modifying the bill "so as to make it acceptable to the coal-fired utilities." Boucher helped win coal companies' support in part by ensuring the bill would offer "free allowances" for emissions, "as opposed to having the emissions be auctioned," which would have forced polluters to pay for their emissions. The committee's reduction in the total emissions target was a direct response to industry demands, in this case personal pressure from Duke Energy CEO Jim Rogers.[36]

Other key Democratic players on the committee included steel industry allies Mike Doyle of Pennsylvania and Jay Inslee of Washington, who raised the specter of capital flight if the government mandated cuts in carbon emissions. John Dingell of Michigan, the committee's immediate past chair, was the House's second-leading recipient of auto industry cash and third-leading recipient of energy industry donations. He was "fully capable of organizing a deadly blockade inside the committee" if the demands of these sectors were not honored, notes journalist Eric Pooley.[37] In June 2009, the bill, replete with industry-sponsored compromises, passed the House by a slim 219–212 margin.

35   Eric Pooley, *The Climate War: True Believers, Power Brokers, and the Fight to Save the Earth* (New York: Hyperion, 2010), 370, 376–7.

36   Boucher in Louis Peck, "A Veteran of the Climate Wars Reflects on U.S. Failure to Act," *Yale Environment 360*, January 4, 2011; Pooley, *Climate War*, 335, 370, 376.

37   Pooley, *Climate War*, 329 (quote), 344.

In the Senate, only one of the several bills that had survived the earlier filtration process stood a realistic chance of passage: the Kerry-Graham-Lieberman bill (later "Kerry-Lieberman," after Graham dropped out). In that earlier process polluters had been able to exclude most of the unacceptable elements from consideration. Now they sought to further dilute it or kill it altogether. With its passage in doubt due to senators' industry loyalties, Kerry and Lieberman at the last minute decided to restrict the bill's regulations to power plants only. Yet even this limited bill failed, as the utilities mobilized the manufacturing sectors with warnings of price increases and power grid disinvestment. The American Chemistry Council, for instance, publicly complained that even "a utility-only cap" would "stall economic recovery" and potentially lead to capital flight.[38] Since the bill did not include price controls, the freedom to threaten price hikes allowed the utilities to enlist the aid of industries that had just been exempted from the bill.

The bill's proponents conjured the prospect of EPA regulation if congressional efforts failed, thinking that polluters would want to avoid the more uncertain outcome associated with EPA intervention. But this counter-threat was ineffective. Democratic senator Ben Nelson, a leading opponent of climate reform, said confidently in late July, "I have such a view of the balance of power between the three branches of government that I don't feel like the EPA's in any position to threaten us."[39]

Nelson's comment is worth dissecting. He was ostensibly invoking the Constitution's checks-and-balances system of government, implying that the courts or Congress would prevent the EPA from taking unilateral action. The problem with his statement, however, was that there was no obvious counter-power that would check the EPA. The Supreme Court in 2007 had already affirmed the EPA's legal right to regulate carbon emissions under the Clean Air Act, the Obama White House was rhetorically committed to reducing carbon emissions, and Congress would have lacked the two-thirds Senate majority needed to override a presidential veto on a bill to constrain the EPA.[40] But Nelson

---

38   Josh Voorhees and Robin Bravender, "Clock Winding Down on Carbon Cap Efforts," E&E Daily, July 16, 2010.

39   Quoted in Evan Lehmann, "Senate Abandons Climate Effort, Dealing Blow to President," NYT online, July 23, 2010.

40   A congressional effort to prohibit EPA regulations failed soon after the climate reform legislation failed; Geof Koss, "Key Senate Vote of 2011: Prohibition on EPA Regulations," CQ Weekly, January 3, 2011: 51.

was right in another sense: the "most affected" industries had multiple chokepoints for blocking reforms they disliked, and therefore could frustrate unilateral EPA action. Those chokepoints derived less from the three-branch structure of government than from business's proven ability to threaten, implement, and sustain capital strikes while delaying EPA action through endless lawsuits.[41]

As the threat of any new environmental legislation receded, polluters became more emboldened to reject reform altogether. As Pooley notes, "The threat of onerous EPA regulation had caused many corporations to swing behind cap and trade" in 2007–09, "but now, both on the Hill and in the executive suites, opponents were saying, Let EPA come ahead with regulation . . . [T]he corporate lawyers figured they could keep EPA tied up in the courts for years."[42]

Unlike the healthcare and financial reforms of 2010, the climate reform bills failed. Though they had made it through the initial stage of the legislative process, when the basic list of ingredients had been negotiated between corporate and congressional leaders, the subsequent congressional sausage-making failed to produce a recipe acceptable to all the corporate stakeholders. The ultimate reason was not that the sausage-makers were inept at deal-making, but that polluters did not have a compelling enough reason to consent to *any* deal. There was no external threat capable of making legislative reform a lesser-evil option for them. The potential for EPA regulation had played that role for a time, convincing some corporations to get behind reform. But their history of successful litigation against the EPA and their success at defeating new provisions within Congress emboldened them to scuttle reform altogether. An obstreperous mass movement targeting polluters and their profits might have made reform into a lesser evil. But no such movement existed, or at least the disruptive activities targeting polluters were far too few and too scattered. The failure of climate legislation in 2010 highlights the importance of mass disruption that targets corporations' bottom lines, even when there is a congressional majority publicly supporting regulation.

---

41   Although the Supreme Court had already ruled carbon dioxide an air pollutant subject to EPA regulation, lawsuits could still be launched on an almost infinite array of technical grounds.

42   Pooley, *Climate War*, 350.

Recalibrating the Corporate Compromise

The three cases examined in this chapter illustrate the legislative approach of the administration and congressional Democrats during Obama's first term. On issue after issue, the White House and Democratic Congress declined to confront entrenched corporate power. Instead they sought to craft reforms that minimized regulatory constraints, preserved corporate profit levels, and maintained corporate control over capital flows. As a result, progressive legislation was far more modest than Democratic voters had anticipated. The president himself understood this disjunction. As one Beltway journalist noted shortly before the 2012 election, "Obama wants voters to cast their ballots based on the platforms of the two candidates, not on the record of his first term."[43] Little had changed after his second term.

More surprising, however, is the fact that Obama-era legislative reforms allowed specific industries to maintain privileges at the expense of other corporate sectors. Price gouging by healthcare companies and the "too-big-to-fail" nature of the top banks are detrimental to those sectors' corporate clients as well as the public at large. Many members of the 1% were ultimately hurt by the lack of more robust regulatory reform. Despite Obama's commitment to serving the corporate elite "as a whole," his administration ultimately failed to stop predatory industries from preying on the rest of the business world. How can we explain this outcome?

In societies where business is the most powerful force, most successful policy reforms require careful renegotiation of the "corporate compromise." Physicians David Himmelstein and Steffie Woolhandler coined this term to describe the negotiation of health policy. Politicians, they said, must find policies that serve both the "cost-conscious corporate purchasers of care"—that is, businesses that provide healthcare to their employees—"and corporate health care providers struggling to expand profitability and assert control of medicine." They argued that the growth of Health Maintenance Organizations (HMOs) in the late twentieth century was an arrangement "uniquely acceptable to both." HMOs ensured robust profits for both constituencies, in part by incentivizing the exclusion of sick and poor patients. Beginning with the Nixon administration, the US government sought to promote the HMO

---

43   Ryan Lizza, "The Second Term," *TNY*, June 18, 2012: 54.

model in part as a way of massaging the intercorporate tensions around healthcare cost and provision.[44]

Like most compromises, intercorporate compromises tend to be unstable, since no party is getting everything they want, and each may seek to circumvent the original deal, using whatever tools they can. Corporate employers may continue to be resentful of, say, galloping healthcare costs or the plethora of state subsidies to large banks. These conflicts are typically assuaged in two ways.

First, intercorporate relationships often mute or suppress such conflict. Business coalitions, think tanks, interlocking corporate directorates, and policy advisory committees all help resolve potential conflicts and preserve unstable compromises.[45] The financial industry has had particular success in drawing upon its dense network of intercorporate relationships and its control of investment capital to rally or even coerce other corporate sectors to support its demands.[46] The big banks' mobilization of corporate customers in opposition to derivatives regulation is an example of how a parasitic business sector can often persuade other sectors to rally behind its agenda (in this case, by raising the specter of price increases).

Second, tensions are mitigated by externalizing costs onto those who lack access to the sausage-making process: workers, the sick and elderly, most communities of color, foreigners, future generations, and other vulnerable constituencies. The congressional modifications to the legislation that became the Affordable Care Act offer numerous examples.

44 David U. Himmelstein and Steffie Woolhandler, "The Corporate Compromise: A Marxist View of Health Maintenance Organizations and Prospective Payment," *Annals of Internal Medicine* 109, no. 6 (1988): 494, 498. For a detailed historical account of the corporate compromise on health policy see Colin Gordon, *Dead on Arrival: The Politics of Health Care in Twentieth-Century America* (Princeton, NJ: Princeton University Press, 2003), esp. 210–60.

45 Mark S. Mizruchi, *The Structure of Corporate Political Action: Interfirm Relations and Their Consequences* (Cambridge, MA: Harvard University Press, 1992); Dan Clawson, Alan Neustadtl, and Mark Weller, *Dollars and Votes: How Business Campaign Contributions Subvert Democracy* (Philadelphia, PA: Temple University Press, 1998); Michael Dreiling and Derek Darves, "Corporate Unity in American Trade Policy: A Network Analysis of Corporate-Dyad Political Action," *AJS* 116, no. 5 (2011): 1514–63; Tarun Banerjee and Rebekah Burroway, "Business Unity and Anticorporate Protests: The U.S. Fortune 500 in 2010," *Mobilization* 20, no. 2 (2015): 179–206; Joshua Murray, "Interlock Globally, Act Domestically: Corporate Political Unity in the 21st Century," *AJS* 122, no. 6 (2017): 1617–63.

46 Beth Mintz and Michael Schwartz, *The Power Structure of American Business* (Chicago, IL: University of Chicago Press, 1985); Kevin L. Young and Stefano Pagliari, "Capital United? Business Unity in Regulatory Politics and the Special Place of Finance," *Regulation and Governance* 11, no. 1 (2017): 3–23.

Because the architects had rejected major cost-containment measures, someone outside the health industries had to bear the brunt of rising costs. Rising insurance premiums, fueled largely by providers' price-gouging, were one result.[47] Non-health industries were partly shielded from this harm by the law's tax on union-won health plans. As critics of the tax noted, it gave employers an excuse "for cuts they wanted to implement anyway" as well as a strong incentive "to dump more costs onto workers by offering lower-premium, higher-deductible" (and higher co-pay) plans.[48] A 2014 survey found that, among Fortune 500 companies, nearly three-quarters had devised plans to shift more of their health costs onto their workers. The survey analysts noted that most of the cost-reducing measures being pursued by the companies "are being shouldered by employees."[49]

The ACA and Dodd-Frank survived the Congressional sausage-making process and were signed by Obama because the engineers found a mix of ingredients consistent with the logic of the corporate compromise. In both cases all the major players found the balance of gains and losses at least acceptable, in that their profits would be protected, their investment autonomy would not be seriously compromised, and the costs of the parasitic health industries would mostly be borne by unrepresented stakeholders. Climate legislation failed in Congress precisely because this fragile fine-tuning was too difficult, largely because the key sectors had little to lose if they refused to compromise.

However, even successful renegotiations of the corporate compromise are inherently unstable. In the case of the ACA, few of the elite participants in the sausage-making process were fully satisfied with the new arrangement, and some of them sought to reopen negotiations afterwards. Soon after passage, the health insurers began complaining that the ACA's individual mandate had not delivered them as many new customers as predicted. Corporations in the non-health sectors registered their discontent with rising prices. In 2018 billionaire Warren

47   Alex Wayne, "Big Pharma Has a New Way to Limit Drug Costs," *BW*, March 16–22, 2015: 23–4; Robert Langreth with Jared Hopkins, "Demystifying Drug Pricing," *BW*, June 27–July 3, 2016: 40.

48   Jenny Brown, "Obamacare Opens for Business, Shuts Out Labor," *LN*, August 2013: 3–4.

49   Peggy Binette, "Survey: Fortune 500 Employees Can Expect to Pay More for Health Insurance," Darla Moore School of Business at the University of South Carolina, September 18, 2014. See also Mark Dudzic, "Employers Keep Shifting Costs under Affordable Care Act," *LN* online, November 25, 2014; Reed Abelson, "High-End Health Plans Scale Back to Avoid 'Cadillac Tax,'" *NYT*, May 27, 2013: B1.

Buffett declared that "the ballooning costs of health care" were "a hungry tapeworm" that threatened the profitability of major industries.[50]

Sometimes the key players cannot be brought to support the final recipe of the sausage, and congressional negotiations fail entirely. In the case of the climate bills, the corporations that signed on to the US Climate Action Partnership in 2007 brokered the backstage compromises necessary to get the bills considered in Congress. But they were only weakly committed to reform. They came to the table mainly to protect their interests against the threat of electorally popular environmental reforms. The same logic has led many polluters to rhetorically support a price on carbon in the years since. As the congressional debate progressed, and as polluters were able to win repeated concessions without significant resistance, their positions began to change: some demanded further relaxation of the proposed regulations, and others became convinced they could kill reform entirely. The lukewarm and superficial support from a few corporations was insufficient to counter the intense opposition from top polluters.

The limited success of Donald Trump's legislative agenda as president can largely be traced to his failure to abide by the logic of the corporate compromise. Trump and the Republican Party of recent years have proven less committed to, in Obama's words, serving the corporate elite "as a whole," and more committed to serving the interests of favored corporate sectors, even when it harms others. This favoritism has often involved giant giveaways to particular industries. Trump's 2018 tariffs on steel, aluminum, and certain other imports have spurred significant corporate opposition. Sometimes he has pursued those disruptive policies anyway, empowering one corporate sector at the expense of others, as the example of tariffs suggests. But for the most part, policy reforms that divide the corporate elite have only been possible when the changes have not required new legislation.

The repeated Republican failures to repeal the ACA are revealing in this regard.[51] Trump could not offer an alternative proposal for healthcare policy that would accommodate all the corporate stakeholders. His efforts to eliminate subsidies that enabled poor people to purchase health insurance incurred stiff opposition from health insurers, because congressional Republicans were politically unable to *also* cut

50   Quoted in "Backporch," *AB*, March 2018: 24.
51   The primary motivations behind this effort seem to have been both material (reversing the ACA's small tax increases on the wealthy) and electoral (fulfilling a Republican campaign promise to repeal "Obamacare").

down the third pillar of the "three-legged stool," the requirement that insurers must cover patients with preexisting conditions. Throughout late 2016 and 2017, health industries threatened massive market disruption, warning that providers would close medical facilities, that pharmaceutical companies would discontinue product development or raise drug prices, and that insurers would jack up premiums even faster or withdraw from the ACA marketplaces altogether.[52] Insurance industry spokesperson Marilyn Tavenner warned that eliminating the ACA's subsidies would force insurance companies to completely disinvest at "the next logical opportunity." Consequently, the *Times* reported that many Republicans privately "voiced concern that their efforts to undo the law could have harmful consequences, such as inadvertently destabilizing insurance markets—a concern shared by Democrats and insurers." The CEO of the American Hospital Association protested the 2017 Senate bill that would strip 22 million people of health insurance (thus depriving hospitals of needed revenue) by warning that "the underpayment on one side" would mean that "everybody else pays."[53] These threats constrained congressional Republicans and the Trump administration.

In the end, in the absence of an alternative corporate compromise, they opted to sabotage the ACA from within. They slipped a repeal of the individual mandate into the December 2017 tax legislation and promoted low-quality insurance plans that would siphon away healthy customers from ACA plans, further raising premiums for remaining customers.[54] The sabotage approach was not optimal from the perspective of health corporations, and they protested it. Trump's healthcare policy also unsettled the broader corporate world, which continued to express displeasure at health industry parasitism, as Warren Buffett's 2018 "tapeworm" comment suggests.

52   Abby Goodnough, Robert Pear, and Thomas Kaplan, "Health Groups United to Oppose Republican Bill," *NYT*, March 9, 2017: A1; Zachary Tracer, "Health Rules Targeted by GOP Could Upset U.S. Insurance Markets," bloomberg.com, March 23, 2017; Reed Abelson, "Anthem Threatens to Leave Health Exchanges if Patient Subsidies Are Ended," *NYT*, April 27, 2017: B4; Reed Abelson and Katie Thomas, "In Rare Show of Unity, Hospitals, Doctors, and Insurers Reject Health Bill," *NYT*, May 5, 2017: A20.

53   Reed Abelson, "Health Insurers List Demands if Affordable Care Act Is Killed," *NYT*, December 7, 2016: A22; Robert Pear and Thomas Kaplan, "G.O.P., in Private, Airs Its Anxiety over Health Act," *NYT*, January 28, 2017: A1; CEO Rick Pollack quoted in "In Brief," *BW*, July 3, 2017: 8.

54   Linda J. Blumberg, Matthew Buettgens, and Robin Wang, "The Potential Impact of Short-Term Limited-Duration Policies on Insurance Coverage, Premiums, and Federal Spending," Urban Institute, February 2018.

Notably, however, the Republican attack on the ACA still allowed health industry firms to retain their standard weapons of market disinvestment and virtually limitless price increases, which would allow them to weather the impact of market disruption with minimal damage to profits. The Trump administration also used its regulatory authority to quietly loosen regulations on insurance companies, enabling them to degrade coverage and to again discriminate against patients with preexisting conditions.[55] The worst costs of health industry parasitism continued to be borne by patients, not by other industries. The Republican healthcare policy thus respected the corporate compromise in many ways, despite acting in a more rash and sloppy manner than business would prefer, and despite failing to resolve the underlying crisis.

Trump's reform agenda was most successful when it did not divide elite stakeholders—when its main victims were vulnerable constituencies like workers, consumers, immigrants, and communities on the front lines of environmental destruction. Some of his most important reforms were accomplished through executive action: scrapping or refusing to enforce protections against predatory industries, and giving the military, police, and anti-immigrant agencies even freer rein to terrorize communities of color.[56] Legislatively, his victories were very limited. By far his most dramatic triumph was the historic giveaway to corporations and the super-rich in the form of the December 2017 tax-cut law. An analysis at the time of passage estimated that 83 percent of the tax savings would accrue to the richest 1 percent over the next decade. The increase in the federal budget deficit that resulted from the $1.5 trillion tax cut would in the future be used to justify cuts to public programs like Medicare and Medicaid, as Republican leaders essentially admitted at the time.[57] While his other legislative efforts failed, Trump was successful in this instance because the legislation directly benefited stakeholders all across the business world and offloaded the costs onto non-elites.

---

55   Robert Pear, "Justice Dept. Acts Against Protections for People With Pre-Existing Conditions," *NYT*, June 8, 2018: A13; Robert Pear, "New Rule Allows Small Businesses to Skirt Obamacare," *NYT*, June 20, 2018: A11; Robert Pear, "Extending Short-Term Insurance, but Not All of Its Benefits," *NYT*, August 2, 2018: A16.

56   See Chapter 3 for more discussion of these non-legislative reforms.

57   Tax Policy Center, Urban Institute, and Brookings Institution, "Distributional Analysis of the Conference Agreement for the Tax Cuts and Jobs Act," December 18, 2017: 5; Jeff Stein, "Ryan Says Republicans to Target Welfare, Medicare, Medicaid Spending in 2018," *WP* online, December 6, 2017.

In a capitalist system unthreatened by disruptive popular protest, all politicians must respect the logic of the corporate compromise. If a major corporate sector is hurt by a policy reform, it must usually be compensated somehow. This imperative can be partially overcome if mass disruption jeopardizes the profitability of key business elites. In such circumstances those elites may be willing to agree to meaningful progressive reforms. This happened with the passage of the Wagner Act in 1935, and in Chapter 4 we will explore some additional examples. Yet the need to preserve the corporate compromise in some form also underscores the inherent limitations of reform under capitalism.

3

The System We Are Beholden to Serve: Business Hegemony in the Executive Branch

The bill creates the outlines for America's financial system of the twenty-first century, but it leaves the regulatory agencies with the job of filling in the blanks . . . It is in the trenches of these agencies where the real skirmishes will begin . . . Here is where it will be determined just how far-reaching or not the legislation will be, and here will be determined the winners and losers.

> Financial consultant Eugene Ludwig, on the Dodd-Frank Act, 2010

I am concerned that the size of some of these institutions becomes so large that it does become difficult for us to prosecute them . . . [I]f you do bring a criminal charge, it will have a negative impact on the national economy, perhaps even the world economy.

> Attorney General Eric Holder, 2013

No government actively enforces all the laws on its books. Some laws go unenforced and others are enforced selectively. In most countries, enforcement is primarily the domain of the executive branch, consisting of the president and/or prime minister, their appointees, and career civil servants.[1] To understand if and how a given law is enforced, we must scrutinize the array of forces that influence executive branch actors. As financial consultant Eugene Ludwig suggested in reference to the Dodd-Frank financial reform, the implementation phase that follows the passage of new legislation is crucial in determining "the

---

1 Legislatures and judicial bodies often circumscribe the executive's freedom of action, as we will highlight.

winners and losers."[2] For Wall Street interests not entirely satisfied with Dodd-Frank itself, the implementation phase offered numerous additional opportunities for reversing or mitigating disagreeable elements, which they did with considerable success in the years that followed.[3]

As in prior stages of the policymaking process, the influence of business does not stem primarily from campaign donations. Rather, corporate leaders are crucial to the successful implementation of most major government policies because of their control over capital flows. For instance, soon after Jimmy Carter's 1976 election, the business press noted that his economic stimulus proposals "aim at making business a full partner in planning and administering manpower programs." Because Carter was committed to stimulating private rather than public investment, he knew that "the private sector [would] have to hire" the unemployed if they were to find jobs, and therefore that the goodwill of business was essential to fulfillment of a central promise of his campaign. Four decades later, the rising electoral hopes of progressives within the British Labour Party prompted similar reflections. According to one government economist in 2018, "If Labour doesn't take business with it," any future Labour government "will be a very short-lived government as the economy will suffer." The party needed "to get this cooperation in place since it has promised a lot of things it won't be able to do otherwise."[4] In both cases, business campaign donations were relatively unimportant: corporate cash heavily favored the opponents of both Carter and the Labour Party progressives. But business was still in a position to call most of the shots.

As we have argued, some state institutions like the military and law enforcement agencies exercise a parallel power over the policies that directly affect them. Their power likewise derives from the fact that their cooperation is crucial to policy implementation. Their power of disruption is wielded not through disinvestment but through non-compliance with the efforts of politicians or other government personnel. We have already discussed how Pentagon officials successfully obstructed President Obama's attempt to transfer prisoners from the

2   Eugene Ludwig, "Now It's Up to the Regulators," *NYT* online, June 25, 2010.

3   For details on this process see Kevin A. Young, Tarun Banerjee, and Michael Schwartz, "Capital Strikes as a Corporate Political Strategy: The Structural Power of Business in the Obama Era," *PAS* 46, no. 1 (2018): 17–19.

4   "Carter's Job Policy: A Key Role for Business," *BW*, December 13, 1976: 63; Vicky Pryce quoted in Thomas Penny, David Hellier, and Svenja O'Donnell, "Taking Tea with Marxists," *BW*, January 22, 2018: 33.

Guantánamo torture camp. Usually this disruptive action is not necessary, since the input of these leaders is institutionalized within the policymaking process. Policymakers normally accord them great respect,
especially in the case of the military and intelligence and law enforcement agencies. But when that respect falters, the power of disruption
can be deployed.

In this context, most top executive branch officials and their appointees possess an almost intuitive appreciation of the need to maintain a
high level of "confidence" among business and institutional leaders. As
President Obama put it, "the most important thing we can do is boost
and encourage our business sector," because only collegial cooperation
from government can "make sure that they're hiring."[5] As we saw in
previous chapters, this concern usually leads policymakers to reject
from the outset any proposal that would compel business to invest or
hire, as well as proposals that would result in government investment
competing with top corporations. Maintaining business confidence
also means abstaining from rigorous regulation and criminal prosecu-
tions against top business leaders, whose retaliation might, as Attorney
General Eric Holder warned, "have a negative impact on the national
economy."[6] In like fashion, the armed forces, the police, and other
powerful state bureaucracies must be treated with deference lest they
engage in disruptive behavior of their own.

These guidelines continue to apply once the legislative sausage-
making concludes and the executive branch takes up the task of implementation. This process typically takes place behind closed doors without the knowledge or input of non-elite stakeholders. Sometimes
explicit negotiation is unnecessary, since policymakers who have gone
through the proper vetting understand the dos and don'ts. An unswerv-
ing commitment to "steady growth in the Pentagon's budgets" is non-
controversial, with debate limited to minor skirmishes over the choice
of different weapon systems and the like.[7] The president, secretary of
state, and other top officials are expected to traverse the globe "opening
new markets" for US-based weapons companies and other

5   Obama quoted in Elizabeth Williamson and James R. Hagerty, "The New
Political Landscape: Executives Await Friendlier Climate," *WSJ*, November 4, 2010:
A6.
6   "Transcript: Attorney General Eric Holder on 'Too Big to Jail,' " *AB*, March 6,
2013.
7   Jen Dimascio, "Robert Gates Meets Defense Industry Heads," politico.com,
January 13, 2010.

corporations, both through lucrative deals for specific firms and through international treaties like the Trans-Pacific Partnership.[8] The most egregious recent expression of these unwritten rules is the executive branch's record of torpedoing or greatly watering down international climate agreements that could infringe on the prerogatives of US fossil fuels producers, utilities, and other major polluters. For all their differences, all recent US presidents have shown basic agreement on these points.

The commitment to these pro-business policy parameters is maintained irrespective of campaign promises. Though candidate Obama pledged aggressive action to combat global warming, President Obama helped ensure that the climate accord that emerged from Paris in 2015 was weak and non-binding, as we will show. Domestically, as well as globally, he pursued an "all-of-the-above" energy approach that included strong support for fossil fuels extraction and infrastructure. Just a year after the historic 2010 Deepwater Horizon oil spill in the Gulf of Mexico, the administration gave the green light to new offshore drilling, which one industry analyst cited "as an example of how CEO pressure helped shape or clarify policies affecting energy companies."[9] In 2012, Obama defended himself against polluters' criticisms by pointing out that "America is producing more oil than at any time in the last eight years. We've opened up new areas for exploration. We've quadrupled the number of operating rigs to a record high. We've added enough new oil and gas pipeline to circle the Earth and then some." By the end of his time in office, fossil fuel companies had added enough pipeline to encircle the globe almost *seven* times, all with the approval of the executive branch.[10] As Obama told a business audience in 2016, "Our production

8   Hillary Clinton, "America's Pacific Century," *Foreign Policy*, November 2011: 57. See also Elizabeth Dwoskin with Indira A. R. Lakshmanan, "Secretary of Commerce," *BW*, January 14–20, 2013: 22–5; "America's #1 Weapons Salesman: Trump Promotes U.S. Arms Manufacturers and Weakens Export Rules," *Democracy Now!* April 18, 2018.

9   Mike Beard of Hodges Capital Management quoted in Joshua Green, "CEOs Can't Get Enough of the Capital," *BW*, October 14–20, 2014: 34. See also Edward Klump, "The Rush Back to the Gulf," *BW*, November 8, 2013–January 2, 2014: 58.

10   Between 2008 and 2016 the country added 170,854 net miles of petroleum and gas pipelines. Calculated from Pipeline and Hazardous Materials Safety Administration, "Annual Report Mileage for Hazardous Liquid or Carbon Dioxide Systems," "Annual Report Mileage for Natural Gas Transmission & Gathering Systems," and "Annual Report Mileage for Gas Distribution Systems," November 1, 2017. For Obama quote see White House, Office of the Press Secretary, "Remarks by the President on Increasing Oversight on Manipulation in Oil Markets," April 17, 2012.

of traditional fossil fuels has exceeded all expectations."[11] The Obama EPA even went so far as to distort scientific findings in order to justify these policies, by hiring "experts" from the fossil fuel industry and by censoring results on the harmful impacts of fossil fuels.[12]

Campaign financing alone cannot explain these policies, nor the many other realms in which policy diverged from campaign promises. The energy and natural resources sector accounted for less than one percent of Obama's corporate donations in both 2008 and 2012, and its donations to his campaign dropped significantly in 2012 as compared to 2008. Campaign donations from the weapons industry were even less important.[13] The state bureaucracies that Obama treated with such deference—the armed forces, the anti-immigrant and antidrug agencies, and other law enforcement—had still less financial control over the administration, and Obama was the commander-in-chief of most of those entities, at least in theory. Much of the explanation for the administration's behavior lies in the structural power of business and key state institutions, which was used to obstruct progressive policy change.

This structural power is amplified by other mechanisms, such as campaign finance, that help to elect a certain kind of president and to ensure a certain kind of appointee for key cabinet and regulatory positions in the executive branch. Those personnel then interpret threats according to the logic of business and institutional confidence, and tailor their enforcement actions to avoid disruption. While this pattern is similar to that seen in the prior stages in the policymaking process, the "most affected" institutions also have several additional weapons at their disposal for shaping enforcement. In this chapter, we analyze three of these: the institutionalization of "cost-benefit" requirements that force regulators to avoid any reduction in profits among affected industries, the defunding of the agencies charged with regulating business, and the use of lawsuits to obstruct implementation and drain regulators of scarce resources.

---

11   Interviewed in John Micklethwait, Megan Murphy, and Ellen Pollock, "'Don't Gamble, Invest,'" *BW*, June 27–July 3, 2016: 45. See also Bill McKibben, "Obama's Catastrophic Climate-Change Denial," *NYT* online, May 12, 2015; Sonali Prasad, Jason Burke, Michael Slezak, and Oliver Milman, "Obama's Dirty Secret: The Fossil Fuel Projects the US Littered around the World," *Guardian* online, December 1, 2016.

12   Elisabeth Rosenthal and Dan Frosch, "Pipeline Review Is Faced with Question of Conflict," *NYT*, October 8, 2011: A11; Ramit Plushnick-Masti, "EPA Changed Course after Oil Company Protested," *AP*, January 16, 2013. The administration's belated and reluctant halting of the Keystone XL and Dakota Access pipelines in 2015–16 was the exception that proves the rule: those decisions came in response to disruptive and sustained mass resistance.

13   Calculated from CRP data on contributions coded by industrial sector.

To underscore the leverage available to corporations, we concentrate on legislated reforms intended to restrain business power. In the following two sections we analyze two patterns of behavior by the executive branch. The first is the simple non-enforcement of laws, which entails ignoring existing regulations and sometimes moving to eliminate them entirely. The second is selective enforcement, which we illustrate through examination of the 2010 Dodd-Frank Act, the 2010 Affordable Care Act, and Obama-era environmental regulations. In the third section, we step back from these specific examples to consider the broader logic that informs executive branch enforcement, which has shown a strong degree of consistency across Democratic and Republican administrations. The concern for systemic prosperity, meaning the prosperity of all large firms, is a common priority of all presidential administrations. In Obama's words, the executive's main purpose "is to make sure that the overall system is stable."[14] That means promoting the profitability of all major corporations and preventing individual capitalists or industries from doing things that hurt the rest of the capitalist class.

The Trump administration is often seen as an exception to the normal rules of US politics. In fact, Trump allows for a further test of our argument about the structural roots of business power, because his campaign was much less dependent on broad support from capitalist donors than other presidents' campaigns. In the final section of the chapter, we show that, despite Trump's lesser reliance on corporate funding, his vehement assertions of independence from "special interests," and his erratic and megalomaniacal personality, corporate and institutional power have continued to be exercised in many of the same fundamental ways that they were under Obama. The constraints have been especially visible when Trump has failed to respect the concept of the "corporate compromise," according to which policymakers must accommodate the interests of diverse capitalist industries. In these moments, key segments of the corporate elite have intervened to restrain what they view as reckless behavior benefitting narrow elite segments at the expense of the rest of their class. They have often been successful in thwarting or modifying the policies they dislike. The ways in which the Trump administration is *not* exceptional reinforce our argument about the structural bases of elite power.

---

14   Quoted in Micklethwait et al., " 'Don't Gamble, Invest,' " 46.

Non-Enforcement

The most dramatic expression of the power of elite institutions over the executive branch is when they prevent laws from being enforced. We already noted one major example: the non-prosecution of criminal actions by bank executives following the 2008 financial meltdown, which the nation's top law enforcement official freely acknowledged. Despite clear evidence of illegal actions by financial institutions, the Department of Justice opted not to prosecute for fear of damaging business confidence. That is, banks would intensify their disinvestment from the US economy in protest of any criminal charges brought by the Obama administration. A decision to prosecute could have had "a negative impact on the national economy," with dire political repercussions as well. This sort of decision—not to take legally-mandated criminal or civil action—is one of several common forms that non-enforcement takes.

Environmental regulations go unenforced with particular frequency. Consider, for example, the $787 billion American Recovery and Reinvestment Act of 2009, commonly known as the Obama stimulus plan. Congressional deliberations involved an extended debate over the applicability of the National Environmental Policy Act (NEPA), passed in 1969, to the projects funded by the new legislation. Surprisingly, the environmental advocates of full enforcement of NEPA regulations prevailed over the industries that had lobbied for a blanket exemption. However, the executive branch reversed Congress's decision during the implementation phase. NEPA guidelines allow the president to grant occasional exemptions. The Obama White House used this power to award over 179,000 "categorical exclusions," exempting virtually *all* (96 percent) of the stimulus money from NEPA rules. The process by which it granted exemptions is also telling: it gave the contractors themselves the discretion to judge their own eligibility for exemptions, based on information they volunteered to government overseers. Eligibility for exemption was supposedly based on whether the enforcement of environmental regulations would inhibit the economic stimulus by restricting investment. But the answer to that question had no definitive, objective answer. Since business investment does not simply depend on the immutable laws of economics, no one could predict with certainty whether the recipients of stimulus money would delay or withhold new investments in protest of the environmental regulations or other policies they disliked. It is no surprise, then, that in 96 percent of cases, the firms receiving stimulus money declared that environmental enforcement would indeed limit the stimulus. The administration approved 100 percent of businesses' judgments.[15] In other words, the executive branch ceded decision-making authority to the corporations. In doing so, the administration was also reaffirming the business-friendly conceptualization of cost-benefit analysis that has become institutionalized within the US government in recent decades. It was saying that the costs of regulations to corporations—even minor costs—outweighed the health and other benefits that the regulations would deliver to the public. We will return to this point later.

Most non-enforcement decisions pass unnoticed. A comprehensive 2014 study by *The Crime Report* offered a stunning finding: the EPA almost *never* prosecutes business violations of environmental law. "More than 64,000 facilities are currently listed in agency databases as being in violation of federal environmental laws, but in most years, *fewer than one-half of one percent* of violations trigger criminal investigations." The executive branch has full legal authority to prosecute any violation under the Clean Air and Water Acts, but actively chooses not to pursue criminal charges in all but a handful of cases. Thus, the study notes, "the vast majority of corporate environmental transgressions—even cases that involve the releases of large amounts of toxic chemicals—are relegated to civil and administrative enforcement." The resulting fines are seldom a major deterrent, and executives often factor them into their budget projections.

The decline in EPA criminal investigations is a long-term, bipartisan trend: the number of annual investigations was significantly lower during the Obama years than during the early 2000s, under George W. Bush's EPA. The EPA's non-enforcement is also shaped by racism: in over three hundred cases of alleged environmental racism at the state level since the 1990s, it has never confirmed a single violation. Toxic lead levels in the Flint, Michigan, water supply (and before that, lethal air pollution caused by Flint industry) were possible because the EPA declined to intervene.[16]

Non-enforcement is, however, a weak form of protection from prosecution. Unenforced regulations that remain on the books carry the

---

15   Kristen Lombardi and John Solomon, "Polluters Freed from Environmental Oversight by Stimulus," Center for Public Integrity, November 29, 2010.

16   Graham Kates, "Environmental Crime: The Prosecution Gap," *The Crime Report*, July 14, 2014 (quotes; emphasis added); Zoë Carpenter, "How the EPA Has Failed to Challenge Environmental Racism in Flint—and Beyond," *Nation* online, January 28, 2016.

risk that pesky members of the public will take legal action to demand enforcement. Thus, under pressure from nervous corporate miscreants, executive branch officials often seek to scrap existing regulations altogether. Midway through his first term, Obama appointed former JPMorgan Chase executive Bill Daley as his chief of staff and expanded the domain of Cass Sunstein, the business-friendly head of the Office of Information and Regulatory Affairs (OIRA).[17] Soon after these changes, "the president issued an executive order . . . [to] review hundreds of federal regulations to ensure they aren't hampering business efforts to grow and hire." Acting on this initiative, Sunstein "launched a review of existing rules and ultimately proposed killing hundreds of them." Daley ordered regulators to give greater weight to "the impact on jobs when proposing new regulations."[18] Individuals whose appointment owed much to business power were thus eliminating regulations on business's behalf. Their arguments against regulation cited both the need to restore business confidence and the alleged costs to business, while downplaying the benefits of regulation for the public.[19]

New proposals for regulation within the executive branch must also pass through the "cost-benefit" gauntlet. In one case, the Obama White House blocked a high-profile EPA proposal for stricter controls on smog-forming ozone emissions. The EPA had recommended lowering the smog limit from 84 to 65 parts per billion, citing the costs of smog to public health, worker productivity, and public budgets. It calculated that "as many as 7,200 deaths, 11,000 emergency room visits and 38,000 acute cases of asthma would be avoided each year." Yet Obama scuttled the proposal since a "consensus with industry" could not be reached.[20]

---

17   OIRA approves and amends rules submitted by other regulators. On Sunstein see Kristin Shrader-Frechette, "Flawed Attacks on Contemporary Human Rights: Laudan, Sunstein, and the Cost-Benefit State," *Human Rights Review* 7, no. 1 (2005): 92–110.

18   According to a senior Chamber of Commerce official speaking in fall 2011, "Mr. Daley had 'changed the climate' at the White House" and "Mr. Sunstein is far more visible than during the first two years of the administration." Elizabeth Williamson and Jonathan Weisman, "Obama Courts Business Support," *WSJ*, January 19, 2011: A4; Laura Meckler and Carol E. Lee, "White House Regulation Shift Is a Political Bet," *WSJ*, September 12, 2011: A6.

19   One measure of Obama-era deregulation came in July 2017, when the Trump administration "published a list of almost 500 pending regulatory actions it classified as inactive." But as business observers noted, "the vast majority of those were put on hold under Obama." Alan Levin and Jesse Hamilton, "Trump's Red Tape Cuts Are Overblown," *BW*, December 18, 2017: 39.

20   John M. Broder, "Re-election Strategy Is Tied to a Shift on Smog," *NYT*, November 17, 2011: A1; Meckler and Lee, "White House Regulation Shift." In 2015, the administration adopted a weaker standard.

That is, industry claimed that enforcement of the Clean Air Act would harm the economy. As we saw in previous chapters, the administration made this and many other decisions in the context of a historic disinvestment crisis, with business continuing to withhold trillions of dollars in hoarded cash. In making his announcement, Obama stressed "the importance of reducing regulatory burdens and regulatory uncertainty, particularly as our economy continues to recover."[21] Since the hoarders held the investment capital needed to jump-start the economy, recovery depended on their goodwill. The administration hoped that scrapping life-saving regulations would cajole them into investing again. Again, it was reaffirming the corporate-friendly version of cost-benefit logic: some minor costs to polluters were deemed more important than thousands of annual fatalities and millions of dollars in costs to the public.

The Trump administration accelerated this deregulatory trend, killing scores of health and safety, financial, and environmental regulations. When it was unable to eliminate protections entirely, the administration often simply stopped enforcing them. It did "less to enforce existing rules, leading to a dramatic decline in fines for bad actors," reported Bloomberg at the end of Trump's first year. The EPA, for example, became even more polluter-friendly in its enforcement patterns. The Consumer Financial Protection Bureau (CFPB), which had survived the congressional sausage-making machine with some important regulatory power, virtually ceased to enforce consumer protections.[22] This shift was overseen by numerous personnel with close ties to the most destructive sectors of business, from fossil fuels figures like Scott Pruitt at the EPA and Scott Angelle and David Bernhardt at the Department of the Interior, to Wall Street bankers like Stephen Bannon (White House chief strategist), Gary Cohn (National Economic Council), Steve Mnuchin (Treasury secretary), and Wilbur Ross

---

21   Quoted in Juliet Eilperin, "Obama Halts Tighter Rules on Ozone Emissions," *WP*, September 3, 2011: A1.

22   Levin and Hamilton, "Trump's Red Tape Cuts" (quote); Eric Lipton and Danielle Ivory, "E.P.A.'s Polluter Playbook Takes a Turn to Leniency," *NYT*, December 11, 2017: A1; Nadja Popovich, Livia Albeck-Ripka, and Kendra Pierre-Louis, "95 Environmental Rules Being Rolled Back Under Trump," *NYT* online, updated December 21, 2019; AP, "Under Trump, a Voice for the American Consumer Goes Silent," April 10, 2018; Sheelah Kolhatkar, "When Wall Street Writes Its Own Rules," *NYT*, February 11, 2018: SR5; Alan Rappeport, "Lenders See Rules Easing Under Trump," *NYT*, February 5, 2018: A1; Robert Schmidt and Jesse Hamilton, "Banks Win Big in Trump's Washington," *BW*, February 12, 2018: 39–40; Public Citizen, *Corporate Impunity: "Tough on Crime" Trump Is Weak on Corporate Crime and Wrongdoing* (July 2018).

(Commerce secretary).[23] These officials explicitly sought to make cost-benefit analysis even more business-friendly and to use it as a way to prevent or eliminate regulations.[24]

The examples of Daley and Sunstein, and virtually the entire cast of the Trump administration, highlight the role of pro-business appointees in ignoring or eliminating existing regulations. Like lobbyists, such personnel act as conduits for business demands. They can normally be counted on to interpret their enforcement duties in ways that prioritize profits over public welfare. The embeddedness of these personnel within the state and corporations' structural control over economic investment are thus mutually reinforcing, amplifying the power of business threats and promises and ensuring that policymakers' cost-benefit analyses will be decisively skewed in favor of business.

Selective Enforcement

Selective application of the law is more common than outright non-enforcement, and takes various forms. For example, the executive branch often delays the implementation of regulations mandated by law, weakens the stringency of those regulations, and carves out exemptions for particular industries or certain business practices. These patterns are apparent in the Obama administration's enforcement activities in the three major policy realms we have analyzed: financial, healthcare, and environmental policy. In each, the pattern of enforcement was shaped by business disinvestment threats and policymakers' efforts to boost business confidence.

Financial Regulations Far Less Onerous Than Anyone Envisioned

The executive branch's response to the 2008 financial crisis was strongly influenced by the crisis of ongoing disinvestment from the economy.[25] Starting with George W. Bush and continuing under Obama, the executive delivered policies demanded by Wall Street in exchange for promises that banks would start investing in Main Street again. The major initiative was the Bush and Obama

---

23   See Chapter 1, note 33.
24   See for instance Coral Davenport and Lisa Friedman, "E.P.A. Aims to Revalue Human Health in Its Review of Mercury Rules," *NYT*, September 10, 2018: A15.
25   This section is partly based on Young et al., "Capital Strikes."

administrations' Troubled Asset Relief Program (TARP), or bank bailouts. TARP entailed massive government assistance to Wall Street on extremely generous terms. According to Obama's treasury secretary Timothy Geithner, neither the low interest rates nor the gargantuan size of the bailouts were essential for a successful rescue. But the administrations and Congress understood that if they priced the rescue loans "too punitively, we would have risked undermining the effectiveness of the emergency response."[26] In other words, the banks made clear that they would not reinvest in Main Street in the form of home mortgages and loans to small businesses unless the government granted them terms far more generous than what they could find on the market—and far more generous than was needed to assure their recovery.

Congress and the executive responded accordingly. As a sign of good faith, the Bush and Obama administrations even invited Wall Street representatives to write most of the TARP plan.[27] They also tailored the implementation of the legislation to avoid measures that might reduce banks' confidence. For instance, although the TARP legislation itself suggested that the most important category of "troubled assets" was "residential or commercial mortgages," Bush's Treasury allocated nothing to acquiring and modifying home mortgages, and the Obama administration allocated only about 7 percent of the $700 billion in TARP funds to this purpose.[28] Thus, just a tiny fraction of the TARP money was used to aid struggling homeowners, even as the foreclosure crisis impeded national economic recovery. Infringements on banks' privileges and prerogatives were also carefully avoided. In former Federal Reserve official Alan Blinder's analysis, both the Bush and Obama administrations avoided forcing banks to accept reductions on mortgage debts for fear of violating lenders' "property rights." They instead opted for purely "voluntary" and "industry-led" initiatives on housing which, though predictably ineffective, would not provoke Wall Street's wrath and would avoid exacerbating its disinvestment.[29]

---

26   Timothy Geithner, "On the Politics of the Crisis Response," Document PTX-667, amazonaws.com, May 11, 2013: 4.

27   Robert Kuttner, *A Presidency in Peril: The Inside Story of Obama's Promise, Wall Street's Power, and the Struggle to Control Our Economic Future* (White River Junction, VT: Chelsea Green, 2010), 61, 64.

28   Alan S. Blinder, *After the Music Stopped: The Financial Crisis, the Response, and the Work Ahead* (New York: Penguin, 2013), 332.

29   Blinder, *After the Music Stopped*, 328–9; Kuttner, *A Presidency in Peril*, 49–59.

The popular justification for the TARP bailouts was that they were needed to provide lenders with capital to revive the home mortgage and small business markets. Federal Reserve chair Ben Bernanke promised that TARP would relieve banks of "illiquid assets," which in turn would "reduce investor uncertainty" and "help to restore confidence in our financial markets," allowing "credit to begin flowing again, supporting economic growth."[30] In practice, however, this prediction was inaccurate at best. Despite the rapid and profitable revival of the nine major Wall Street firms that received TARP funds, they did not restore lending to Main Street. Even the Congressional Oversight Panel in charge of monitoring TARP, which was not inclined to be overly critical, concluded that the program had only rescued Wall Street and not Main Street. After several months of TARP, "hundreds of billions of dollars have been injected into the marketplace with no demonstrable effects on lending."[31] The banks were keeping the bailout money. Their confidence had not yet been restored, and so further government action would be needed.

The lack of "demonstrable effects on lending" was a sign of things to come. In the years that followed, Wall Street would continue to withhold investments from Main Street in an effort to extract a host of further policy changes from government, some of which had no relation to the original causes of the 2008 crash. The Fed noted this collective withholding of investment capital when it reported that the rescued banks had actually "slowed down lending" even more than the "banks that didn't receive TARP funds."[32] The lack of new investments was not merely a result of low demand for loans or other market conditions. It was, in large part, a strategy to wrest further pro-business concessions from policymakers.

The transcripts of the 2009 Federal Reserve Board meetings show how the negotiation of these added concessions occurred.[33] The reports by board members, based on their continuous

---

30   Ben S. Bernanke, "Current Economic and Financial Conditions," speech at the National Association for Business Economics meeting, Washington, DC, October 7, 2008.

31   "Accountability for the Troubled Asset Relief Program: The Second Report of the Congressional Oversight Panel," January 9, 2009.

32   Matt Taibbi, "Secrets and Lies of the Bailout," *Rolling Stone*, January 17, 2013: 38.

33   Transcripts of the eleven meetings that the Federal Open Market Committee held with the Board of Governors of the Federal Reserve are available at amazonaws.com.

conversations with business executives, attributed the post-TARP drag in investment to insufficient business confidence. "The key underlying weak factor that I hear about from CEO after CEO," said Dallas Fed president Richard Fisher in March, "is a lack of confidence."[34] Members made clear that large companies would only be willing to restart lending and hiring if the Obama adminis- tration modified or abandoned a wide range of policies, many in areas unrelated to the original disinvestment from Main Street. At the December meeting, multiple participants remarked on the "tremendous amount of political uncertainty" among executives "about health care reform, financial reform, and tax policy," as well as "new environmental regulations." The "general lack of confi- dence" about potential reforms in these areas was explicitly cited by business executives as a reason for their disinvestment: "In talking to our directors, they make it very clear that this is a factor influ- encing their hiring behavior." With respect to lending, "their will- ingness to make new loans is driven at least in part by regulatory considerations." Board member Elizabeth Duke told the group in March that "I've never, ever talked to bankers where the conversa- tion was so much about government and so little about the banking business."[35] As Duke's comment suggests, business confidence does not simply mean the business world's expectations of profitable returns on future investments, as it is conventionally defined. Its practical definition is much broader, referring to business predic- tions of government policy across many realms.

The way that corporations were using their disinvestment to influ- ence federal policies was also a topic of discussion at a Board meeting in November 2009. Having canvassed key investors, Richard Fisher reported that the "uncertainty among business decision makers," created by "the plethora of new economic and regulatory initiatives" on the horizon, "appears to be retarding commitments to expansions of the workforce and to a commitment to cap-ex [capital expenditures] in the United States." Specifically,

I am finding a good many CEOs and CFOs who are planning to commit to cap-ex and deploy that $1 trillion in build-up in cash, plus additional cashflows, but very few—in fact none out of the somewhat 30 that I

---

34   Federal Reserve Board of Governors, 2009 meeting transcripts, 472.
35   Ibid., 1541, 1536, 1400, 500.

spoke to—are planning to commit it here in the United States, unless there is greater clarity about future policy initiatives.[36]

Fisher's contacts were engaged in a massive capital strike: the withholding of one trillion dollars of investment capital, coupled with a demand for "greater clarity." Translated into plain English, "greater clarity" meant favorable policies with regard to healthcare, financial reform, tax policy, and environmental regulation. House Speaker John Boehner was more direct when he commented:

> My worry is that for American job creators, all the uncertainty is turning to fear that this toxic environment for job creation is a permanent state. *Job creators in America are essentially on strike.* The problem is not confusion about the policies . . . the problem is the policies.[37]

The policies about which Boehner was complaining were the various proposals still on the Obama reform agenda.

These statements offer a window into the behavior of US business in the aftermath of the 2008 crisis. Having pocketed the generous government rescue loans, Wall Street executives continued their disinvestment, as did executives in other industries. Whereas their initial disinvestment had been a more or less automatic response to the mortgage crisis, they now used their disinvestment as leverage to try to extract a whole smorgasbord of policies from the Obama administration. What had started as a natural response to adverse market conditions had become a full-fledged capital strike. This coordinated action allowed corporate leaders to extract further concessions—in this case, modifications in healthcare, financial regulation, and other pending policies— that had little or nothing to do with the profitability of potential investments in Main Street.

Business continued to wield this power as financial regulatory initiatives got underway during Obama's first term. Wall Street representatives had been unable to block the 2010 Dodd-Frank Act from passing into law, but they had successfully blocked many of the measures they found most objectionable. And, given the complicated implementation process associated with all such legislation, the bill's passage was only

---

36 Ibid., 1368.
37 "Boehner's Jobs Speech" (transcript), *NYT* online, September 15, 2011. Emphasis added.

"halftime," in the words of the chief lobbyist at the Financial Services Roundtable. As executive-branch agencies began writing the 390 rules that would make the new law operational, commercial banks increased their lobbying expenditures.[38]

Throughout the implementation process, the threat of new or continued capital strikes was a central negotiating tool for Wall Street spokespersons, including many inhabiting government positions. The routine claim was that the new law would have a negative "impact on lending," therefore "retarding growth and employment," unless implementation incorporated various exceptions and exemptions.[39] These dire warnings were a constant refrain throughout the contentious rulemaking process. They helped ensure that the new law would be selectively enforced, producing a variety of exemptions, delays, and modifications for the benefit of industry.

The rulemaking involved several different agencies, including the Federal Reserve, the Federal Deposit Insurance Corporation (FDIC), the Securities and Exchange Commission (SEC), the Commodity Futures Trading Commission (CFTC), the Comptroller of the Currency, the Treasury Department, and the newly created Consumer Financial Protection Bureau (CFPB). Most rules required the participation of more than one of these entities. Since rulemaking required agreement among all involved agencies, Wall Street had multiple chokepoints for blocking or weakening most rules. Particular Wall Street interests enjoyed greater influence with particular regulators, with this influence often amplified and protected by congressional allies who could join the negotiations to defend their favored sectors and firms. Secretary Geithner noted that the rulemaking debates were rarely restricted to the opinions of regulators: "The affected agencies all had congressional defenders looking out for their turf, as well as influential supporters in the financial industry."[40]

Corporations' ongoing hoarding of trillions in capital, including $1 trillion by banks, made the voice of Wall Street particularly salient.

---

38   Gary Rivlin, "Wall Street Fires Back," *Nation*, May 20, 2013: 11–12 (Scott Talbott quoted).

39   Quote from Financial Services Forum CEO Rob Nichols, in Donna Borak, Victoria Finkle, and Joe Adler, "Consensus Is Elusive on TBTF, Big-Bank Subsidies," *AB*, April 23, 2013. For other threats see Williamson and Hagerty, "The New Political Landscape"; Elizabeth Williamson and Joann S. Lublin, "Obama's Overture to Business Gets Wary Reception from CEOs," *WSJ*, November 17, 2010: A4; Andrew Ackerman, Jamila Trindle, and Michael R. Crittenden, "President Presses Regulators on Financial Rules," *WSJ*, August 20, 2013: A4; Ryan Tracy, Victoria McGrane, and Justin Baer, "Fed Tells Big Banks to Shrink or Else," *WSJ*, July 21, 2015: A1.

40   Timothy F. Geithner, *Stress Test: Reflections on Financial Crises* (New York: Crown, 2014), 400.

JPMorgan CEO Jamie Dimon spoke for the financial industry in 2011 when he threatened that the hoarded funds would not be invested in the US economy unless Dodd-Frank regulations were curbed or eliminated: "Has anyone looked at the cumulative effect of all these regulations, and could they be the reason it's taking so long for credit and jobs to come back?" In 2014 *American Banker* observed that Dimon's comment had become "a rallying cry by the industry," repeatedly conveyed to regulators during the rulemaking negotiations.[41]

The banks treated the implementation process as another chance to weaken the impact of the regulations that had survived the congressional battles. The threat of new or continued capital strikes was essential to that effort. For example, one key issue was "capital ratios." The failure of major banks to maintain sufficient capital as a buffer against crisis was a central factor contributing to the 2008 crash. Because Dodd-Frank mandated an unspecified increase in banks' retained capital, the amount of this increase became a focal point for negotiation. Speaking for eighteen major lenders, Financial Services Forum CEO Rob Nichols delivered one of many disinvestment threats intended to limit the increase: "There is a tradeoff with higher capital ratios, and that is the impact on lending and economic growth."[42] Nichols was asserting that investors would respond to increased capital ratios by continuing or amplifying their boycott of domestic lending markets.

If the banks did react by withholding investments, it would not be a response to market forces, but rather a capital strike. FDIC chair Sheila Bair cited academic studies showing that an increase in mandated capital levels had no automatic impact on the money available for lending, and subsequent studies have confirmed that finding.[43] Bair called the lenders' threats "self-serving nonsense" and insisted on a major increase

---

41 Donna Borak, "Four Years Later, Economic Cost of Dodd-Frank Remains Elusive," *AB*, July 18, 2014.

42 Quoted in Borak et al., "Consensus Is Elusive on TBTF."

43 Increased capital ratios imply no inevitable cost to banks, since banks can maintain their lending by issuing new shares and/or reinvesting profits. See Anat R. Admati and Martin F. Hellwig, *The Bankers' New Clothes: What's Wrong with Banking and What to Do About It* (Princeton, NJ: Princeton University Press, 2013), 7; Jonathan Bridges, David Gregory, Mette Nielsen, Silvia Pezzini, Amar Radia, and Marco Spaltro, "The Impact of Capital Requirements on Bank Lending," Bank of England Working Paper No. 486, January 2014; Juliane Begenau, "Capital Requirements, Risk Choice, and Liquidity Provision in a Business Cycle Model," Harvard Business School Working Paper no. 15-072, March 2015. In 2015 the Fed modestly raised requirements on the largest US banks, prompting Financial Services Roundtable president Tim Pawlenty to threaten that "this rule will keep billions of dollars out of the economy" (quoted in Tracy et al., "Fed Tells Big Banks to Shrink").

in capital ratios. But Bair was overruled by the Wall Street loyalists who had been appointed to other regulatory bodies.[44]

Another key example of selective enforcement was the implementation of "risk retention." The law sought to prevent lenders from granting a loan that was likely to default and then selling it to an uninformed investor. It thus required banks to bear 5 percent of the risk associated with securitized loans, which are loans guaranteed by mortgaged property like homes and automobiles. *American Banker* spoke for the financial community when it promised that banks would respond by passing on the costs of these rules in "the form of higher interest rates and fees," which would price many borrowers out of the market.[45] These threats led to a negotiated settlement. The ultimate risk-retention rule kept the 5 percent requirement, but exempted the category of "qualified residential mortgages." The final definition of this category was then negotiated to include mortgages with no down payment, meaning that the 5 percent requirement would not apply to many of the riskiest loans. Someone else would therefore bear the cost if the banks' loans ended in default.[46] Financial analyst Isaac Boltansky reported a similar outcome in almost all the "mortgage-related" regulations: "The rules have been far less onerous than anyone originally envisioned."[47]

In all these instances, industry and its allies used the logic of cost-benefit analysis (CBA) to weaken the regulatory bite of the new legislation. In each case they claimed that regulation would impose costs on the industry and thus reduce its profitability. They backed up this argument by threatening to exercise their investment autonomy: if policy-makers did not selectively tailor the new law to their wishes, they would continue their capital strike against Main Street. Sympathetic personnel within government then cited the banks' predictions of lost profits and threats of continued disinvestment as justification for their compliance with industry demands.

44   Sheila Bair, *Bull by the Horns: Fighting to Save Main Street from Wall Street and Wall Street from Itself* (New York: Free Press, 2012), 225.

45   "Six CFPB Rules That Will Increase Consumer Costs," *AB*, April 25, 2013; Victoria Finkle, "Mortgage Lending at Risk Thanks to New Rules, Small Banks Say," *AB*, April 6, 2013.

46   Joe Adler, "Fed, Other Agencies Finalize Risk Retention Rule," *AB*, October 22, 2014.

47   Quoted in Rachel Witkowski, "Obama Signals Support for Easing Mortgage Rules," *AB*, August 8, 2013. In 2017 Bloomberg reported that "subprime lending is booming—this time for autos," and "Wall Street loves it." Gabrielle Coppola and Jamie Butters, "It's Happening Again," *BW*, July 24, 2017: 23.

Cost-benefit analysis had become a formal part of regulatory implementation during the last decades of the twentieth century.[48] Its early usage was based on the idea that the rulemaking process should be informed by rigorous estimates of the impact of regulation on the economy as a whole. Over the years, the focus narrowed to the costs absorbed by the corporations subject to regulation. For two of the key agencies in charge of Dodd-Frank implementation, the SEC and CFTC, CBA was institutionalized in 1996 legislation signed by President Clinton. The 1996 law required CBA to give special weight to the potential impact of a new rule on "efficiency, competition, and *capital formation*" (i.e., profitability and investment flows) in the regulated sector.[49] By the time President Obama took office, CBA had largely come to be understood as the avoidance of any decline in profits for affected businesses. This definition of CBA focused on the alleged costs to companies facing regulation while deemphasizing the benefits to the public, the workforce, and other industries. By demanding that regulatory rules avoid constraints on "capital formation" for the regulated firms, and by relying on testimony from industry representatives about the negative impact of regulation, CBA effectively conferred on large corporations a form of veto power over the implementation of regulations. It further institutionalized business-confidence logic within government, empowering corporations to pursue legal redress when that logic was not adequately respected.

In 2012, CFTC commissioner Bart Chilton pointed to the distorting effects of the narrow definition:

> There are a bevy of bellowers booing about the "costs" of regulation. To those catcalls, I'd simply ask, what were the complete "costs" of the $414 billion taxpayer funded bailout? What are the "costs" of families losing their homes, or of folks who can't get a job? . . . My view is that there is not a single benefit to not doing these regulations, but there are unacceptable costs if we don't go forward. Without these rules and

48   Cass R. Sunstein, *The Cost-Benefit State: The Future of Regulatory Protection* (Chicago, IL: American Bar Association, 2002); David M. Driesen, "Is Cost-Benefit Analysis Neutral?" *University of Colorado Law Review* 77 (2006): 335–65; Paul Rose and Christopher J. Walker, "The Importance of Cost-Benefit Analysis in Financial Regulation," Report for US Chamber of Commerce Center for Capital Markets Competitiveness, March 2013.
49   H.R. Rep. No. 104–622, Section 106 (1996), quoted in Eugene Scalia, "Why Dodd-Frank Rules Keep Losing in Court," *WSJ*, October 4, 2012: A25. Emphasis added.

regulations, there will be unacceptable costs to consumers, to businesses, to markets, to our economy and our country.[50]

Chilton accused Wall Street of demanding that regulatory CBA "go beyond a 'consideration' of costs and benefits for the industry . . . to making their narrow conception of costs . . . the crucible for judging all financial regulations."[51] As he implied, the narrow definition of CBA that prevails in the twenty-first century both reflects and enhances corporate power over policymaking. Not surprisingly, the use of CBA in regulatory rulemaking has usually weakened protections for workers, consumers, and the environment, irrespective of whether a Democrat or Republican holds the presidency.[52] In 2016, the business press noted that "the Obama administration has been particularly vigilant" in its adherence to regulatory CBA. The Trump administration would be even more vigilant, explicitly deploying CBA on behalf of industry.[53]

CBA works hand-in-hand with two other corporate weapons: lawsuits and the defunding of regulators. When the rulemaking process resulted in regulations that might constrain Wall Street profits, the industry often brought lawsuits based on CBA, arguing that the rules violated the 1996 law or other legislation. In court, regulatory agencies' ability to defend themselves was further hampered by prior congressional budget cuts. During Dodd-Frank rulemaking both the SEC and CFTC publicly complained that underfunding impaired their ability to respond to financial firms' judicial challenges.[54]

Defunding the regulators had become a central weapon for business starting in the 1980s, not just for bankers but for polluters, tax evaders,

---

50   Bart Chilton, "The Thing Is," speech before Americans for Financial Reform, Washington, DC, May 9, 2012.

51   Ibid.

52   Lisa Schultz Bressman and Michael P. Vandenbergh, "Inside the Administrative State: A Critical Look at the Practice of Presidential Control," *Michigan Law Review* 105, no. 1 (2006): 47–99; Driesen, "Is Cost-Benefit Analysis Neutral?"; Rena Steinzor, Michael Patoka, and James Goodwin, *Behind Closed Doors at the White House: How Politics Trumps Protection of Public Health, Worker Safety, and the Environment* (Center for Progressive Reform White Paper #1111, November 2011).

53   "The Problem with Ryan's Reforms," *BW*, June 27–July 3, 2016: 14. Trump's first CFPB appointee, Mick Mulvaney, promised even more intensive use of CBA. "There is a lot more math in our future," he said. Quoted in "Backporch," *AB*, March 2018: 24. See also Davenport and Friedman, "E.P.A. Aims to Revalue Human Health."

54   Corey Boles and Jamila Trindle, "Global Finance: CFTC Budget Request Cut by Lawmakers," *WSJ*, November 15, 2011: C3; Victoria Finkle, "SEC, CFTC Blame Funding Woes for Slow Dodd-Frank Implementation," *AB*, July 30, 2013.

and employers in dangerous occupations.[55] Regulators therefore suffered from a chronic lack of resources, which accelerated the transfer of rule-enforcement responsibility to the regulated firms themselves. Firms were often allowed to decide how, and whether, rules would apply. Underfunded regulators could then choose to either trust the companies' claims or expend scarce resources to make an independent judgment. If they did make an independent assessment, disagreement with the companies' interpretation could trigger a resource-intensive administrative hearing, with the promise of an expensive appeal to the courts if the regulators prevailed.

Their resource advantage over poorly-funded regulatory agencies yielded considerable success for the banks in the early battles over Dodd-Frank implementation. Six challenges to SEC rules based on CBA primacy were litigated before the DC Court of Appeals, with the SEC losing each time. This record, along with many other costly challenges, created strong pressure for regulators to capitulate. As Chilton put it, Wall Street was wielding CBAs "as a Sword of Damocles over regulatory agencies. We are virtually paralyzed by intimidation—or, indeed, the reality—of lawsuits brought (haphazardly, in my assessment) on the foundations of allegedly poor CBAs."[56]

Disputes over derivatives regulation show how this Sword of Damocles worked in conjunction with capital-strike threats. In one drastic gesture, several of the smaller players declared that "they won't participate in the U.S. swaps market" as a result of Dodd-Frank.[57] The dominant firms echoed this threat in a more tempered fashion. JPMorgan, Bank of America, Morgan Stanley, Citigroup, and Goldman Sachs offered a CBA-based rebuttal to most of the specific rules governing derivatives. Their response to a rule designed to ensure that "the

---

55   At least 37,994 US workers died on the job during Obama's time in office, according to the Bureau of Labor Statistics' Census of Fatal Occupational Injuries. Since 1981 the Occupational Safety and Health Administration has suffered major cuts. A 2013 report from the Center for Effective Government found that "it would take federal OSHA inspectors 131 years to visit every U.S. workplace." Cited in Josh Eidelson, "Using the Web to Police Dangerous Workplaces," *BW*, September 22–8, 2014: 34.

56   Scalia, "Why Dodd-Frank Rules Keep Losing"; Rose and Walker, "The Importance of Cost-Benefit Analysis"; Chilton, "The Thing Is." See also Rivlin, "Wall Street Fires Back," 20; Paul M. Barrett, "Wall Street Chips Away at Dodd-Frank," *BW*, April 25–May 1, 2016: 41–2; Victoria Finkle, "Proposed Legislation Would Add Scrutiny of Wall Street Regulators," *NYT*, January 20, 2016: B3.

57   "Dodd-Frank's Financial Outsourcing" (editorial), *WSJ*, November 6, 2010: A16.

failure of one party does not lead to a systemic collapse" illustrates their strategy: "the banks warned that trading would become more expensive for companies and funds." They recruited nonfinancial companies that used derivatives to echo the same line.[58] A similar dispute arose over the mandate for multiple price quotes prior to swaps trades, aimed at protecting against price-fixing and concealment of risk from clients.[59] As *American Banker* reported, the banks responded with "the curious (if not spurious) story" that "too many price quotes will increase trading costs and reduce liquidity."[60] Here again, they were asserting that maintaining banks' high profit levels was more important than protecting their clients and the larger economy. They were saying that regulation was impermissible, and often illegal, if it resulted in lower profits for regulated companies, regardless of the benefits accruing to other institutions, the public, or the economy as a whole. In these two cases the banks forced key compromises that limited the protection for buyers and maintained the higher prices charged by banks.[61] As these and other rules were being finalized, former Federal Reserve official Alan Blinder concluded that Dodd-Frank as implemented "exempts the vast majority of derivatives."[62] Thus the protective intent of the legislation was largely negated.

The defunding of regulatory agencies, CBA, lawsuits, and threats of disinvestment had all contributed to that outcome. Wall Street got its congressional allies to starve the regulators of resources. It launched lawsuits based on CBA. And, finally, it threatened disinvestment that

---

58 The rule required the centralized clearing of derivatives trades. Michael Mackenzie and Tom Braithwaite, "Derivatives Trading Safer and More Efficient, Says Citadel," *FT* online, September 10, 2013; Geithner, *Stress Test*, 412; Barney Frank, *Frank: A Life in Politics from the Great Society to Same-Sex Marriage* (New York: Farrar, Straus and Giroux, 2015), 313.

59 Blinder, *After the Music Stopped*, 281–2.

60 Neil Weinberg, "Dodd-Frank Rollback, Pandit's Return, As JPM Turns," *AB*, May 17, 2013.

61 Specifically, the multiple quote requirement was reduced from five to two. The centralized clearing mechanism was enacted, but with undefined exemptions that would be decided in arenas in which corporations had the resource advantage and the law on their side.

62 Alan Blinder, "Five Years Later, Financial Lessons Not Learned," *WSJ*, September 11, 2013: A15. Soon thereafter the US megabanks achieved an almost universal exemption from the restrictions on which funds could be utilized in derivatives trading, with legislation allowing them to speculate on derivatives using FDIC-insured depositors' money. Their allies in Congress attached the exemption, written by Citigroup, to a $1.1 trillion spending bill that President Obama then signed. Peter Eavis, "Wall St. Wins a Round in a Dodd-Frank Fight," *NYT*, December 13, 2013: B3.

could impose enough harm on the economy to offset any benefits stem-
ming from the enforcement of new regulations.

What was the "real" impact of Dodd-Frank regulations on Wall Street?
Though most of the final rules were declared "reasonable" by industry
leaders, a few rules were imposed over Wall Street opposition. A frequent
target of industry criticism were the new reporting requirements, which
would allegedly raise costs that banks would then pass on to their customers (thus pricing less affluent customers out of the market). Nevertheless,
two years after Dodd-Frank's passage, *American Banker* reported that "it
is difficult to discern . . . any explosion in compliance costs."[63] By 2016,
the profits of both large and small banks had increased, with the net
income of commercial banks reaching a record high.[64]

Helping Healthcare Corporations Survive

The implementation of the Affordable Care Act was likewise a process of
continual negotiation between the Obama administration and the "most
affected" industries—but not the most affected consumers or communities.
The administration's selective enforcement involved granting lucrative
exemptions and delays to corporate lobbyists. These included a one-year
delay for major employers to insure all their workers—a concession worth
$10 billion to the affected corporations—and a two-year delay before the
dialysis drug Sensipar would be subject to Medicare price controls, which
would transfer about $500 million to biotechnology giant Amgen. In 2013
and 2014, the administration unilaterally cancelled the ACA's scheduled
reductions in payment to private insurers in the Medicare Advantage
program, which would have saved $156 billion over the first decade by
reducing reimbursements to private insurers to the standard Medicare
reimbursement rates; it then negotiated rate increases that exceeded those
requested by the private insurers. Meanwhile, labor and consumer petitions for temporary reprieve from ACA penalties fell on deaf ears.[65]

---

63   Harry Terris, "Evidence Sketchy for Dodd-Frank Boom in Compliance Costs,"
AB, June 21, 2012.
64   Victoria Finkle, "Warren: Dodd-Frank Rules Aren't Hurting Small Banks
Very Much," *AB*, February 12, 2015; FDIC, "Commercial Banks: Historical Statistics
on Banking," Table CB04, accessed November 22, 2017.
65   Eric Lipton and Kevin Sack, "Fiscal Footnote: Big Senate Gift to Drug Maker,"
NYT, January 20, 2013: A1; John Tozzi, "Obamacare: Deadline, Schmedline," *BW*,
March 17–23, 2014: 24–5; Jason Millman, "Obama Administration Reverses Proposed
Cut to Medicare Plans," *WP* online, April 7, 2014; Jenny Brown, "Obamacare Opens
for Business, Shuts Out Labor," *LN*, August 2013: 1.

The health industries won these and other concessions by utilizing (or threatening to utilize) their almost unfettered ability to raise prices and the insurance and hospital industries' ability to disinvest from specific markets—two freedoms safeguarded during the earlier stages of the healthcare reform process. Pharmaceuticals seized upon the lack of price control: according to Bloomberg, twenty-nine of thirty-eight top-selling drugs "logged price increases of more than double the rate of inflation from 2009 to 2015."[66] Hospitals threatened to close facilities that they claimed had lower-than-expected profits, and used these threats to help justify their own price increases. Practitioners threatened to refuse Medicaid unless their price increases were fully reimbursed, and many followed through on the threat.[67] As drugmakers and providers raised their prices, insurance companies followed suit. The insurers' first reaction was to raise premiums, copays, and deductibles while reducing benefits.[68] They fended off the reduction in reimbursements in the Medicare Advantage program by threatening "that seniors will see reduced benefits and fewer health care choices."[69] In each case industry exploited the logic of CBA, which since the 1990s had come to mean that no regulation could result in reduced profits for the regulated sector, even if it improved overall healthcare or reduced costs for other parties.

In 2016 and 2017, several insurers escalated the pressure by withdrawing altogether from the state insurance exchanges established by the ACA. At first glance, the decisions by Aetna, UnitedHealth, and Humana to stop offering coverage in those markets reflected straightforward financial logic: they had reported significant losses on the exchanges given that not enough healthy customers had purchased plans to fund their coverage of the sick, whom they were now barred from turning away. However, short-term losses often make good business sense. As Aetna CEO Mark Bertolini noted in an April 2016

66   Robert Langreth with Jared Hopkins, "Demystifying Drug Pricing," *BW*, June 27–July 3, 2016: 40.

67   "Only half of family doctors accepted Medicaid in 2013, down from 65 percent four years earlier": John Tozzi, "More Patients, Less Money for Doctors," *BW*, December 22–8, 2014: 31. See also Margot Sanger-Katz and Katie Thomas, "Data Shows Large Rise in List Prices at Hospitals," *NYT*, June 2, 2015: B6; Sabrina Tavernise, "Cuts in Hospital Subsidies Threaten Safety-Net Care," *NYT*, November 9, 2013: A1; Elisabeth Rosenthal, "Patients' Costs Skyrocket, Specialists' Incomes Soar," *NYT*, January 19, 2014: A1.

68   On insurance prices see the annual reports from the Kaiser Family Foundation (kff.org).

69   Millman, "Obama Administration Reverses Proposed Cut."

earnings call, entering new markets is initially very expensive, but the investment can pay off down the road. Despite the temporary losses that Aetna was incurring, the exchanges remained "a good investment."[70]

Aetna's withdrawal was therefore not dictated by simple market logic, but by a broader political-economic calculus. Its exit was a reaction to the Department of Justice's prevention of its planned merger with Humana. In a July 2016 letter, CEO Bertolini had privately warned that "if the DOJ sues to enjoin the transaction, we will immediately take action to reduce our 2017 exchange footprint," including cancelling plans to expand to five new states and withdrawing "from at least five additional states."[71] It was a political strategy for coercing the government to give ground on policies that had nothing to do with the exchanges—a classic capital strike. And as in all capital strikes, there was a promise of a quid pro quo if government did as it was told. Aetna accompanied its threat with a promise to expand into new markets if the DoJ allowed its merger with Humana. When the DoJ nonetheless blocked the merger, Aetna made good on its threat.[72]

Though the administration actually rebuffed the corporate threat in this case, there are clues that insurers' withdrawals continued to shape the executive's selective enforcement of the ACA. Just after Aetna's exit, Obama reached out to health insurance executives to "emphasize the Administration's commitment to working with them," while privately describing the actions it would soon take "to help them survive."[73] The specific actions were not publicly disclosed.

These outcomes were foretold in the original law itself, which had scrupulously avoided any regulation of prices or of private companies' power over investment decisions. The law further entrenched private interests' powers of disruption and thus guaranteed its own uncertain future. The ACA's long-term fate was still unclear as Trump took office, and particularly after the December 2017 Trump tax reform repealed the individual mandate. At best, the ACA would continue to hobble

---

70   "If we were to build out 15 markets, it would cost us somewhere between $600 million to $750 million to enter those markets . . . So in the broad scheme of things, we are well, well below any of those numbers from the standpoint of losses we've incurred in the first two-and-a-half years of this program. So we see this as a good investment." April 28, 2016. Transcript available at seekingalpha.com.

71   Mark T. Bertolini to Ryan M. Kantor, July 5, 2016, at big.assets.huffingtonpost.com.

72   Gregory A. Freeman, "Obama Meets with Payers in a Bid to Boost Obamacare," healthleadersmedia.com, September 14, 2016.

73   Ibid.

along, constantly threatened by rising prices, degraded coverage for patients, and tens of millions of uninsured people.

Environmental Regulations That Polluters Can Live With

The consequences of safeguarding corporate profits and decision-making power were even more lethal in the realm of environmental regulation. Although congressional climate legislation failed in 2009–10, the Obama administration itself initiated several notable environmental reforms in its last six years. The most important new regulations were those mandated by the 1970 Clean Air Act, which requires the executive branch to regulate air pollutants. They included modest new rules on vehicle fuel efficiency, limits on the emission of localized pollutants like ozone and mercury, and several measures to reduce the emission of the greenhouse gases that contribute to global warming. Most notable was the 2015 Clean Power Plan (CPP), which was designed to cut power plant emissions and which formed the basis for US pledges under the 2015 Paris global climate accord. The impetus for these initiatives came from a combination of considerations: electoral pressures, environmentalists' lobbying efforts, the escalating public health costs of pollution, and perhaps the administration's concern for the business world "as a whole," which could be disrupted by climate chaos.

These executive policy initiatives were much less ambitious than news coverage implied. As with its financial and healthcare policies, the administration abstained from imposing regulations based on independent studies of the consequences for public wellbeing. Instead, it sought to forge a "consensus with industry" before finalizing any new rules, and often made further adjustments when implementing the rules to accommodate the affected industries. Throughout, the administration's regulatory approach took for granted the corporate monopoly over investment capital and adhered to the CBA logic that new regulation should not result in any decline in corporate profits. Undergirding this principle was the threat, constantly reiterated by energy companies, that aggressive regulations would trigger retaliatory actions by the polluters that would disrupt the flow of investments into the energy sector on which the economy depended.

The making of Obama-era environmental regulations thus obeyed a consistent pattern: the administration made a modest initial proposal that had the potential to make a small dent in the growing ecological crisis, then weakened that proposal following consultation with polluters. A 2011 study of the White House's Office of Information and Regulatory Affairs (OIRA) found that Obama's OIRA was about as likely to weaken EPA-proposed regulations as George W. Bush's OIRA, changing EPA rules over 80 percent of the time. The report concluded that OIRA under both administrations had been a "one-way ratchet that only weakens agency rules."[74] A mass movement directly targeting business might have countered polluters' pressures, but mass disruption was virtually absent early in Obama's presidency and only began to spread in his second term.

The EPA's tightening of fuel efficiency standards in 2012 illustrates this pattern. The new standards did "mandate an average fuel economy of 54.5 miles per gallon for the 2025 model year" for cars and light trucks, but only after "lengthy negotiations" with the "Big Three" US automakers (Ford, General Motors, Chrysler) and other industry leaders. The negotiations sought to maintain or enhance the automakers' profit levels. The final deal included more lenient standards for large trucks and SUVs. Since these larger vehicles are more profitable to manufacture than smaller vehicles, and since the Big Three were increasingly concentrated in these markets, the deal constituted a major subsidy to the profits of the Big Three. It also created added incentive for automakers to shift investments into more gas-guzzling and dangerous vehicles.[75]

The pattern also applied to ozone emissions, as we mentioned earlier. After delaying new regulations on ozone in 2011 (when "a consensus with industry" could not be found), the administration finally tightened emission limits in 2015. However, the final standard was significantly weakened as a result of business resistance. The *New York Times* reported that the leading manufacturing and energy industry coalitions "waged an all-fronts campaign to persuade the Obama administration to make the new standard as weak as possible." Industry enlisted "dozens of mayors and local lawmakers, including many Democrats" and conservative labor officials, to relay the threat of disinvestment to the EPA and White House. Their threat was clear: "a strict new ozone rule could lead to the closing of factories and power plants across the country." Following close consultation with lobbyists from fossil fuel and

---

74   Steinzor et al., *Behind Closed Doors*, 60.

75   Bill Vlasic, "U.S. Sets High Long-Term Fuel Efficiency Rules for Automakers," *NYT*, August 29, 2012: B1; Peter Coy, "Get out the Way," *BW*, February 23–March 1, 2015: 26–7. George W. Bush had initiated this change, and Obama reaffirmed it.

other industries, the administration raised the previous EPA proposal for ozone limits from 65 to 70 parts per billion.[76]

Industry also succeeded in shaping the most heralded of Obama's environmental reforms, the Clean Power Plan. The CPP was finalized in August 2015 after years of negotiation. It set emissions limits for power plants, giving each state the flexibility to determine how it would reduce emissions. The emissions goals themselves were far from ambitious. The target—a 32 percent reduction in power plant emissions by 2030 (based on 2005 levels)—was much more modest than what was scientifically mandated.[77] The CPP's ceilings on emissions also primarily affected coal-fired plants, which had already become much less economical than gas-fired plants following the natural gas boom.[78] It thus "follows a shift that is already unfolding in the electric power market," noted the *Times*—hardly the mark of an aggressive regulatory initiative. In fact, utilities had already advanced halfway to the EPA's reduction targets before the CPP was even finalized. Ultimately, many fossil fuel executives "said they could live with the new policy" (nevertheless, the Trump administration moved to repeal it in 2017).[79]

Modesty was taken to an extreme at the Paris climate summit later in 2015. The reduction pledges of the rich countries, with the US at the helm, were much weaker than necessary to keep global warming below 2 degrees Celsius, let alone the 1.5 degrees that many scientists urged.[80] And rather than enacting binding rules that would give governments

---

76   Coral Davenport, "New Limit on Smog-Causing Emissions Is Not as Strict as Expected," *NYT*, October 2, 2015: A21 (quotes); Juliet Eilperin and Joby Warrick, "New EPA Ozone Limits Criticized from Both Sides," *WP*, October 2, 2015: A20.

77   Furthermore, the benchmark year commonly accepted around the world was 1990, not 2005. By moving the benchmark to 2005, when US carbon emissions were 20 percent above 1990 levels, the administration was disguising the modest ambitions of its plan.

78   Even so, the CPP was hardly a "war on coal," as industry propagandists alleged. It explicitly assumed that "coal and natural gas will remain the two leading sources of electricity generation in the U.S." for decades into the future. (Quoted in David Biello, "How Far Does Obama's Clean Power Plan Go in Slowing Climate Change?" *Scientific American* online, August 6, 2015.) The administration also made significant concessions to coal and coal-fired utilities during the revision process, for example by extending the deadline for compliance from 2020 to 2022.

79   Felicity Barringer, "For New Generation of Power Plants, a New Emission Rule from the E.P.A.," *NYT*, March 28, 2012: A13 (first quote); Clifford Krauss and Diane Cardwell, "Hopes Modest for Carbon Rules," *NYT*, June 3, 2014: B1 (second quote); Coral Davenport, "Energy Trends Outpace Plans for the E.P.A.," *NYT*, December 9, 2016: A1; Mark Drajem with Jim Polson, "Coal Lobbies for More Time to Burn," *BW*, November 10, 2014–January 6, 2015: 84.

80   See Introduction, note 20.

the power and responsibility to regulate investment decisions or make large public investments, negotiators took the prerogatives of private capital as givens. They aimed to send a "signal to global financial investors that they should move money away from fossil fuels and toward clean-energy sources" in light of the "trillions of dollars in profit to be made." Global investors, not governments, were the "people who decide where the dollars go," said an economist who had advised the Obama administration. Since governments did not plan to undertake major public investments in alternative energy, they had to figure out "how to get their industries to go along" through a "signal" that could cajole them.[81] Control over the investment capital needed to carry out the accord gave business a central place in the negotiations. An official with the We Mean Business Coalition, composed of over five hundred global corporations, said that his organization had "indicated to governments not only the type of agreement we would like to see, but also where the text should be placed."[82]

This deferential approach to private investors stemmed from multiple sources of pressure on the Obama administration. An obvious one was the diehard intransigence of the Republican-controlled US Congress, which would not even publicly concede the reality of anthropogenic global warming, let alone approve a binding treaty or commit major funds for public investment. Another key factor was polluters' regular lawsuits based on cost-benefit analysis. As in the case of Dodd-Frank regulations, corporations regularly challenged regulations such as emissions controls based on the allegation that the government had not properly weighed the costs to the regulated industries, and business-friendly judges often agreed to delay or revoke new rules.[83] A related factor was the severe shortage of resources at the EPA and other regulatory agencies, which limited their ability to enforce rules and to defend those rules against legal challenges.

---

81 Coral Davenport, "Key to Success of Climate Pact Will Be Its Signals to Global Markets," *NYT*, December 11, 2015: A18 (second quote from US secretary of state John Kerry, third from Nathaniel Keohane); last quote from Clifford Krauss and Keith Bradsher, "Climate Deal Is Signal for Industry to Go Green," *NYT*, December 14, 2015: A1.

82 Edward Cameron quoted in G. Ananthakrishnan, "Progressive Paris Agreement Will Unlock Green Funds, Says We Mean Business Coalition," *Hindu*, December 6, 2015.

83 See for instance Adam Liptak and Coral Davenport, "Justices Block the Obama Administration's Limits on Power Plant Emissions," *NYT*, June 30, 2015: A12.

These factors amplified the constant background reality: private investors' structural control over the economy was the fundamental root of policymakers' deference. Corporations controlled the flow of energy on which the entire economy and a substantial proportion of employment depended. This power conditioned the behavior of policymakers at all levels, from the federal to the local. Even the communities most harmed by environmental destruction often opposed harsh punishment of the perpetrators for fear that the polluters would respond with retaliatory disinvestment. In its study of EPA non-enforcement, *The Crime Report* cites the case of a lethal oil refinery explosion in Oklahoma. The explosion killed two workers, but no punitive or regulatory action was taken, since "no one wants to put the small town's main employer at risk."[84]

Serving the System

Policymakers' deference to the decision-making power of private capital was a central feature in all these stories. Their sensitivity to the disruptive power of disgruntled capitalists reinforced their determination to ensure business confidence. This concern for business confidence had two types of policy impacts. First, it led the executive branch to take proactive measures on behalf of business, exemplified by the free-trade deals and corporate tax cuts discussed in Chapter 1, and the administration's quiet gifts to pharmaceuticals and health insurers in the aftermath of the ACA's passage. Second, it helped define the range of acceptable policy options, as in the many moments when the executive branch decided to avoid enforcement options that were permitted by congressional legislation. Environmental policy provides the most catastrophic examples of the constraints under which executive action is formulated. Whereas Obama's "all-of-the-above" energy policy was acceptable to polluters, favoring renewables or punishing fossil fuel industries would not have been.

Maintaining business confidence means maintaining or enhancing the high profit levels of regulated companies and industries, even if it means not enforcing legislation passed by Congress. Again, environmental policy features numerous examples. Between 2008 and 2015, oil-train shipments increased by 4,000 percent, and devastating derailments and explosions had killed scores of people in the United States

---

84   Kates, "Environmental Crime."

and Canada. Yet, as railroad safety analyst Fred Millar observed, for most of his time in office Obama limited action to "quiet back-door meetings with the railroads and oil companies" to determine "what they'll agree to do voluntarily." When Obama's Transportation Department finally issued new rules, the Transportation secretary acknowledged that their light touch reflected the need to ensure industry prosperity: his department could have "been more aggressive, but at some point, the manufacturers aren't going to be able to produce the tank cars we need." The private companies' control over the manufacture of critical products gave them a virtual veto power. Thus, they were central to the regulatory negotiations, and "industry input was very important" in the eventual rules, reported *The Hill*.[85]

This light touch is preferred even when corporations are found to have systematically flouted the law. The Volkswagen emissions scandal during Obama's second term is a telling example. For years the company had violated regulations on emissions from its diesel-fueled vehicles. An estimated 1,200 people in Europe alone were predicted to die prematurely as a result.[86] The violations were so egregious that the Obama administration seemed to have the upper hand in negotiating a settlement. Nevertheless, officials chose not to order full compliance with the violated standards. They instead engaged in "talks with the automaker" to negotiate its compliance. After months of talks, regulators reported that no "agreement [had] been reached," and so the company was excused from full compliance. The final agreement announced in July 2016 did not require Volkswagen to meet the emission standards for the recalled vehicles that had violated the law; scientists at the EPA and California Air Resources Board predicted that the repaired vehicles would "emit as much as 40 times the permitted amounts of nitrogen oxides." Government negotiators justified this result by arguing that equipping the vehicles with "a urea-tank system, which most diesel cars use to detoxify exhaust fumes, was deemed prohibitively expensive" for the company.[87]

85   First quote (Fred Millar) in Matthew Philips, "Trains That Go Boom," *BW*, February 17–23, 2014: 36; for statistic and second quote (Anthony Foxx) see Timothy Cama, "Obama Cracks Down on Oil Trains," *The Hill* online, May 1, 2015.

86   Guillaume P. Chossière, Robert Malina, Akshay Ashok, Irene C. Dedoussi, Sebastian D. Eastham, Raymond L. Speth, and Steven R. H. Barrett, "Public Health Impacts of Excess NO_x Emissions from Volkswagen Diesel Passenger Vehicles in Germany," *Environmental Research Letters* 12, no. 3 (2017) (online).

87   Jeff Plungis with Kartikay Mehrotra and Erik Larson, "A Big Settlement That Won't Fix the Problem," *BW*, July 25–31, 2016: 22.

This outcome was the logical conclusion of the regulatory pattern that had evolved over recent decades. Since corporate profitability was the primary priority, and since the corporate right to determine invest-ment decisions was sacrosanct, the government could not enforce a law that was on the books if it would reduce Volkswagen's profits or constrain the company's investment decisions—even if non-enforcement would result in thousands of deaths.

The mandate to protect the profitability of regulated firms and indus-tries sometimes runs counter to the imperative of ensuring prosperity for the capitalist class as a whole. Seldom was this conflict more conse-quential than in the 1998 executive decision to deregulate financial derivatives, a policy that helped enable the Wall Street meltdown a decade later. A meeting of top Clinton administration officials consid-ered a proposal by Brooksley Born, the chair of the Commodity Futures Trading Commission, to regulate "credit default swaps" and other "over-the-counter" (OTC) derivatives.[88] These forms of financial speculation were highly volatile and added nothing of value to the real economy, but they had become increasingly popular and highly lucrative. Born had drafted a "concept release" that would publicly air her proposal to regulate derivatives.

Other administration officials not only opposed her idea, they vehe-mently opposed the public release of the proposal, which would have promoted debate on the matter. Federal Reserve chair Alan Greenspan, Secretary of the Treasury Robert Rubin, and Deputy Secretary of the Treasury Lawrence Summers—all staunch promoters of Wall Street—were the key opponents within the administration. Summers spoke for the three of them, asserting that "Treasury, Fed, SEC, & industry view concept release as being disastrous for market." Rubin added that the financial world was "petrified" that the idea would even be considered. Greenspan warned that regulation "might suppress OTC derivatives business," and raised the specter that the "OTC derivatives market could flee to London (or Europe)." Greenspan conceded that unregulated swaps were dangerous, but said that the Fed had nevertheless decided "not to deal with this issue (avert eyes & let it continue)," because nurturing the profitability of the derivatives market was its primary concern. He said explicitly that the dangers associated with unregulated

---

88   Our account is based on the handwritten notes documenting the meeting. See "Re: Financial Markets Working Group Principals Meeting," April 21, 1998, in "FOIA 2010-0673-F—President's Working Group on Financial Markets," Clinton Digital Library, clinton.presidentiallibraries.us.

derivatives "shouldn't induce us to do things that will undercut the system that we are beholden to serve."

The "system" to which the regulators were "beholden" was Wall Street, which viewed credit default swaps as a promising sector. Although Born published the concept release anyway, Greenspan, Rubin, Summers, and other top officials nevertheless prevailed, and her proposal was defeated. To ensure against the revival of Born's proposal, Congress subsequently passed, and President Clinton signed, legislation guaranteeing unregulated derivatives markets.[89] The preservation of the unregulated market resulted in the diversion of capital from productive investment to derivatives, and was a prime cause of the 2008 crash.

This episode highlights the way in which business-friendly personnel within government magnify the power of capital strike threats, and vice versa. The best way for business to ensure that government safeguards corporate profits and investment decision-making is to place its own representatives directly into the relevant government agencies. Brooksley Born was a career lawyer and regulator, not a Wall Street loyalist. Her opponents were much more closely tied to finance capital: Greenspan and Rubin had long worked on Wall Street prior to entering government, and Summers had a well-established reputation as a neoliberal economist and would later direct a top Wall Street hedge fund. Their backgrounds predisposed them to embrace the logic of business confidence and the protection of industry profits. What ultimately gave Greenspan, Rubin, and Summers the power to defeat Born was the banks' threat of disinvestment from the derivatives market. The three men acted as interpreters for that threat, using their economic expertise to enhance its credibility as they relayed it to other policymakers.

The showdown highlights competing visions of policymaker responsibilities in a capitalist economy. All the key players agreed on the need to serve "the system," not just particular companies—in Barack Obama's words, "to make sure that the overall system is stable." But the trio's understanding of that "system" differed from Born's. The three men thought the system consisted of the leading financial institutions, whereas Born defined it to include the business world as a whole. In their aggressive action to boost the profitability of Wall Street firms, the

---

89   The Commodity Futures Modernization Act of 2000, Publ. L. No. 106-554, 114 Stat. 2763 (2000).

three Wall Street transplants paved the way for the destabilization of the broader business world that Born wanted to protect.

Only rarely do government officials take actions that favor specific companies or industries with such devastating system-wide consequences. They generally respect the logic of the corporate compromise. When they do not, their attempted violations of the compromise can run into great difficulty, as Donald Trump's presidency would demonstrate.

Murder and Normality in the Trump Era

In many ways, Donald Trump's record is extreme by the standards of his predecessors. It's also starkly at odds with the vague populist promises of his campaign. Though Trump the candidate often said that Wall Street banks, pharmaceuticals, and offshoring manufacturers were "getting away with murder," he filled his administration with business representatives intent on eliminating the few rules that protected workers, consumers, and the environment.[90] He eviscerated key Obama-era regulations on Wall Street, took no meaningful action to regulate drug prices, and did nothing to punish corporate offshoring.[91] His much-touted negotiation to (temporarily) stop a Carrier manufacturing plant in Indiana from relocating to Mexico was in fact a bribe to the company in the form of money and promises of access to government policy discussions, and did nothing to alter the overall pattern of offshoring.

In contrast, he largely fulfilled his most pernicious promises—the ones that enhanced the profits or autonomy of large elite institutions. The most lethal was his environmental policy, with his deregulation of

90 For his use of the phrase in reference to Wall Street and drug companies see Donna Borak and Henry Williams, "Clinton vs. Trump: Where They Stand on Wall Street," *WSJ* online, October 25, 2016; Anna Edney and Jared S. Hopkins, "Trump Spoils Pharma Chiefs With No More Bad News on Drug Pricing," bloomberg.com, January 31, 2017.

91 Elizabeth Dexheimer, "Trump Signs Biggest Rollback of Bank Rules Since Dodd-Frank Act," bloomberg.com, May 24, 2018; Hannah Lang, "What's Left of the Volcker Rule after the Final Rewrite?," *AB*, August 20, 2019; Edney and Hopkins, "Trump Spoils Pharma Chiefs"; David Lazarus, "This Is Wrong Guy for Health Chief," *Los Angeles Times*, January 12, 2018: C1; Robert Pear, "Drug Plan Drops Populist Designs, Not the Rhetoric," *NYT*, May 12, 2018: A1. As of this writing (September 2019) Trump had maintained his public criticisms of drug companies, but his proposals for new regulations were very modest and likely to be stopped by industry opposition. See Katie Thomas and Abby Goodnough, "Goal to Rein In Prices of Drugs Faces Setbacks," *NYT*, July 12, 2019: A1.

polluters predicted to kill 80,000 people per decade in the United States alone and untold hundreds of thousands around the world.[92] Trump explicitly used presidential power to "take the shackles off" the most authoritarian state entities, including the military, law enforcement, and the anti-immigrant agencies.[93] He greatly increased the rate at which foreigners are murdered by US air strikes, scrapping even the pretense of concern for civilian casualties.[94] In all these areas, Trump delivered what business and/or powerful state entities had been demanding under Obama; if they had gotten 90 percent of what they wanted from Obama, Trump aimed to give them 110 percent.

At the same time, Trump's early record with regard to corporate stakeholders was qualitatively distinct from Obama's, in two ways. First, personal enrichment played a significant role in driving his policies, with corruption reaching cartoonish proportions within Trump's family and inner circle, even when the negative publicity threatened to disrupt business confidence.[95] Second, Trump violated the principle of the corporate compromise when he sought to advance the interests of certain business sectors and state agencies over others. He attempted to sabotage the ACA subsidy system and individual mandate without compensating medical providers and insurers. His March 2018 tariffs subsidized steel at the expense of that sector's many corporate custom-ers, while the much broader tariffs on Chinese goods harmed numer-ous US companies and elicited major complaints.[96] As of this writing,

---

92   David Cutler and Francesca Dominici, "A Breath of Bad Air: Cost of the Trump Environmental Agenda May Lead to 80,000 Extra Deaths per Decade," *Journal of the American Medical Association* 319, no. 22 (2018): 2261–2. See also Popovich et al., "95 Environmental Rules"; Kevin Young, "Will Climate Change Make Family Separations the Norm?," *Truthout*, August 25, 2018.

93   White House Press Secretary Sean Spicer quoted in Michael D. Shear and Ron Nixon, "More Immigrants Face Deportation under New Rules," *NYT*, February 22, 2017: A1.

94   "Reported Civilian Deaths from US-led Coalition Strikes in Iraq and Syria," airwars.org, December 2018.

95   Joy Crane and Nick Tabor, "501 Days in Swampland," *New York Magazine* online, April 1, 2018; David Leonhardt and Ian Prasad Philbrick, "Trump's Corruption: The List," *NYT*, October 29, 2018: A18.

96   See for instance Stephanie Dhue, "Trump's Tariffs Cost US Businesses $3.4 Billion in June, Trade Advocacy Group Says," CNBC.com, August 7, 2019. As the *Times* reported in August 2018, the administration was letting companies "with deep ties to administration officials" profit at the expense of others. In a telling detail, the Commerce department gave the major steel companies veto power over applications for exemption from steel tariffs. In literally *all* the hundreds of cases in which a company applied for an exemption and the Commerce department had issued a deci-sion, the steel companies' objections had "never failed." Jim Tankersley, "Steel Companies with Trump Ties Veto Tariff Relief," *NYT*, August 6, 2018: A1.

the outcomes of these conflicts remained unresolved. In July 2018, JPMorgan CEO Jamie Dimon spoke for many of the impacted sectors when he expressed disagreement with Trump's rash approach to tariffs, but made clear that the good had so far outweighed the bad. In Dimon's words, the tariffs "could offset some of the benefit we've had from the good things he's done," such as corporate tax cuts and regulatory rollbacks. At that moment, he was only "a little worried."[97]

Trump's defiance of certain corporate constituencies on certain matters, and the lack of stronger business opposition in response, suggests that the US president has a significant degree of discretion in designing policies, particularly when seen as "a business cheerleader."[98] Obama was much less willing or able to push the limits of that discretion. Nevertheless, a president's intentions are only a small part of the story. Much more important is the degree to which elite institutions support or reject the president's proposals and their capacity to either facilitate or impede executive action. Despite vast differences in rhetoric and demeanor, Obama's and Trump's policies share major commonalities, resulting from the consistent background forces that constrain all presidents. All face very strong pressure to advance corporate profitability and safeguard the prerogatives of state institutions that wield disruptive power. That means pursuing certain policies and avoiding others. If presidents try to shake things up, elite institutions can usually thwart their efforts, particularly in the absence of counter-disruption from mass movements. While the ultimate outcome of Trump's policies on certain issues (particularly tariffs) is still unclear at this point, there is no question that Trump, like Obama, has been subject to major constraints.

Trump's environmental policies suggest the limits to presidential power, but only when there is systematic resistance by strong corporate or institutional forces. The administration's homicidal policy of dismantling environmental protections and blocking meaningful action on global warming proceeded unhindered, precisely because the policy

---

97   "JP Morgan's Jamie Dimon on Trump's Trade Policies," CNBC.com, July 30, 2018. In a major continuity on trade policy, the North American Free Trade Agreement (NAFTA) that Trump had angrily denounced was subjected to only minor changes. The new "United States-Mexico-Canada Agreement" finalized in September 2018 "is more rebranding than rewrite," as the business press reported: Shawn Donnan with Peter Coy, "NAFTA [*naf*-tuh] USMCA [*naf*-tuh]," *BW*, October 8, 2018: 37.

98   Quote from Mark Hemmeter, head of a Colorado business that rents offices to small business, in Patricia Cohen, "U.S. Businesses Feeling Bullish, Despite Tumult," *NYT*, July 25, 2018: A1.

enjoyed broad corporate support or indifference.[99] But other parts of his agenda were constrained by the parameters of the corporate compromise. An emblematic example came during the fall 2017 negotiations over tax reform. A proposal to scrap a longstanding tax credit for the wind power industry was reversed in the final version of the law following the familiar threat of disinvestment: wind industry representatives had warned that cancellation would erode "the confidence of businesses ready to pour billions of dollars into job-creating American infrastructure."[100] A month later, regulators at the Federal Energy Regulatory Commission (FERC) unanimously rejected a proposal by Trump's Energy Department to grant special price subsidies to the coal and nuclear industries, invoking the familiar cost-benefit logic: the subsidies would reduce profit levels in other energy sectors, which aggressively lobbied FERC to reject the proposal.[101]

Trump's January 2018 proposal to open virtually all US coastal waters to oil drilling met with the same obstacle. The announcement generated fierce opposition from representatives of the tourist and seafood industries in coastal states, who predicted massive disruption to their business if the proposal were enacted. Their concerns were then transmitted through a bipartisan coalition of governors from coastal states, including far-right Trump allies like Rick Scott of Florida and Chris Christie of New Jersey, who sought exemptions from the Department of the Interior and vowed to take legal action if the administration did not grant them. California officials promised to use their power over licenses to block needed pipelines. Less visible resistance came from the Pentagon, which had opposed a more modest proposal under Obama, arguing that increased drilling would disrupt coastal military exercises.[102] This multidimensional opposition appears to have

99   Or halfhearted opposition: business protests of Trump's withdrawal from the 2015 Paris climate accord have been confined to rhetoric, and have not constrained the administration in any real way.

100   Diane Cardwell, "Buffeted by Energy Politics," NYT, May 31, 2017: B1; Brad Plumer, "Tax Bill Largely Preserves Incentives for Wind and Solar Power," NYT online, December 16, 2017; American Wind Energy Association, "US House Misses Opportunity, House Bill Would Cripple Wind Power," November 17, 2017.

101   Ari Natter and Jennifer A. Dlouhy, "Perry's Coal Plan Unites Energy Lobbyists," BW, December 11, 2017: 48–49; Brad Plumer, "Regulators Reject Plan to Rescue Struggling Coal and Nuclear Plants," NYT, January 9, 2018: A16.

102   Darryl Fears, "Administration Plan Would Widely Expand Drilling in U.S. Continental Waters," WP, January 5, 2018: A3; Daniel Brown, "10 Industries at Risk from Trump's Offshore Oil and Gas Drilling Proposal," businessinsider.com, February 2, 2018; Tom DiChristopher, "California Just Gave Coastal States a Blueprint to Block Trump's Offshore Drilling Plan," CNBC.com, February 8, 2018.

influenced a federal judge's March 2019 ruling against the proposal, as well as the administration's decision to respect the ruling while it appealed.[103] The conflict highlights the limits of Trump's freedom to advance particularistic elite interests. He could eliminate safety regulations for existing offshore drilling in the Gulf of Mexico, but he was unable to take actions on behalf of oil companies that would harm other corporate sectors and potentially constrain the military.[104]

Elite institutions' capacity to implement or obstruct the president's policies also determined how much Trump could do. For example, the administration was very successful at terrorizing, imprisoning, deporting, sexually assaulting, and sometimes killing immigrants. One prerequisite for that success was lack of resistance from relevant business sectors (such as agribusiness) and the support of relevant law enforcement agencies like ICE and the Border Patrol.[105] The other prerequisite was institutional capacity. As immigrant rights advocates have often noted, Trump's predecessors, both Republicans and Democrats, handed him a massive detention and deportation apparatus that he could deploy. The number of Border Patrol agents was increased from 4,000 in 1994 to 8,500 in 2001, to 20,000 before Trump took office. ICE, created in 2003, boasted some 20,000 employees and over four hundred offices by 2017.[106] Presidents prior to Obama could never have attempted ethnic cleansing on the scale of Trump, for they lacked the institutional capacity. But these expanded agencies were both eager and able to carry out Trump's agenda.

103   Timothy Puko, "Offshore-Drilling Plan Delayed Indefinitely," *WSJ*, April 26, 2019: A2.

104   On deregulation see Eric Lipton, "Targeting Rules 'Written with Human Blood,'" *NYT*, March 11, 2018: A1; Miranda Green, "Trump Administration Eases Obama-Era Offshore Drilling Safety Rules," *The Hill*, May 2, 2019. In yet another example, Trump's plan to rescind Obama-era auto emission standards drew resistance from many automakers, who feared that the administration's rescinding of the standards while California continued to enforce them would "upend their business by splitting the United States into two car markets, one with stricter emissions standards than the other." See Coral Davenport and Hiroko Tabuchi, "Carmakers' Pact to Cut Emissions Saps Trump Plan," *NYT*, August 21, 2019: A1.

105   US agribusiness might be expected to protest. Yet in the midst of 2018's public outrage over family separation on the US-Mexico border, the top industry lobbying group was "choosing to stay on the sidelines, hoping to solve an ongoing worker shortage through separate agricultural legislation"—that is, trusting that their acquiescence to Trump's policy would pay dividends in the form of future legislation and increased temporary visas. Deena Shanker, "Farmworkers Clash with Farm Lobby amid Immigration Crackdown," bloomberg.com, June 21, 2018.

106   Todd Miller, *Border Patrol Nation: Dispatches from the Front Lines of Homeland Security* (San Francisco, CA: City Lights, 2014), 17; U.S. Office of Immigration and Customs Enforcement, "History." ice.gov/history.

Some clear patterns were apparent after several years of the Trump presidency. Executive branch actions were subject to most of the same rules that had constrained Obama and his predecessors. Trump's regressive and violent agenda generally succeeded only when it did not generate resistance among the ranks of business and institutional elites. Those elites agreed on certain things, such as tax cuts for corporations and the ultra-wealthy and further deregulation of business activities. Other Trump policies, like the assault on immigrants and the increased use of violence against foreign civilians, rewarded particular institutional interests—the Pentagon, intelligence agencies, defense contractors, Border Patrol, and so on—without harming competing elite interests. When those policies *did* stand to impinge on other elite interests, they were often "quietly but pragmatically" modified to accommodate them.[107] In contrast, Trump was often defeated when he violated the corporate compromise by seeking to advance the particularistic interests of certain elites at the expense of others.[108] Murder is only okay when it does not threaten the rest of the corporate and institutional elite.

This pattern, ironically, confirms one of the central arguments of this book: that all politicians in capitalist societies must operate within relatively narrow parameters, even if they are narcissistic billionaires who seem to disdain the ordinary rules of politics. Obama and Trump were very different, but they also were not.

Conclusion

If reforms survive Congress's sausage-making process, their targets still have ample opportunities to weaken or overturn them as they pass into

---

107   A striking example is the racist E-Verify system, which requires employers to check the residency status of potential employees. Since reactionary Southern state governments enacted the system in 2011, it has gone almost universally unenforced, with states "quietly but pragmatically bowing to business interests": "None of the Southern states that extended E-Verify to the private sector have canceled a single business license ... Most businesses caught violating the laws have gotten a pass." Margaret Newkirk, "The South's Pretend War on Immigration," *BW*, August 27, 2018: 36–7.

108   Trump's tariffs are one possible exception, but as of this writing it is too early to tell whether the cost to business will be high enough for business leaders to turn against him. Corporations no doubt worry that opposing Trump could jeopardize their ability to get more "good things" (Jamie Dimon) from the administration. Turning against Trump could also help open the door to a Bernie Sanders–style social democrat, who would be a greater evil from their perspective.

the implementation phase. The reforms must still survive the slicing and dicing of the sausage that is performed by the executive branch.

As in prior stages, unelected elite institutions wield enormous power over policy implementation regardless of which party controls the White House. Changes in the executive branch's enforcement of the law, whether progressive or regressive, must usually safeguard the interests of all elite stakeholders. Business power, at this stage, derives largely from the same combination of weapons that we analyzed in prior chapters, namely campaign funding and the threat or reality of capital strikes. We have highlighted several complementary strategies that business uses when pressuring the executive branch: the institutionalization of cost-benefit analysis into regulatory rulemaking (and a narrow, business-friendly conception of it), litigation based on regulators' alleged failure to properly weigh the costs of regulation to business, and the defunding of regulatory agencies. Each of these strategies works in conjunction with the more general tools of campaign financing and disinvestment. Business campaign donations and control over investment led to the congressional decisions that institutionalized cost-benefit analysis in the first place. They also help ensure that business-friendly individuals are appointed to regulatory positions and judgeships, where they hold the power to adjudicate the costs and benefits. Thus the struggle over policies that constrain corporate or institutional autonomy continues into the indefinite future.

Yet, as in previous stages, there are also real limits to elites' power during the implementation phase. Sometimes popular resistance alters the equation. We now turn to some of the most notable instances of US social movements shaping implementation.

4

Attacking the Substance: How Mass Resistance Can Shape the Implementation of Laws

Why can the city of Birmingham abrogate the US Constitution with impunity? One of the reasons is that the most powerful men in the country are willing that they should. Ten US corporations employ over 35 percent of the manufacturing workers of Birmingham. The directors of these corporations are among the top corporate elite of America. If they chose to act to change things in Birmingham, things would change.

Student Nonviolent Coordinating Committee,
Birmingham, Alabama, 1963

I'm still a segregationist, but I hope I'm not a damn fool.

Sidney Smyer, president of the Birmingham
Chamber of Commerce, 1963

In the normal routine of politics in capitalist societies, the government is mostly "run by a few big interests looking out for themselves."[1] Previous chapters have shown when and how corporations and a handful of state institutions exercise power over the executive and legislative branches of government. But this process is never smooth: it involves constant pushing and pulling by elites and non-elites in a perpetual war to shape policy. At times, resistance from mass constituencies like workers, consumers, and soldiers becomes a powerful factor influencing

---

1 Pew Research Center, "Beyond Distrust: How Americans View Their Government," November 23, 2015, 35, and "Most Say Government Policies since Recession Have Done Little to Help Middle Class, Poor," March 4, 2015, 1.

policymaking. That resistance is sometimes organized and sometimes spontaneous, often subtle and gradual in its buildup but sometimes sudden and explosive. We believe that the influence of non-elite actors is potentially most powerful at two stages: in the initial definition of the legislative agenda, which we have already discussed, and in determining how laws are implemented, which we discuss in this chapter. Though these moments are also subject to the full force of those "few big interests," mass constituencies nevertheless possess significant *potential* leverage that, cultivated and deployed effectively, can decisively alter the trajectory of government policy.

The fundamental source of this leverage lies in the ability to disrupt "business as usual," and to convince corporate and political elites that the disruption cannot be ended without some concessions. This means that elites' most common reactions to protest—repression and endless stalling—must cease to be viable options. We will consider some major historical instances in which mass resistance compelled elites to make concessions, in order to determine which strategies and conditions allowed that resistance to be effective. We focus on how resistance can shape the implementation of existing laws since we have already discussed how similar rules apply to the earlier stage in which the legislative agenda is defined.

Numerous factors affect a social movement's chances of success, many of which are out of activists' control. For instance, different governments and industries are vulnerable to different types of pressure. A strategy that works in one setting may be useless in others, meaning that another means of pressure is necessary. A boycott might work against a company that depends on household consumers, but it might be less effective against a company that relies on government contracts or sales to other companies. Also important are the cultural understandings and social relationships within the communities that organizers seek to mobilize. For example, both the US civil rights movement and the Central American revolutionary movements of the 1970s and 1980s drew upon a reading of the Bible that emphasized human liberation from earthly suffering; church congregations then served as key sites for organizing and for shielding activists from repression. Much also depends on the strategy that a movement adopts, which encompasses many questions. Whom does a movement seek to recruit? Once it recruits them, does it empower them by allowing them to participate in internal decision-making? Whom or what does it pressure, and how? The answers to such questions have major bearing on a movement's efficacy and sustainability.[2]

Most scholars of social movements, and even many organizers, simply assume that "collective action will be most productive if it focuses on elected officials."[3] We disagree. Our primary argument in this chapter is that social movements of the oppressed are most powerful when they focus their disruptive energies not on politicians but on "the few big interests" that shape government policies. Non-elites wield the greatest influence over policy when they engage in sustained action that threatens the functioning of the businesses and state institutions that exercise routinized control over policy behind the scenes. If, as John Dewey wrote in 1931, politicians are "the shadow cast on society" by those interests, then targeting the shadow will not bring real change. It makes more sense to target the "substance" of business and state institutions. Force a change in the substance, and the shape of its shadow will change accordingly.

The most successful movements have focused their disruptive energy on the institutions that are most vulnerable to the pressures of collective

---

2 For an overview of the literature on some of these questions see Kevin Young and Michael Schwartz, "A Neglected Mechanism of Social Movement Political Influence: The Role of Anticorporate and Anti-Institutional Protest in Changing Government Policy," *Mobilization* 19, no. 3 (2014), esp. 239–42. Among many additional recent works on strategy see Amanda Tattersall, *Power in Coalition: Strategies for Strong Unions and Social Change* (Ithaca, NY: Cornell University Press, 2010); Eric Mann, *Playbook for Progressives: 16 Qualities of the Successful Organizer* (Boston, MA: Beacon, 2011); Andrew Boyd with Dave Oswald Mitchell, eds., *Beautiful Trouble: A Toolbox for Revolution* (New York: OR Books, 2012); Kate Khatib, Margaret Killjoy, and Mike McGuire, eds., *We Are Many: Reflections on Movement Strategy from Occupation to Liberation* (Oakland, CA: AK Press, 2012); Steve Williams, *Demand Everything: Lessons of the Transformative Organizing Model* (New York: Rosa Luxemburg Stiftung, 2013); Stellan Vinthagen, *A Theory of Nonviolent Action: How Civil Resistance Works* (London: Zed, 2015); Mark Engler and Paul Engler, *This Is an Uprising: How Nonviolent Revolt Is Shaping the Twenty-First Century* (New York: Nation Books, 2016); Jane F. McAlevey, *No Shortcuts: Organizing for Power in the New Gilded Age* (New York: Oxford University Press, 2016); Juman Abujbara, Andrew Boyd, Dave Mitchell, and Marcel Taminato, eds., *Beautiful Rising: Creative Resistance from the Global South* (New York: OR Books, 2017); George Lakey, *How We Win: A Guide to Nonviolent Direct Action Campaigning* (Brooklyn, NY: Melville House, 2018); Lisa Fithian, *Shut It Down: Stories from a Fierce, Loving Resistance* (White River Junction, VT: Chelsea Green, 2019).

3 Edwin Amenta, Neil Caren, and Sheera Joy Olasky, "Age for Leisure? Political Mediation and the Impact of the Pension Movement on US Old-Age Policy," *ASR* 70, no. 3 (2005): 522. Some studies note that many movements target multiple entities, but do not assess the relative efficacy of confronting different targets. E.g., Nella Van Dyke, Sarah A. Soule, and Verta A. Taylor, "The Targets of Social Movements: Beyond a Focus on the State," *Research in Social Movements, Conflicts, and Change* 25 (2004): 27–51.

protest. Some elites are always more vulnerable than others, and different elites are vulnerable to different types of pressure. The trick lies in identifying which elites to target with which tactics, so as to maximize the costs of disruption and to foster or exacerbate divisions among elites. Faced with enough sustained disruption, one or more groups of elites will come to favor concessions to the movement—not out of the goodness of their hearts, but as a lesser-evil option. They will then push for changes in government policy, potentially countering the obstructive power of other elites. The most successful movements search for the potential fault lines among elites and then build disruptive campaigns that can break those fault lines wide open.

Finding the most effective strategy is easier when a movement is internally democratic. Democracy does not just mean holding competitive elections within a protest organization. It also means structuring an organization in a decentralized way that allows for rank-and-file autonomy, participation in strategizing, and direct engagement with both allies and adversaries. That participation may be informal, as when a local branch of a national organization pioneers a new tactic which then spreads to other branches. If members are able to experiment with different strategies and tactics, and then communicate the lessons to the rest of the membership, the whole movement will benefit.

We support these arguments by analyzing four moments when social movements have decisively shaped how US laws were enforced: the implementation of the 1935 National Labor Relations Act ("Wagner Act") that guaranteed workers' right to unionize, the end of formal racial segregation in the US South, the black-led struggles for economic justice that shaped the "War on Poverty" of the late 1960s, and the end of the US war in Vietnam. In each instance, progressive reform was implemented as a result of disruption that directly threatened the institutions that shaped policy. In the first three examples, the movements' disruption of key businesses led business owners to push government to make concessions. This was also the case in the withdrawal from Vietnam, but there the US military was also a key force: the combined resistance of the Vietnamese people and angry US soldiers severely undermined the military's capacity to continue fighting, leading top commanders to join business elites in demanding withdrawal. Facing sustained threats to their profits, and in the military's case its viability as an institution, leaders chose the lesser-evil option of withdrawing from Vietnam.

The internal organization of the resistance movements varied significantly, from the member-driven unions of the 1930s to the loosely coordinated civil rights movement, to the tightly structured Vietnamese armed resistance. In all cases, however, the local autonomy of the rank and file was critical to finding and implementing an effective disruptive strategy. Sometimes, this autonomy took the form of factions competing with one another for members' allegiances, as in the rivalry among Depression-era unions. With or without formal competitive elections, though, local organizers took the initiative on many occasions, from the factory sit-down strikes of the late 1930s to numerous local boycotts in Southern counties in the 1960s. Even within the Vietnamese resistance, which was not internally democratic in any conventional sense, local initiative was crucial to the initiation of the guerrilla struggle in the South in the late 1950s and remained crucial throughout the war. Usually effective disruption required careful organization, but not always. Sometimes uncoordinated mass action effectively interfered with "business as usual," as in the case of declining military enlistment in the late 1960s and early 1970s.[4]

US social movements of the twenty-first century have yet to achieve the same kind of results. Among the many reasons, we argue, is a widespread misreading of how these past struggles succeeded.

Disruption of Industry Wins Workers' Rights

Most of the business world initially opposed the New Deal labor reforms. As we have noted, employers ignored the 1933 National Industrial Recovery Act requiring good-faith bargaining with unions, were generally opposed to the 1935 Wagner Act when it passed, and initially refused to comply with its requirement to recognize new unions. When faced with workers' demands for recognition or negotiation, they challenged the Wagner Act in court. The new National Labor Relations Board (NLRB), which was tasked with supervising labor-management relations, lay dormant throughout 1935 and 1936.

By the end of the decade, however, many employers had grudgingly shifted toward at least partial acceptance of independent unions, and had even come to rely on NLRB authority to settle disputes. They also greatly reduced their use of violence and intimidation against

---

4 On the concept of mass action see Shuva Paul, Sarah Mahler, and Michael Schwartz, "Mass Action and Social Structure," *Political Power and Social Theory* 11 (1997): 45–99.

labor activists. In explaining this shift, scholars have typically cited the landslide victories of the Democrats in the 1936 elections and the Supreme Court's 1937 confirmation of the Wagner Act's constitutionality as the two key developments that forced recalcitrant employers to comply with the law. These accounts stress the importance of liberals in the three branches of government.[5] Others have cited employers' ideological embrace of "corporate liberalism" in the midst of the crisis to explain their growing acceptance of unions in the late 1930s and 1940s.[6]

These explanations miss the mark. The government was neither willing nor able to impose the law on employers, and noncompliance was virtually universal even after the Supreme Court's April 1937 ruling. Given the strong corporate presence within the Roosevelt administration, federal efforts at enforcement were negligible and might have been postponed indefinitely.

What led employers to accept the Wagner Act and the NLRB was a sustained upsurge of working-class disruption—including nearly 9,000 strikes in 1935–1937—that had threatened their profitability or even survival.[7] Corporate leaders decided that consenting to independent unions was preferable to continued chaos in the factories. They began conceding to workers' demands and even inviting the NLRB into their workplaces to oversee union elections.

Major aspects of the Wagner Act were simply unenforceable without employers' consent. The NLRB was responsible for ensuring that management and labor bargained "in good faith." But how could it prove that one party was not negotiating in good faith, much less compel them to change their behavior? Seeking enforcement through the federal court system might require years or even decades of costly legal battles.

Nor could the Supreme Court force employers to accept unions. As *Businessweek* commented a month after the court's ruling, "the

---

5   See for instance Irving Bernstein, *Turbulent Years: A History of the American Worker, 1933–1941* (Boston, MA: Houghton Mifflin, 1969), esp. 318–51, 641–6; Theda Skocpol, "Political Response to Capitalist Crisis: Neo-Marxist Theories of the State and the Case of the New Deal," *PAS* 10, no. 2 (1980): 192.

6   E.g., Ronald Radosh, "The Myth of the New Deal," in *A New History of Leviathan: Essays on the Rise of the American Corporate State*, eds. Ronald Radosh and Murray N. Rothbard (New York: Dutton, 1972), 146–87.

7   On the strikes see Frances Fox Piven and Richard A. Cloward, *Poor People's Movements: How They Succeed, Why They Fail* (New York: Vintage, 1979 [1977]), 131–47.

antagonists dug in for a showdown test of strength." The act's passage and court's approval had only been the "first battle" between business and labor. Though labor had won an apparent victory, now "the second battle is on to decide if the winners really won anything."[8] Historian Irving Bernstein, who gives much credit to the liberals in government, nonetheless observes that effective implementation of good-faith bargaining hinged on workers' own organization and militancy: "The realistic sanction lay not in the order or its ultimate enforcement by the courts but in the power of the union. A strong union got bargaining from the employer; a weak one often did not."[9] The contest of forces within the workplace—the confrontation between employers and the organized disruptive power of workers—was more important than any act of Congress or ruling from the Supreme Court.

Implementation in the auto industry was crucial. The process by which this violently anti-union sector came to accept the Wagner Act was central to the law's national implementation, since other industries looked to the auto giants for guidance. Auto companies' acceptance of unions began gradually in 1937. The immediate catalyst was the wave of sit-down strikes centered in General Motors plants in the winter of 1936–1937, which forced the largest company in the world to temporarily recognize the United Auto Workers (UAW) union in February, two months before the Supreme Court ruling. The sit-down tactic was replicated on the local level by workers across the country, some seven hundred times by the end of 1937.[10]

While the sit-down strikes are famous, what happened over the ensuing three years is much less known. By 1939, the auto employers had gone beyond grudging recognition of the UAW to demanding that the hated NLRB intervene in their workplaces. They now called upon the board to enforce the Wagner Act's "exclusive representation" principle, which provided for all the eligible workers in a workplace to be represented by a single agent, and which the companies had strongly resisted in the past. Reports from the business press at the time illuminate the logic behind their change in position. Between 1936 and 1939,

---

8   "Steel Interprets Wagner Act," *BW*, May 15, 1937: 15.
9   Bernstein, *Turbulent Years*, 651.
10   Sidney Fine, *Sit-Down: The General Motors Strike of 1936–1937* (Ann Arbor: University of Michigan Press, 1969); Joshua Murray and Michael Schwartz, "Moral Economy, Structural Leverage, and Organizational Efficacy: Class Formation and the Great Flint Sit-Down Strike, 1936–1937," *Critical Historical Studies* 2, no. 2 (2015): 219–59.

the companies were plagued by an intense rivalry between the UAW factions associated with the American Federation of Labor (AFL) and the more militant Congress of Industrial Organizations (CIO). In January 1939, the UAW split into two separate unions, the UAW-AFL and UAW-CIO, which then began engaging in alternating work stoppages as they competed for jurisdiction. The stoppages drastically reduced output, threatening the industry's otherwise fabulous profits and shattering the hopes for labor peace that had arisen after GM's 1937 recognition of the UAW. Moreover, inter-union rivalry increased union democracy, which spelled disaster for the companies. Labor leaders competing for rank-and-file support were pushed to make more radical demands on their employers and to support more militant action on the shop floor.[11]

First GM and eventually the other companies decided that NLRB intervention to establish exclusive representation was the only hope for ending the disruption in the factories. By August 1939, the *Wall Street Journal* reported that auto industry executives "unanimously express satisfaction with the National Labor Relations Board decision to hold elections" in workplaces where unions requested them.[12] After General Motors and Chrysler had conceded, even the legendarily anti-union Henry Ford gave in. The auto giants had chosen the lesser evil. The NLRB, with all its constraints on management prerogatives, was preferable to endemic disruption.[13]

Other large employers began to follow suit. *Businessweek* reported in 1938 that companies in diverse industries increasingly "looked to the government for help" when confronted with strikes and inter-union rivalries.[14] By 1939, *Fortune* magazine's polling of business executives found that outright opposition to the Wagner Act had fallen below 50 percent, with a plurality seeking modifications rather than repeal. The magazine interpreted the results to mean that business had increasingly come to accept the basic principle of "collective bargaining under

---

11 Jonathan Cutler, "'To Exercise Control over the Men': Rival Unionism, Corporate Liberalism, and the Wagner Act," unpublished manuscript.

12 Quoted in Cutler, "'To Exercise Control,'" 32.

13 As Cutler's account makes clear, the NLRB's enforcement of exclusive representation was a very mixed blessing for labor. For example, it reduced the potential for democratic competition among union factions. While conventional wisdom holds that factionalism weakens a movement, it can also make a movement more democratic and more powerful—thus the auto companies' distaste for it. On the positive impacts of factions see also Judith Stepan-Norris and Maurice Zeitlin, *Left Out: Reds and America's Industrial Unions* (Cambridge: Cambridge University Press, 2003), esp. 159–88.

14 "Union Rivalry Hurts Portland, Ore.," *BW*, January 8, 1938: 32.

federal supervision."[15] With the wave of disruptive strikes continuing through the 1940s (with only a temporary decline at the beginning of World War II due to the "no-strike" pledge), the NLRB became an accepted part of the unionization process, empowered to impose union elections on recalcitrant companies. It remained a major resource for labor for decades into the future, regardless of which political party held the presidency.

Movement pressure on business, not on politicians, had been the decisive factor in business's shift. Millions of workers had exercised their structural power to create sustained disruption of industry. Corporate adversaries then softened their hostility to the law's implementation and even sought out NLRB intervention in the unionization process, as a lesser evil compared to the expensive process of crushing strikes. This intervention led to progressive changes within government, as a new regulatory agency was empowered to enforce the law. In short, the Wagner Act by itself had limited practical value. It was the class struggle in US workplaces that determined if and how the law would be enforced.

However, corporations' shift of position did not mean they had given up their quest to dominate and exploit their workers. They sought to outlaw the sit-down strike tactic that had been so powerful.[16] After 1939, they continued trying to shape how the Wagner Act would be implemented. On the legislative front, they relentlessly sought amendments to the new law, culminating in anti-labor measures like the 1947 Taft-Hartley Act that greatly constrained workers' rights. They also pursued the familiar corporate strategy of pushing Congress to defund the regulator, the NLRB. Decades later, they would succeed in greatly weakening the Board and packing it with business-friendly appointees.[17]

As the NLRB's trajectory suggests, the implementation of laws is a never-ending war in which the contending parties constantly try to move the needle closer to their side. Business "dug in," largely behind the scenes, and gradually succeeded in eroding the Wagner Act and the

15   "What Business Thinks," *Fortune*, October 1939: 52, 90, 95. Business leaders' public expressions need to be interpreted cautiously, as we noted in Chapter 1. The magazine was attempting to showcase leaders' alleged enlightened attitudes. But the shift in attitudes was real.

16   Joshua Murray and Michael Schwartz, *Wrecked: How the American Automobile Industry Destroyed Its Capacity to Compete* (New York: Russell Sage, 2019).

17   James A. Gross, *Broken Promise: The Subversion of U.S. Labor Relations Policy, 1947–1994* (Philadelphia, PA: Temple University Press, 1995).

board. It used the same strategies we saw in the last chapter: pressing for the appointment of its allies to regulatory agencies, mounting expensive lobbying campaigns to shape specific regulatory rules, filing lawsuits to get judges to overturn regulatory constraints, and threatening to disinvest if regulators disobeyed.

Labor, on the other hand, did not dig in. Unions certainly tried to prevent the Taft-Hartley Act and other employer offensives, but their strategy had changed. They increasingly relied on electoral activism and lobbying, instead of creating and sustaining direct pressure on their corporate adversaries. They adopted a "business unionist" outlook that stressed the common interests between workers and their bosses. This shift in strategy was consolidated by the purge of most radical union leaders by the late 1940s and by the merger of the AFL and CIO in 1955. Business unionists also set out to extinguish the local autonomy that had been central to the successful mass disruption of the 1930s and 1940s.[18]

As this process advanced, the political results became more and more apparent. The NLRB gradually lost its orientation in favor of the working class. Successive generations of Democratic politicians failed to deliver on their promises to remove some of the legal roadblocks to unionization, most recently under Obama.[19] Labor's weakness since the 1940s reinforces the key lesson of the Wagner Act: without sustained pressure on business, government is unlikely to deliver pro-labor reforms, and past reforms will be subject to constant erosion. The implementation process is a never-ending war, in which business constantly tries to gain ground. Without sustained disruption on the other side, it is more or less free to do so.

Disruption of Business Wins Desegregation

The Jim Crow system of segregation was ended in much the same way that unionization rights were achieved: mass pressure on key business interests was a prerequisite for the effective implementation of desegregation. By 1954, the Supreme Court had declared school segregation

---

18   Paul Buhle, *Taking Care of Business: Samuel Gompers, George Meany, Lane Kirkland, and the Tragedy of American Labor* (New York: Monthly Review, 1999); Stepan-Norris and Zeitlin, *Left Out*.

19   Steve Early, *The Civil Wars in U.S. Labor: Birth of a New Workers' Movement or Death Throes of the Old?* (Chicago, IL: Haymarket, 2011), 255–80.

illegal, and lower courts continued to rule against segregation in other realms.[20] But, like the Wagner Act, the *Brown v. Board of Education* ruling was unenforceable until mass disruption compelled its implementation. Activists directly targeted schools, bus lines, retailers, banks, and other key institutions in the South. In many cases, these locally-organized movements were able to impose high enough costs on local businesses that business owners not only ended segregation in their own facilities but also sought changes in local and federal policy. This process eventually even softened the opposition of Southern Democrats in Washington.

The civil rights movement's disruption of business, and the political responses that disruption elicited, remains an understudied topic. Many narratives of the movement continue to stress the role of white liberals in allowing it to succeed. The movement won, we are told, because it provoked massive racist violence, which produced outrage among the Northern white public and triggered intervention by sympathetic Northern Democrats in the White House and Congress. Even accounts that seek to highlight "the purposive agency of movement activists" tend to stress the importance of "mobilizing public opinion" behind their cause.[21] The implication for other social movements is clear: they must focus on convincing the broad public and its elected officials if they hope to achieve their goals.

Other studies have instead emphasized the internal strengths of the movement itself. In these accounts, white opinion and Northern Democrats are much less consequential than the movement's own organizational strength, strategic creativity, and resilience.[22] Some of these

---

20   See for instance the testimony of Southern judge Elbert Tuttle in Howell Raines, *My Soul Is Rested: The Story of the Civil Rights Movement in the Deep South* (New York: G.P. Putnam's Son, 1977), 345.

21   Taeku Lee, *Mobilizing Public Opinion: Black Insurgency and Racial Attitudes in the Civil Rights Era* (Chicago, IL: University of Chicago Press, 2002), 7; Jeffrey C. Alexander, *The Civil Sphere* (New York: Oxford University Press, 2006).

22   Aldon D. Morris, *The Origins of the Civil Rights Movement: Black Communities Organizing for Change* (New York: Free Press, 1984) and "Birmingham Confrontation Reconsidered: An Analysis of the Dynamics and Tactics of Mobilization," *ASR* 58, no. 5 (1993): 621–36; Belinda Robnett, *How Long? How Long? African-American Women in the Struggle for Civil Rights* (New York: Oxford University Press, 1997); Kenneth T. Andrews, *Freedom Is a Constant Struggle: The Mississippi Civil Rights Movement and Its Legacy* (Chicago, IL: University of Chicago Press, 2004); Charles M. Payne, *I've Got the Light of Freedom: The Organizing Tradition and the Mississippi Freedom Struggle* (Berkeley: University of California Press, 2007 [1995]); Joseph E. Luders, *The Civil Rights Movement and the Logic of Social Change* (New York: Cambridge University Press, 2010).

studies note the centrality of boycotts, sit-ins, and other economic disruption within the movement's strategic repertoire. Economic elites were often the first to capitulate, and they then exerted pressure for other segregationists to do the same. Historian Charles Payne comments that, among Southern whites confronted with disruptive protests, "the group most consistently playing the progressive role turns out to have been businesspeople," since protests "were not healthy for the bottom line." At most of the key sites of disruption, from the Montgomery bus boycott in 1955 to various boycott campaigns of the late 1960s, business owners were the first element of the white power structure to urge concessions. In many cases they advocated changes in public policies, such as integration of schools and public parks, in addition to integrating their own businesses.[23]

Movement organizers understood this dynamic. The most successful local campaigns throughout the South did not focus on public officials. When they did, they were much weaker. In the Albany, Georgia, campaign of 1961–62, the local branch of the Student Nonviolent Coordinating Committee (SNCC) and other Albany-based organizers targeted downtown businesses and local bus services. However, Martin Luther King Jr.'s Southern Christian Leadership Conference (SCLC) did not throw its weight behind those efforts. As a result, the economic disruption campaign remained somewhat haphazard, which was one of several reasons for the movement's defeat.[24] The Albany campaign is widely said to have failed because of the restraint of the local police chief, who quietly arrested protesters rather than creating violent spectacles. But King's own conclusion was somewhat different:

> All our marches in Albany were marches to the city hall trying to make them negotiate, where if we had centered our protests at the stores, the businesses in the city, [we could have] made the merchants negotiate . . . If you can pull them around, you pull the political power structure because really the political power structure listens to the economic power structure.[25]

23   Steven F. Lawson and Charles Payne, *Debating the Civil Rights Movement, 1945–1968* (Lanham, MD: Rowman and Littlefield, 1998), 117; James C. Cobb, *Industrialization and Southern Society, 1877–1984* (Lexington: University Press of Kentucky, 1984), 110; Luders, *Civil Rights Movement*, 60–4; Elizabeth Jacoway and David R. Colburn, eds., *Southern Businessmen and Desegregation* (Baton Rouge: Louisiana State University Press, 1982).

24   Morris, *Origins*, 239–50.

25   Interviewed by Donald Smith in November 1963, quoted in David J. Garrow, *Bearing the Cross: Martin Luther King, Jr., and the Southern Christian Leadership Conference* (New York: Vintage, 1986), 226.

King and others would take that lesson to heart as they geared up for the Birmingham, Alabama, campaign of spring 1963.

Birmingham was the most iconic local campaign of the entire movement, so its success merits close scrutiny. From the start, economic disruption was the key element of the strategy. Reverend Fred Shuttlesworth and his local SCLC affiliate group had pioneered this strategy locally, and the 1963 SCLC campaign built on it.[26] Wyatt Walker, a close adviser to King, said that "we decided we would concentrate on the ebb and flow of the money downtown." SCLC leaders had spent months researching specific business targets in the city before they launched the campaign on April 3.[27] The mass demonstrations and sit-ins that accompanied the boycott deprived downtown businesses of not only black customers but also many white customers, who were deterred from venturing downtown in the midst of black protests. Retailers lost an average of $750,000 a week.[28] The conscious goal was to get business to "pull around" the politicians. According to Birmingham organizer Abraham Woods, "We had the pressure on [the merchants] in order that they might pressure the city."[29]

The execution of the strategy was facilitated by two factors that had not been present in Albany. First, mass disruption was possible because of the preexisting level of community organization. SCLC leaders had chosen Birmingham in part because it was already home to a strong local organization, led by Shuttlesworth.[30] Second, the movement achieved a greater cohesion and unity of purpose than in Albany. While strategic disagreements and rivalries between SNCC and SCLC had hampered the Albany effort, they were not a major factor in Birmingham. Although SNCC lacked a strong base in the city, it helped amplify SCLC's efforts by promoting a nationwide boycott of well-known corporations that operated in the city. Their logic was the same as that of SCLC: if the business elite "chose to act to change things in Birmingham, things would change."[31] Thus, internal disagreements within the movement did not prevent strategic unity when it was needed.

26   Morris, *Origins*, 50, 252.
27   Morris, "Birmingham Confrontation," 625.
28   "The Boycott Road to Rights," *Time*, June 7, 1963: 117; Morris, *Origins*, 269.
29   Walker quoted in Morris, *Origins*, 258; Woods quoted in Raines, *My Soul Is Rested*, 152.
30   Morris, *Origins*, 250.
31   Student Nonviolent Coordinating Committee, "Big Business Supports Segregation in Birmingham," undated flyer available at crmvet.org.

After five weeks of the campaign, business leaders publicly agreed to desegregate lunch counters, restrooms, and certain other public accommodations. These concessions were the result of two factors that converged to make capitulation the most desirable option. One was the direct economic disruption wrought by the movement. The other was the failure of repression. Repression took many forms, including mass arrests, physical violence and terror, and retaliation by white bosses against black workers. But the efficacy of mass arrests had been greatly reduced by prior movement efforts. By early May, the jails were filled to capacity with black protesters, limiting police freedom to make arrests. Unlike in Albany, Birmingham authorities were unable to secure a federal injunction against black protest: the federal judiciary refused to grant it, and also refused to allow the indefinite detentions and draconian punishments that white supremacists were seeking.[32] The NAACP's longtime legal work, in conjunction with escalating mass protest, had fostered a split within the federal government. That work paid off in Birmingham.

Other forms of repression also proved ineffective. One reason was activists' extraordinary perseverance. The immediate tipping point for many business leaders had come on May 7, when the police use of dogs and fire hoses—necessary because the jails were full—failed to deter black protesters.[33] Another reason was the Kennedy administration's concern about the US global image. Third World peoples were expelling their colonizers and considering alternatives to capitalism. Endless racist violence, publicized around the world, would make it harder to secure their allegiance to capitalism and the United States. Concerns about the US image required the federal government to put at least some pressure on Southern segregationists, just as they had earlier led the White House to pressure the Supreme Court to rule against desegregation.[34] After a month of inaction, the administration finally made vague threats of federal intervention if disruption and violence continued.[35] For all these reasons, repression had ceased to be a viable option for Southern elites.

Economic disruption and the failure of repression had induced a change of opinion among business elites both nationally and locally.

---

32 Morris, *Origins*, 264.
33 Ibid., 270.
34 See Mary L. Dudziak, *Cold War Civil Rights: Race and the Image of American Democracy* (Princeton, NJ: Princeton University Press, 2000), 169–71.
35 Raines, *My Soul Is Rested*, 163–4.

Sociologist Aldon Morris concludes that "Northern capitalists who owned businesses in Birmingham" urged settlement "because the boycott and political crisis ensured that profits would cease until a solution was reached." They and their colleagues within the Kennedy administration thus urged local business to concede. Of the local business leaders, the most willing to concede were "merchants, industrialists, corporation and bank presidents, [and] prominent insurance and real-estate men," reported movement negotiator Vincent Harding.[36] Many of these leaders had advised desegregation of public recreation in response to a federal court order and movement agitation in 1961, but only the spring 1963 crisis gave them the will and the power to impose desegregation on recalcitrant political leaders.[37]

Real-estate mogul Sidney Smyer, head of Birmingham's chamber of commerce, personified business's change of position. Smyer led the business faction that negotiated with the movement and then forced local politicians and law enforcement to cease violent repression. He stressed the need to promote "a good image" of Birmingham as a site for investment. Describing his colleagues' decision to yield, he said "it was a dollar-and-cents thing. If we're going to have a good business in Birmingham, we better change our way of living." Smyer was no antiracist. He had helped organize Strom Thurmond's 1948 Dixiecrat candidacy for president and had attended rallies of the white supremacist Citizens Council in the 1950s. In 1963 he was "still a segregationist." But he was "not a damn fool."[38] Giving in to the movement had become the lesser-evil option.

Smyer and his coalition represented the sectors of business that were most vulnerable to economic disruption. In a study of business responses to civil rights protests across the South, Joseph Luders divides Southern business leaders into four groups: accommodators, conformers, vacillators, and resisters. The resisters were the most intransigent group, and were often led by the big planters in each locale. At the other end of the spectrum, the accommodators were

36   Morris, *Origins*, 271 (second quote from Harding).
37   Robert Corley, "In Search of Racial Harmony: Birmingham Business Leaders and Desegregation, 1950–1963," in Jacoway and Colburn, eds., *Southern Businessmen*, 182–3.
38   Smyer quoted in Don McKee, "Peace Leader at Birmingham Explains," *WP*, May 18, 1963: A4, and in Raines, *My Soul Is Rested*, 165 (see p. 162 on Smyer's background). For additional individuals see Claude Sitton, "Birmingham Pact Picks Up Support," *NYT*, May 16, 1963: 1.

generally drawn from the "relatively immobile, local consumption, service, and growth-dependent sectors" such as retail, transportation, and real estate—the sectors from which Smyer and other key figures came. These businesses were particularly vulnerable to black boycotts, sit-ins, and demonstrations that scared away customers. Once they became convinced that disruption would continue and that repression was failing, they began calling for concessions.[39] The accommodators were a key force in toning down the repressive policies of local governments, and also softened somewhat the recalcitrant posture of Southern Democrats in Congress.

The success of local campaigns was therefore largely contingent on the choice of targets and the choice of strategies. Luders shows that campaigns like Birmingham succeeded because they exploited the susceptibility of specific local elites to disruption, assessing "the differences in target vulnerabilities" and "the likely struggles among them over the decision to yield."[40] Mass resistance had created serious divisions among economic and political elites. While intra-elite conflicts had normally remained subtle and suppressed, the movement had split them wide open.

The victory in Birmingham confirmed this insight in the minds of many organizers throughout the South, who continued their use of economic disruption through the rest of the decade. Boycotts often succeeded where other tactics had failed. The 1967 boycott campaign in Holmes County, Mississippi, led the local chamber of commerce to push the mayor of Lexington, the county seat, to concede to some movement demands. In nearby Greenwood, local organizers' victories came only after they started their boycott of business. As Luders notes, "rising economic distress compelled merchants and other interests concerned about economic development to make concessions, and finally, in 1969, to unseat the mayor associated with planter intransigence." According to Payne, "most Greenwood activists feel strongly that the immediate cause of real change, change that they could feel in their daily lives, came in response to economic pressure."[41] In Durham, North Carolina, writes Francis Redburn, a six-month boycott in

39   Joseph Luders, "The Economics of Movement Success: Business Responses to Civil Rights Mobilization," *AJS* 111, no. 4 (2006): 991.

40   Luders, *Civil Rights Movement*, 95n45; "Economics of Movement Success," 963.

41   Andrews, *Freedom Is a Constant Struggle*, 86; Luders, "Economics of Movement Success," 976; Payne, *I've Got the Light of Freedom*, 328.

1968–69 led local business leaders to "become actively involved on behalf of the boycotters." Business was then "able to negotiate policy changes" with city officials, which had been the conscious intention of the local movement.[42] In Birmingham itself, organizers would revive boycotts in the late 1960s in response to police murders of black residents.[43] Again and again, local movements created splits among white elites, honing in on subtle fault lines and breaking them open.

Some national leaders learned the same lesson from the 1963 Birmingham confrontation. A little-known aspect of the voting rights struggle of 1965 was the SCLC call for an economic boycott of Alabama, which King announced on national television three weeks after the racist violence of "Bloody Sunday" in Selma. SCLC proposed an "escalated economic withdrawal" of resources from the state, calling upon business, governments, churches, labor unions, pension funds, and consumers around the country to cease all participation in the Alabama economy. The economic power structure, King reasoned, was the most capable and likely candidate to end "the reign of terror which presently grips the state." He invoked previous local victories: "Our experience from other communities such as Atlanta, Nashville and even Birmingham is that the most immediate and effective means of calling responsible people to the fore is through the implementation of a campaign of economic withdrawal."[44] The boycott idea was angrily attacked by the White House, leading news outlets, and more conservative black leaders.[45] The proposal's impact is hard to assess since it was never fully implemented.[46] King was totally exhausted from recent events, SCLC soon shifted its energies toward organizing in Chicago, and the Voting Rights Act passed Congress a few months later. But the hostile reaction to the idea suggests the threat it posed. Just as business's potential to disrupt the economy lends credence to its threats, the prior demonstration of disruption by a movement can do the same. Sometimes following through is unnecessary.

42   Francis Stevens Redburn, "Protest and Policy in Durham, North Carolina" (PhD diss., University of North Carolina at Chapel Hill, 1970), 161–200, 262 (quote).
43   "Killings By Birmingham Cops Spurs Negroes To Launch Boycott of Stores," *Chicago Defender*, March 25, 1967: 5.
44   Martin Luther King Jr., "Alabama Boycott: Here's Plan in King's Own Words," *Norfolk Journal and Guide*, April 17, 1965: 11. See also Garrow, *Bearing the Cross*, 414–30.
45   Garrow, *Bearing the Cross*, 414–15.
46   At least one Wall Street firm, the Childs Securities Corporation, joined the boycott. "Ala. Already Feels Boycott," *Afro-American* (Baltimore), April 10, 1965: 1.

Many Southern business leaders had also learned the dangers of movement disruption, and sought to prevent a repeat of the 1963 Birmingham confrontation in their own locales. In Atlanta, the mayor and former chamber of commerce president, Ivan Allen Jr., told his colleagues that "if Atlanta didn't solve its racial problems it would suffer economically just as Birmingham had." Business leaders' efforts to attract corporate investment in the city had led many of them to support desegregation in the early 1960s, much earlier than other Southern cities. As Allen himself acknowledged, "there was substance to the charge that the liberalism of the white business community was motivated purely by pragmatism" and not "a genuine sympathy toward the suffering of the Negro."[47] Again, the movement had created a split among elites, pushing one elite segment to see desegregation as the lesser evil and motivating it to "pull around" the others.

In sum, civil rights disruption was most powerful when it targeted economic elites. Politicians typically acted only once business had already shifted. This pattern was apparent to all observers of Southern politicians. The change in business attitudes also helped generate action from Northern Democrats. Faced with the crisis in Birmingham, the Kennedy administration had done nothing for a full month. It only took tangible action—deploying the National Guard—after the May 7 agreement between local business and the movement, as a means of ensuring local extremists' compliance. The administration showed little interest in a new civil rights bill until several weeks later.[48] As Martin Luther King Jr. and others had predicted, the White House was reluctantly "pulled around" by the needs of business, while Southern politicians were dragged kicking and screaming. The political power structure had listened, however begrudgingly, to the economic power structure.

The movement's success in creating fissures among political elites themselves played a supplementary role in movement victory. Most important, perhaps, was the judiciary's increasing unwillingness to support racist violence and segregation, which reduced the efficacy of state repression in the South. Court rulings constrained the power of Southern politicians and police. Judges' opinions were changing in

---

47   Ivan Allen Jr., *Mayor: Notes on the Sixties* (New York: Simon and Schuster, 1971), 93. See also Alton Hornsby Jr., "A City That Was Too Busy to Hate: Atlanta Businessmen and Desegregation," in Jacoway and Colburn, eds., *Southern Businessmen*, 120–36.

48   Morris, *Origins*, 273; Raines, *My Soul Is Rested*, 163–4; Garrow, *Bearing the Cross*, 267–9.

response to movement pressures, including the long-term legal efforts of NAACP lawyers and plaintiffs. In all likelihood, many judges were also driven in part by the pragmatic concern for US global control that helped motivate the executive branch to begin taking steps against segregation and terror.

The history of US desegregation thus suggests the inadequacy of electoral strategies, even at the federal level where black voters supposedly had some influence. Which party controlled the White House and Congress was relatively unimportant in determining the government's position on racial segregation. Almost all of the federal judges appointed by Republican president Dwight Eisenhower were relatively supportive of civil rights demonstrators, while twelve of the thirteen Kennedy administration appointees to Southern courts were die-hard segregationists. The Republican administration of Richard Nixon desegregated more public schools in the South than the Eisenhower, Kennedy, and Johnson administrations combined.[49] This difference did not stem from Nixon's own sympathies, but from a political context that left him little room to maneuver. Thus, though only indirectly focused on the federal government, the 1960s movements, like the 1930s labor movement, led to the development of government capacity and willingness to enforce progressive policies that would have been unthinkable ten years earlier. In the case of desegregation, the combination of social movement offensives and the resulting decline in resistance from Southern elites enabled the construction of a civil rights enforcement apparatus, including a resourceful civil rights desk within the Justice Department, the appointment of pro-integration judges, and the relaxation of FBI collusion with white supremacist violence. When Nixon took office he was constrained by a range of institutions dedicated to policies he had publicly opposed, just as Obama, Trump, and all his other successors would be.

Disruption of Business and the War on Poverty

Black political organizing of the 1960s sought much more than just "civil rights." For most community organizers, the struggle against

---

49   Laura Anker, Peter Seybold, and Michael Schwartz, "The Ties That Bind Business and Government," in *The Structure of Power in America: The Corporate Elite as a Ruling Class*, ed. Michael Schwartz (New York: Holmes & Meier, 1987), 101–2.

white supremacy was inextricable from the struggle for economic justice. Most of the civil rights protests against segregation had economic goals, including the right to education, decent housing, equal employment opportunities, public services, and social programs. This economic focus became more pronounced after the civil rights legislation of 1964–65, as both local organizers and some national leaders, including Martin Luther King Jr., began to attack poverty and exploitation more aggressively.

The "War on Poverty" that President Johnson launched in 1964 must be understood in this context. The 1964 Economic Opportunity Act established an Office of Economic Opportunity (OEO) that would dispense federal grants to Community Action Agencies (CAAs), to be constituted by residents, public officials, and representatives of community groups and businesses at the local level. The act itself resulted from elite fears of disorder and unrest, including both urban "delinquency" and the political agitation of the early 1960s.[50] Richard Boone, who served on the President's Task Force, acknowledged that the portion of the act that called for "maximum feasible participation" of poor people "could not have been written before the flowering of the Civil Rights Movement. In a substantial degree it was written because of that movement."[51]

While the impetus for the act came from the administration's efforts to respond to (and control) the groundswell of black activism, most important for our analysis is the implementation of the act. Specifically, we examine funding for local Community Action Programs (CAPs), the principal institutional vehicle for implementing the plans of each county's CAA. As the flagship program, local CAPs received two-thirds of all grants dispensed by the OEO from 1965 to 1968, a cumulative $2.64 billion. Across the South, these programs constituted "a 25 percent increase . . . [in] local government welfare expenditures" over previous funding levels. In many of the poorest counties, CAP grants more than

---

50   The act was largely modeled on a preexisting Ford Foundation initiative called Gray Areas, which had sought to target the economic roots of crime. The theory behind Gray Areas came from Richard Cloward and Lloyd Ohlin, *Delinquency and Opportunity: A Theory of Delinquent Gangs* (Glencoe, IL: Free Press, 1960). See also Joseph Helfgot, *Professional Reforming* (Boston, MA: Lexington Books, 1980).

51   Cited in Susan Youngblood Ashmore, *Carry It On: The War on Poverty and the Civil Rights Movement in Alabama, 1964–1972* (Athens: University of Georgia Press, 2008), 60. Boone called for "maximum feasible participation of the poor" in OEO programs.

doubled social service budgets when compared to 1962 expenditures.[52] In the Southern states CAAs were organized in about two-thirds of the counties, covering about four-fifths of the population.[53] As a result, CAAs became "almost synonymous with the War on Poverty."[54]

By scrutinizing funding decisions at the OEO, we can judge among competing explanations for the implementation of progressive policy. One explanation holds that OEO decisions were apolitical and represented the best intentions of the Johnson administration to further civil rights for black and poor people. For example, a study on OEO funding across all US counties found that poorer counties and those with greater proportions of nonwhite people were funded at higher rates. The study concluded that the antipoverty effort was "a sincere attempt" by President Johnson "to champion change."[55]

Other observers argue that implementation of the program was fundamentally political. There are two variants of this explanation, electoral and non-electoral. The electoral variant holds that features of the electoral process—including the election of sympathetic politicians, the competitive nature of elections, and voter registration rates—drove policy implementation. Scholars who favor this explanation argue that Johnson and Northern Democrats allocated OEO funding in the South to areas with emerging blocs of black voters.[56]

The second "political" perspective argues that the implementation of progressive policy is shaped less by elections than by non-institutional pressures, chiefly from social movements. Some scholars, and many activists themselves, argue that antipoverty funding was a way of placating the poor and thus averting greater disruption to local white business and society. By these accounts, antipoverty programs were an outcome of movement agitation, even if activists themselves had not

---

52   Martha J. Bailey and Nicolas J. Duquette, "How Johnson Fought the War on Poverty: The Economics and Politics of Funding at the Office of Economic Opportunity," *Journal of Economic History* 74, no. 2 (2014): 360. CAP usually referred to the national program, but we use CAA and CAP interchangeably here.

53   Authors' analysis based on data described below.

54   Andrews, *Freedom Is a Constant Struggle*, 138.

55   Bailey and Duquette, "How Johnson Fought the War on Poverty," 383. See also David C. Colby, "Black Power, White Resistance, and Public Policy: Political Power and Poverty Program Grants in Mississippi," *Journal of Politics* 47, no. 2 (1985): 579–95; Andrew T. Cowart, "Anti-Poverty Expenditures in the American States: A Comparative Analysis," *Midwest Journal of Political Science* 13, no. 2 (1969): 219–36.

56   Colby, "Black Power, White Resistance, and Public Policy"; Bailey and Duquette, "How Johnson Fought the War on Poverty."

necessarily demanded those specific programs.[57] As Kenneth Andrews argues in his study of CAAs in Mississippi, these "programs can be treated as an outcome not because the movement explicitly demanded federal antipoverty programs. Rather, once the War on Poverty was initiated, local movements . . . attempted to secure resources and shape programs."[58]

What can funding decisions of the War on Poverty tell us about the implementation process? There was a wide variety of responses to the OEO in Southern communities, including complete refusal to participate, misallocation of funding, cautious programs that met modest goals, and in some cases the radical reworking of local services.[59] This range of programs and outcomes reflected both the broad mandate to advance black civil rights and the fact that there were few institutional constraints on the OEO. Most important, it was largely free from the requirement to coordinate with other federal government agencies. This autonomy allowed the OEO to channel (or not channel) federal funds directly to local communities, and to implement (or not implement) its mandate to encourage "maximum feasible participation of the poor" in the programs.

The seemingly haphazard results of this process become more coherent when we factor in the history and activities of the civil rights movement. Our analysis of CAP funding patterns shows that funding was particularly concentrated in areas where the civil rights movement exercised pressure from below, while areas with weak or no social movement activity received little or no funding. In other words, implementation of the War on Poverty depended on social movement pressure.[60]

To understand the dynamics that shaped implementation, we analyzed the distribution of CAP funds from 1965 to 1968 for the 736

---

57   Frances Fox Piven and Richard A. Cloward, *Regulating the Poor: The Functions of Public Welfare* (New York: Vintage, 1971); Andrews, *Freedom Is a Constant Struggle*, 136–54. Many activists nonetheless participated in the programs, despite their skepticism of elite motives.

58   Andrews, *Freedom Is a Constant Struggle*, 137.

59   See Andrews, *Freedom Is a Constant Struggle*; Ashmore, *Carry It On*; Robert Francis Clark, *Maximum Feasible Success: A History of the Community Action Program* (Washington, DC: National Association of Community Action Agencies, 2000).

60   This influence by social movements over the implementation of legally mandated government programs has been documented in a variety of circumstances. For consideration of the civil rights movement in Mississippi, see Andrews, *Freedom Is a Constant Struggle*; on the role of social movements in shaping the implementation of Clinton-era welfare reform see Ellen Reese, *They Say Cut Back, We Say Fight Back! Welfare Activism in an Era of Retrenchment* (New York: Russell Sage, 2013).

counties in eight key Southern states.[61] For each county we determined whether a local CAA was established and, if so, the amount of funding received per person in poverty.[62] We assessed the influence of black activism by examining the protest and organizing presence in each county, while accounting for key demographic, political, and economic features. In the interest of readability, we present most of the technical material in the Appendices.[63]

We begin by noting that a sizeable minority of Southern counties (14 percent, or 102 counties) had prominent civil rights activity in the years before the passage of the Equal Opportunity Act, with many of these still active when implementation began in 1965.[64] On the other hand, the vast majority of the counties (86 percent) had not generated civil rights activism that attracted national media attention. When CAP funds became available, about two-thirds of the counties without a strong movement (64 percent) established CAAs (see Table 2) and ultimately received an average of 20 dollars in federal funds for each poor person residing in their counties. Notably, over a third (36 percent) of these counties likely did not apply, refusing to accept the federal dollars that could have dramatically increased their local social spending.[65] This reflects the steadfast racism of governments in those locales, which were determined to maintain the Jim Crow system even when the federal government was offering free aid.

---

61 The eight states were Alabama, Florida, Georgia, Kentucky, Mississippi, North Carolina, South Carolina, and Tennessee, and correspond to Region IV in the OEO's administrative classification. We focus on these initial years because, as early as the late 1960s, Congress—in alliance with Northern and Southern institutional resistance to desegregation and the War on Poverty—began to limit the scope of the Economic Opportunity Act and reduce funding for its programs.

62 The OEO stipulated that the scope of projects be "generally . . . coterminous with a major political jurisdiction, such as a city or county"; Clark, *Maximum Feasible Success*, 84. As most CAAs covered one or a few counties, we follow prior studies and treat the unit of analysis as the county. For CAAs serving multiple counties, we follow the process recommended by Andrews (*Freedom Is a Constant Struggle*, 233n9), dividing multi-county grants "among the counties proportional to the number of households with an income below $3,000 in a county," which is our poverty threshold.

63 See Appendix A for data sources, Appendix B for a listing of variables and summary statistics, and Appendix C for our statistical modeling strategy and complete results.

64 These were counties with civil rights protest activity that were prominent enough to receive coverage in the *New York Times*. See Appendix A for details.

65 The exact number of applicants is hard to determine as the OEO did not maintain comprehensive files on unsuccessful CAA applications. But case studies confirm that the OEO tended to work closely to fund counties whose CAAs put in applications, suggesting that the figure for counties that did not apply is quite close to the number of counties that did not put in successful applications.

But here we also see the first signs of the civil rights movement's impact on implementation. Among the 102 counties that had an active civil rights presence, the refusal rate dropped to one-fifth (20 percent). Moreover, those same activist counties received almost double the allocation compared to the non-movement counties ($37 per poor person versus $19).[66]

Table 2: CAP funding by civil rights movement presence

	No movement presence	Movement presence
% counties funded***	64%	80%
Funds per person in need $***	19	37
Number of counties	634	102
***p<0.001 for 2-tailed tests of significance with independent group t-tests		

To isolate the impact of movement mobilization, we performed additional statistical analyses that controlled for a broad range of factors. These included demographic features such as a county's population, poverty rate, and urban and racial makeup; political factors such as local government revenues and debt, public welfare expenditures, and federal government presence; and economic features including the manufacturing and retail base and capital investment in the county (see Appendix C). When all factors are taken into account, counties where the civil rights movement was present were 54 percent more likely to receive CAA funding, and they received 28 percent more funding per poor person than counties without movement presence. Moreover, counties with great movement strength—which we measured as the number of protests per 1,000 people in the county—were even more likely to be funded, and to be funded at still higher rates.[67]

In practice, this meant that, all else being equal, counties where the civil rights movement was present received $29.80 per poor person compared to $20.40 for those without movement activity, an almost 50 percent increase. Moreover, the more active the movement presence was, the more funding was received, rising to $34.70 for the most active counties, a 70 percent increase in funding over inactive counties (see Figure 2).

---

66   One study of 791 counties found that CAP funding during this period "more than doubled" the total money that the local white power structure had spent on social programs in 1962. (Bailey and Duquette, "How Johnson Fought the War on Poverty," 360.)

67   See Models 1 and 2 in Appendix C, Table [C.1].

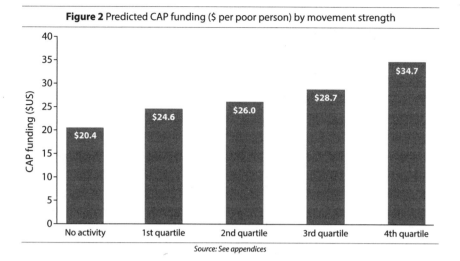

Figure 2 Predicted CAP funding ($ per poor person) by movement strength

Source: See appendices

This data also helps us understand the mechanisms that allowed the movement to impact the implementation of the poverty program. We evaluated the effect of movements' choice of protest targets, and found that targeting government and business were both highly effective strategies: the success rate in obtaining CAP funds was approximately 75 percent among counties that targeted either institution, and rose to 80 percent when both were targeted simultaneously. In contrast, in counties where movement activism was directed only at civic institutions like schools and colleges, or was diffused without clear institutional targets, the success rate was a mere 50 percent.[68] Counties where activists targeted both business and government also received almost twice the funding as counties where activists' targeting was more diffuse ($39 to $22 per poor person).

In the full statistical analysis, we found that counties with black activism targeting the government were 8.6 times more likely to be funded, while those targeting business institutions were 36 percent more likely to receive funding.[69] This meant that counties with activism directed at business interests saw the OEO allocate 41 percent more funding (rising from $20.90 to $29.50), while targeting the state resulted in almost twice as much funding as other counties ($38.90 compared to $21.10) (see Figure 3).

---

68   As there were only ten counties in which local economic and political elites were not targeted, this difference is statistically unstable. But the differences are so dramatic that we believe they are substantively meaningful. Moreover, the efficacy of this strategy is reinforced in our full statistical analysis.

69   See Model 3 in Appendix C, Table [C.1].

Figure 3 Predicted CAP funding ($ per poor person) by targeting strategy

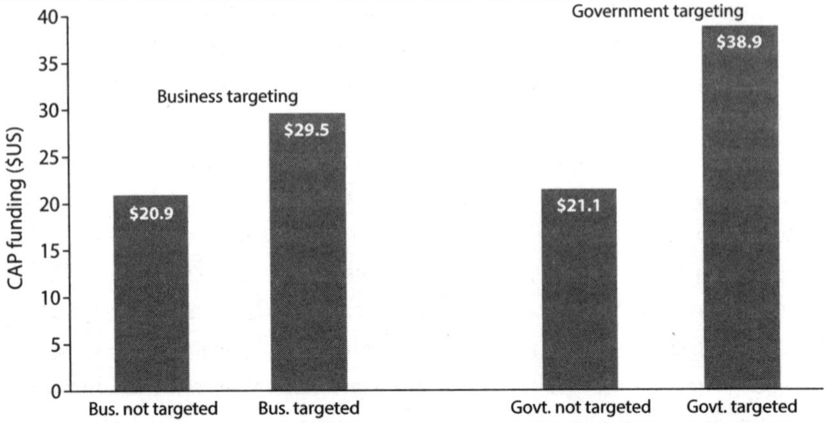

Source: See appendices

What do these findings tell us about the implementation process? As we have noted, some observers insist that funding decisions reflected purely electoral considerations of the federal government. For instance, Bailey and Duquette argue that the "Johnson administration invested in its new Democratic constituency by directing OEO funds to Democrat-trending areas as well as to Democratic strongholds."[70] Yet, as the authors' own data finds, the explanatory power of electoral considerations appears quite small, explaining less than 1 percent of funding decisions in their study. Electoral factors appear to play, at best, a very minor role.

What can we make of the common assertion that the War on Poverty was driven by the "humanitarian vision" of the Johnson administration to address the plight of poor and black Americans?[71] On the face of it, this claim is not entirely unreasonable. When advised to focus on piece-meal programs instead of major civil rights legislation, Johnson reportedly disagreed, asking "What the hell's the presidency for?"[72] Accordingly, the OEO was explicitly tasked with supporting racial integration and did on a number of occasions support black activists, sometimes bypassing hostile racist officials to implement programs directly.[73]

This perceived activism was the very charge levied at the administration by the intransigent white supremacists of the time. Strom Thurmond, the longtime senator from South Carolina, publicly complained that "under the innocent sounding title of 'Community

---

70 Bailey and Duquette, "How Johnson Fought the War on Poverty," 353–54.
71 Ibid., 383.
72 Quoted in ibid., 383.
73 Ashmore, *Carry It On*, 271; Clark, *Maximum Feasible Success*, 93.

Action Program,' the poverty czar ... would have the power to finance the activities of such organizations as the ... NAACP, SNCC, and CORE."[74] Other political elites, including a group of Democratic mayors of large cities such as Chicago, New York City, and San Francisco, accused the OEO of inciting class struggle.[75]

Yet whatever Johnson's intentions may have been, the data undermine the notion that a humanitarian vision shaped the War on Poverty. While the OEO was indeed more likely to fund poorer counties, it was *less* likely to fund black counties than white counties with comparable levels of poverty.[76] How do we explain this? The crucial moderating factor was the pressure from the civil rights movement. In additional analyses, we disaggregated our main statistical models by whether or not a county saw black activism in the years preceding OEO funding.[77] We found that, in poor counties where there was *no* substantial civil rights presence, the funding was highest where the percentage of black residents was *lowest*. In these counties, the US government's racism led it to channel federal money to eligible whites, and to underfund neighborhoods where black people resided.[78] But this traditional pattern did not apply where the civil rights movement was strong. Those counties not only received more per capita dollars than the non-movement counties, but also received more dollars if the percentage of African Americans was higher.[79]

---

74 Quoted in Ashmore, *Carry It On*, 41.

75 Irwin Unger, *The Best of Intentions: The Triumphs and Failures of the Great Society under Kennedy, Johnson, and Nixon* (New York: Doubleday, 1996), 148–97; James T. Patterson, *America's Struggle against Poverty in the Twentieth Century*, 4th ed. (Cambridge, MA: Harvard University Press, 2000 [1981]), 140–3.

76 Average effect of three models in Appendix C, Table [C.1].

77 Not shown but available from the authors.

78 Melvin Oliver and Thomas Shapiro's classic study of racial wealth inequality concluded that "government policies ... paved the way for whites to amass wealth ... [while] simultaneously discriminat[ing] against blacks in their quest for economic security." Whether it is home loan policies through the Federal Housing Administration or tax policy, "[these] policies are not the result of the workings of the free market ... [but] are, rather, a function of the political power of elites." Melvin L. Oliver and Thomas M. Shapiro, *Black Wealth, White Wealth: A New Perspective on Racial Inequality* (New York: Taylor & Francis, 2006), 174.

79 In statistical models that disaggregated counties by whether or not they had a civil rights movement presence, we found that in counties without such presence, increased proportions of black residents were associated with less funding. Yet, among counties with movement activism, such counties instead received 30 percent *more* funding. Moreover, while an increase in poverty rates was associated with 12 percent more funding if there was no movement presence, this rose to a 26 percent increase in counties with black activism.

To be sure, the OEO was under pressure not to be seen as overly supportive of black civil rights.[80] It sought to strike a balance between carrying out its mission to support black and poor communities while trying not to provoke white supremacist backlash.[81] This logic does not, however, explain the funding patterns seen here. The Economic Opportunity Act provided the OEO with a high level of flexibility compared to other federal programs. We see this in four major ways. First, the OEO was constituted within the executive office of the president and dispensed funds directly to local groups. This allowed the program to circumvent many of the traditional federal agencies, like the Department of Labor, which retained their longstanding hostility to civil rights.[82] Second, whereas federal programs had previously been composed largely of work training, the act gave the OEO a good deal of flexibility in the programs it could fund. Local CAAs could apply for grants to fund Head Start programs for schoolchildren, employment services, and a variety of other programs. Third, the act differed from previous initiatives by explicitly calling for the "maximum feasible participation of the poor" in the operation of CAAs. Finally, while tasked with making state-level funding proportionate to the poverty levels among states, the OEO had great discretion over how funds were distributed *within* states.[83]

Thus, the OEO had an unusual degree of freedom to direct funding to areas that needed it most. Strom Thurmond might well have been right that there had never been "such arbitrary and discretionary grants of power, free of congressionally imposed guidelines."[84] Yet, contrary to the accusations of segregationists—and the claims of Democratic apologists—the OEO did not unilaterally direct funding to areas in most need in order to address the plight of black and poor residents. It was movement disruption that shaped the interests of the administration, and thereby the implementation of the antipoverty program.

Together, these results indicate that black activism strongly influenced the implementation of the antipoverty program. Black mobilization resulted in higher likelihoods of a county being funded

80   This pressure came not just from governors, mayors, and other local politicians who objected to the goals of advancing civil and economic rights, but also from Congress, which would spend years systematically limiting the funding and scope of the antipoverty program.

81   Clark, *Maximum Feasible Success*; Ashmore, *Carry It On*, 187–96, 267–8.

82   Andrews, *Freedom Is a Constant Struggle*, 138.

83   Bailey and Duquette, "How Johnson Fought the War on Poverty."

84   Quoted in Ashmore, *Carry It On*, 41.

and of receiving more funding. This is especially consequential given that the OEO was intended to be relatively free of political pressures. These results also demonstrate the importance of movement pressure applied not just to state institutions but to business interests as well. We find that movement targeting of business had an independent effect on which counties were funded through CAP grants and on how much funding they received.

These findings raise two main questions: How exactly did movement pressure influence CAAs? And why was disruption of business—not just of government institutions—an effective path to acquiring antipoverty funding? The histories of specific locales shed light on the dynamics behind the statistics. As Andrews notes for Mississippi, two distinct patterns of movement influence were observable.[85] In one, local activists themselves spearheaded the formation of a CAA and applied for federal funds.[86] Local movement organizations had activists with skills, experience, and a commitment to improving life in their communities. Given that local white elites were often intensely hostile to the program when it began, the strong correlation between the presence of black movement organizations and CAAs makes sense. The South's most well-known early program, the Child Development Group of Mississippi (CDGM), fits this profile. CDGM ran Head Start programs for children throughout the state starting in 1965, enduring constant racist harassment. Its projects were much more common in counties that had witnessed earlier movement activity, and many of its employees had been movement organizers.[87]

In the second pattern, local white elites tried to preempt the threat of groups like CDGM by establishing their own CAAs. A group called Mississippi Action for Progress (MAP) was formed in 1966 as a direct challenge to CDGM, and began competing with it for antipoverty funding in counties across the state. Segregationists insisted the OEO cut off CDGM's funding and designate MAP in its place, and OEO director Sargent Shriver kindly obliged. Commenting on a white-led CAA in Bolivar County, a 1967 US Senate report noted that CDGM's early success had "apparently alerted the county to the possibilities of community action programs. The School Board showed no interest in

---

85   Andrews, *Freedom Is a Constant Struggle*, 145.
86   Ashmore, *Carry It On*, 55–65.
87   Andrews, *Freedom Is a Constant Struggle*, 140. See also Polly Greenberg, *The Devil Has Slippery Shoes: A Biased Biography of the Child Development Group of Mississippi* (London: Macmillan, 1969).

funding Head Start programs, but a group of interested white and Negro leaders decided that the county should organize an agency that would meet necessary requirements to secure funding." White leaders in Alabama similarly reacted to a black-led initiative in Birmingham by forming "all-white antipoverty committees" around the state.[88] Other preemptive efforts included placing black representatives on CAA boards, along with "moderate" middle-class black leaders who had opposed earlier civil rights agitation—leaders whose "moderation," noted one journalist, "was manifested by their invariable habit of agreeing with whatever their white counterparts said."[89]

While data limitations prevent us from distinguishing whether CAAs were formed with active movement support, the results are consistent with both patterns here. Both the initiation of CAAs by movement organizers and white elites' preemptive formation of CAAs ultimately reflect "the organizational capacity of local movements."[90]

These two mechanisms also help explain the efficacy of disrupting business. While political officials would be the logical representatives of a locale vis-à-vis the federal government, more surprising is business leaders' direct involvement in the program. In many cases, white capitalists established CAAs, ran or served on their boards, lobbied Washington for funds, and spent money to sustain local CAAs. Of the three initial board members of the statewide MAP in Mississippi, one was an industrialist and another "a wealthy Delta planter."[91] In Bolivar County the "group of interested white and Negro leaders" who initiated the CAA had included "several planters" and the chamber of commerce, which supplied the staff for grant-writing. When an OEO funding delay led to a shortfall in the Head Start payroll, "a group of businessmen, including the Chairman of the Board, went to the bank and borrowed money," while "merchants and landlords extended credit to the staff."[92]

---

88   John Dittmer, *Local People: The Struggle for Civil Rights in Mississippi* (Urbana: University of Illinois Press, 1994), 375–82; *Examination of the War on Poverty: Staff and Consultants Reports* (US Senate, Committee on Labor and Public Welfare, Subcommittee on Employment, Manpower, and Poverty, September 1967), 4: 1186 (first quote); Marjorie Hunter, "Wallace Defied on Poverty Funds," *NYT*, April 14, 1965: 26 (second quote).

89   Fannie Lou Hamer's response to MAP spared the sarcasm. "We aren't ready to be sold out by a few middle-class bourgeoisie and some of the Uncle Toms who couldn't care less," she told thousands of black protesters in Jackson in October 1966. See Dittmer, *Local People*, 376 (Christopher Jencks quoted), 378 (Hamer).

90   Andrews, *Freedom Is a Constant Struggle*, 145.

91   Dittmer, *Local People*, 377.

92   *Examination of the War on Poverty*, 4: 1186, 1195–6.

In Atlanta, one of the main champions of the program was Ivan Allen, who owned a major furniture company and had been president of the city chamber of commerce before being elected mayor. The local governing board was led by the president of the Woodruff Foundation, which was started by the president of Coca-Cola, and it included various other local businesspeople.[93] These examples point to a larger trend throughout much of the South, wherein white business owners who were feeling (or fearing) the disruption of their profits took action to placate or preempt black activism.

In sum, black militancy helped give rise to the federal antipoverty program, and once the program was created, decisively influenced its implementation. Welfare spending increased dramatically with the infusion of CAP funds, and especially so in the poorest counties where funding was low to begin with.[94] Poverty rates declined from 19.5 percent in 1963 (the year before the act), to 12.8 percent in 1968, and 11.1 percent in 1973.[95]

These gains would not last. The business assault on working people that began in earnest in the 1970s has had devastating results. Today, some 40 million US residents live in poverty, and 18 million live in extreme poverty, even as the Trump administration declares the War on Poverty "largely over and a success."[96] The lesson for today's movement organizers is written in the history of the Community Action Program: the implementation of progressive policies cannot be left to the will of politicians or the workings of government agencies. Instead, imposing accountability requires that movements maintain disruptive pressure on business, the state, and other institutional opponents of progressive reform.

93   Hornsby Jr., "A City That Was Too Busy to Hate," 131; Clarence N. Stone, *Regime Politics: Governing Atlanta, 1946–1988* (Lawrence: University Press of Kansas, 1989), 68; Allen Jr., *Mayor*, 240.

94   Bailey and Duquette, "How Johnson Fought the War on Poverty."

95   Clark, *Maximum Feasible Success*, 81.

96   United Nations Human Rights Council, *Report of the Special Rapporteur on Extreme Poverty and Human Rights on His Mission to the United States of America* (May 4, 2018); Jessica L. Semega, Kayla R. Fontenot, and Melissa A. Kollar, *Income and Poverty in the United States: 2016* (Washington, DC: U.S. Census Bureau, 2017), 10–11; Jim Tankersley and Margot Sanger-Katz, "A Victory Is Declared in the War on Poverty," *NYT*, July 13, 2018: A14 (quote).

Disruption of Business and the Military Ends a War

The implementation of foreign policy is shaped by similar dynamics, as the evolution of the US policy in Vietnam demonstrates. The US escalation of the Vietnam War from the 1950s onward has been the subject of thousands of books and articles, which reveal the roles of state and corporate leaders in shaping US foreign policy in Southeast Asia. The factors leading to US withdrawal have been less studied, but the withdrawal-related decisions that took place between 1968 and 1972 are detailed in leaked documents (courtesy of Daniel Ellsberg, who released the *Pentagon Papers*) and in the writings of policy insiders and journalists. These sources provide a glimpse of how mass movements can frustrate and alter the foreign policy of a major imperial power. In 1968, after two decades of consensus within the US foreign policy establishment, key elite sectors changed their minds and urged withdrawal from Vietnam. The reason is that ferocious popular resistance—mainly in Vietnam, but also in the United States—imposed such severe costs on the institutions that determined US policy that the leaders of those institutions decided withdrawal was the lesser evil.

Following the 1954 French defeat by the Viet Minh resistance and the partitioning of the country, the United States dictated most major aspects of policy in South Vietnam.[97] The neocolonial US policy was driven by the same set of elite institutions that we have seen throughout this book: top corporations and a handful of unelected state agencies. Policy-planning bodies brought together government and economic elites to design policies that would be mutually beneficial for the various interests represented.[98]

---

97   This account of Vietnam policy is based on *The Pentagon Papers: The Defense Department History of United States Decisionmaking on Vietnam* (Boston, MA: Beacon Press, 1971); Carl Oglesby, "Vietnam Crucible: An Essay on the Meanings of the Cold War," in Carl Oglesby and Richard Shaull, *Containment and Change: Two Dissenting Views of American Foreign Policy* (New York: MacMillan, 1967); Marilyn B. Young, *The Vietnam Wars: 1945–1990* (New York: HarperPerennial, 1991); Nick Turse, *Kill Anything That Moves: The Real American War in Vietnam* (New York: Metropolitan, 2013); Christian G. Appy, *American Reckoning: The Vietnam War and Our National Identity* (New York: Viking, 2015); John Marciano, *The American War in Vietnam: Crime or Commemoration?* (New York: Monthly Review Press, 2016).

98   For the origins and functioning of the post–World War II foreign policy establishment, see, among many sources, C. Wright Mills, *The Power Elite* (New York: Oxford University Press, 1956); Gabriel Kolko, *The Roots of American Foreign Policy: An Analysis of Power and Purpose* (New York: Beacon, 1969); Gar Alperovitz, *Cold War Essays* (New York: Doubleday, 1970); G. William Domhoff, *The Higher Circles* (New York: Vintage, 1971); Joyce Kolko, *The Limits of Power: The World and United States*

The key planning body was the Council on Foreign Relations (CFR). Many CFR members bridged the realms of business and government. John Foster Dulles and his brother Allen exemplified the pattern. Both had long histories at or near the peak of the corporate world, and both were founding CFR members with substantial records of "government service." During the 1950s, they connected the CFR and its sponsoring corporations to the respective agencies that they headed, the State Department and the CIA. These latter two institutions exercised preponderant influence in the design of US foreign policy.

President Eisenhower accepted this reality, ceding to the State Department and CIA the responsibility for determining what constituted the "national interest" and how best to advance it.[99] Decisions were made after taking into account the nexus of corporate and state actors who had vested interests in the results. The president, Congress, and the judiciary played decidedly secondary roles and often none at all. Public opinion and electoral concerns were even less important. This policymaking structure, in which politically experienced business representatives formulated and implemented US policies toward the Global South, would endure long past the 1950s.

The foreign policy establishment achieved a consensus on the basic orientation toward the "Third World." Policy toward these countries aimed to install and maintain client regimes that would support US Cold War policies and welcome US private investment and trade. In the case of Vietnam, the fall of the US-installed capitalist dictatorship of Ngo Dinh Diem in South Vietnam would be a clear setback. The Viet Minh resistance movement led by Ho Chi Minh had sought to expel the succession of colonial regimes that ruled the country, starting with the French plantation economy, then the Japanese occupation during

---

Foreign Policy, 1945–1954 (New York: Harcourt Brace, 1972); Laurence H. Shoup and William Minter, *Imperial Brain Trust: The Council on Foreign Relations and United States Foreign Policy* (New York: Monthly Review, 1977); Richard J. Barnet and Ronald E. Muller, *Global Reach: The Power of the Multinational Corporations* (New York: Simon and Schuster, 1979); Gabriel Kolko, *The Politics of War: The World and United States Foreign Policy, 1943–1945* (New York: Pantheon, 1990); G. William Domhoff, *State Autonomy or Class Dominance: Case Studies on Policy Making in America* (New York: Routledge, 1997); Stephen Kinzer, *The Brothers: John Foster Dulles, Allen Dulles, and Their Secret World War* (New York: MacMillan, 2013); Laurence Shoup, *Wall Street's Think Tank: The Council on Foreign Relations and the Empire of Neoliberal Geopolitics, 1976–2014* (New York: Monthly Review, 2015).
99   On the degree to which the State Department and CIA determined both the thrust and the tactics of US foreign policy in general, and with regard to Vietnam, see Kinzer, *The Brothers*, esp. Chapter 7.

World War II, and then the French occupation that resumed after the war. The resistance fighters' plans for land reform and various socialist measures also directly threatened the landed oligarchy. The 1954 Geneva Accords that followed the French military defeat promised reunification of the country, but it was widely recognized that Ho Chi Minh would win a democratic election, and that the new government would oppose the two tenets of US policy for Third World countries: support for capitalism and hostility to the Soviet Union. Thus the United States resorted to a typical measure, installing an autocratic regime in the South and declaring a separate Republic of South Vietnam. The new dictator, Ngo Dinh Diem, refused to participate in the election scheduled for 1956. Washington supported Diem's effort to reimpose the plantation economy that the resistance movement had undermined, a task that entailed the systematic use of terror and thousands of murders.

In response, the guerrilla resistance that had defeated the French began forming again in the South, led by Communist cadres who eluded Diem's repression. By 1961, the resistance had developed into a major insurgent movement known as the National Liberation Front (NLF). There has been much debate about the extent to which the NLF insurgency was directed by the North Vietnamese leadership in Hanoi. While the Communist Party and North Vietnamese army were not democratic in any formal sense, the Communists and other villagers in the South possessed enough de facto local autonomy to enable them to make key decisions on their own. That autonomy was central to the growth of the resistance into a movement capable of challenging the Diem regime.

Hanoi was initially unwilling to support a renewed guerrilla uprising. This reluctance may have derived from the fear of military retaliation by the United States against the North, which was trying to rebuild after thirty years of warfare, and from the adamant opposition of their two principal allies, China and the Soviet Union. The Southern rebellion therefore began as uprisings in many disparate locales, which became more coordinated as small areas were liberated from the violence of the Diem regime. In a detailed examination of the uprising in a particular Southern province (My Tho), historian David Hunt concludes that it was "a decentralized, improvisatory affair."[100] Even

---

100   David Hunt, *Vietnam's Southern Revolution: From Peasant Insurrection to Total War* (Amherst: University of Massachusetts Press, 2008), 29–46 (p. 33 quote).See also David W. P. Elliott, *The Vietnamese War: Revolution and Social Change in the Mekong Delta, 1930–1975*, 2 vols. (Armong, NY: M. E. Sharpe, 2003).

after the Communist leadership in the North endorsed armed action in response to the demands of Southern activists, its directives initially spoke only of "self-defense" and "breaking the grip" of oppression. Local militants in the South reinterpreted these vague pronouncements as an endorsement of revolutionary war. Guerrillas began taking offensive actions against abusive landlords and local political tyrants, creating their own government in areas where they had expelled representatives of the Diem regime. Even after the NLF's official formation in December 1960 and the start of more traditional forms of military engagement against South Vietnamese and US forces, Southern villages retained a degree of autonomy. The mass movement centered in those villages would remain the primary target of the counterinsurgency campaign.

In the years that followed, US policymakers unleashed a brutal war that killed between two and four million Vietnamese, Laotians, and Cambodians, as well as about sixty thousand US soldiers. The aim was to exterminate the resistance in the South and destroy the North economically and militarily. Yet, due to the movement's resilience, officials were compelled to make numerous tactical adaptations throughout the 1960s. The revised tactics included the initiation of aerial bombing of Southern villages under Kennedy, the deployment of over half a million US ground troops under Johnson, the depopulation of entire regions through the creation of "free fire" zones where any living thing would be targeted, a scorched-earth policy targeting farmland and houses with chemical warfare, the herding of peasants into concentration camps, and the carpet-bombing of Northern cities and farms.

At the beginning of 1968, the US military, the State Department, and the CIA were assuring the Johnson administration and the US public that the "police action" in Vietnam was nearing victory. The insurgency in the South was supposedly exhausted and depleted, and the government in the North had supposedly been crippled by US bombing. But beginning on January 30, the Tet Offensive definitively refuted this portrait of the situation.[101] NLF forces and North Vietnamese soldiers invaded five of the six major cities in South Vietnam, including the capital, Saigon. They also attacked 35 of 44 provincial capitals, a quarter

---

101   David F. Schmitz, *The Tet Offensive: Politics, War, and Public Opinion* (Lanham, MD: Rowman and Littlefield, 2005); Chuck O'Connell, "The Significance of the Tet Offensive," counterpunch.org, November 2, 2018; Marciano, *American War*, 91ff.

of the 242 district capitals, and fifty other targets.[102] The offensive inflicted major losses on the US and South Vietnamese militaries and demonstrated that the US military could no longer expect to have a safe zone where its forces were not under constant threat. Most importantly, it demonstrated that the village-based resistance that had initiated the insurgency would not be vanquished in the foreseeable future.

The Tet Offensive also galvanized public resistance to the war within the United States. Among the first signs was its energizing impact on Senator Eugene McCarthy's protest candidacy for the Democratic presidential nomination. McCarthy had announced his campaign as a way of pressuring the Johnson administration to abandon the drive for "victory" in Vietnam. He had not been expected to attract even a double-digit percentage of the vote in the first presidential primary in New Hampshire on March 12. But antiwar activists converged on New Hampshire in unprecedented numbers, citing Tet as proof that the war was unwinnable, and nearly pulled off a victory for McCarthy. The near-upset suggested that the antiwar movement was expanding and reaching large portions of the public.

More consequential than the New Hampshire primary, however, was a private meeting held in Washington two weeks later. It involved the President's Senior Advisory Group on Vietnam, known informally as the Wise Men. The group was composed mainly of top-ranking corporate leaders from the banking, insurance, telecommunications, and other industries, including many who had served in government and military leadership positions. Johnson had consulted with the group periodically since 1965, and less than five months earlier they had strongly endorsed the full-on military strategy.[103] But the devastating setbacks from the Tet Offensive had exposed the unreliability of the reports coming from the military, CIA, and State Department and had motivated more accurate reports of the situation, some of which found their way to the Wise Men during their March 1968 conference. The Tet Offensive and those new reports dramatically changed the Wise Men's assessments.

Tet had a similar impact on the broader world of US business leaders. Though some capitalists had already expressed frustration about

---

102   For these figures see John Prados, *Vietnam: The History of an Unwinnable War, 1945–1975* (Lawrence: University of Kansas Press, 2009), 239, cited in O'Connell, "Significance of the Tet Offensive."

103   Schmitz, *Tet Offensive*, 58–64. For a list of names and affiliations see Anker et al., "The Ties That Bind," 114.

declining profit rates, the tight labor market, rising budget deficits, the weakening of the dollar, and other grievances that they associated with the war, business opposition to the war had lacked "open support by big-name corporations."[104] Tet changed that, convincing top corporate leaders that de-escalation was preferable to the exorbitantly expensive alternative of total military commitment.[105] The Wise Men forcefully conveyed this change of opinion at their March 26 meeting with Johnson. According to an aide, Johnson was "deeply shaken" by the changed posture, particularly among some of the group's most vocal hawks. The defection of Dean Acheson and McGeorge Bundy carried special weight because they had been advocates and architects of the US strategy during their time in the Kennedy administration. Johnson left that fateful meeting with "no doubt that a large majority" of the Wise Men "felt the present policy was at a dead end."[106]

On March 31, Johnson gave a televised speech announcing a unilateral de-escalation, including a halt to bombing in most of North Vietnam and a rejection of the top military commanders' demand for 205,000 additional soldiers. He also announced his abstention from the 1968 presidential race. The speech was a shocking break from his bellicose public comments two weeks earlier, when he had promised "a total national effort to win the war."[107]

The Wise Men's judgment on March 26 set them apart from most top officials then serving in government. The executive branch

104   "The Bad Business of War 'Prosperity,'" *BW*, August 13, 1966: 144–6; "Executives Step up War on War," *BW*, March 16, 1968: 36 (quote). Wartime spending was not the only or even the primary cause of all these "problems." But business leaders widely believed that the near-full employment of the late 1960s "was cutting into their profits" by giving workers more power. See Dean Baker, Robert Pollin, and Elizabeth Zahrt, "The Vietnam War and the Political Economy of Full Employment," *Challenge*, May–June 1996: 35–45 (quote, 43). Moreover, ending the war was the easiest way to address the problems.

105   *Businessweek* greeted the March 31 de-escalation announcement with approval: "A Whiff of Peace", April 6, 1968: 21–22.

106   Hedrick Smith and William Beecher, "'68 Shift on Vietnam—II," *NYT*, March 7, 1969: 14 (aide quoted); Townsend Hoopes, *The Limits of Intervention: An Inside Account of How the Johnson Policy of Escalation in Vietnam Was Reversed* (New York: David McKay Co., 1969), 217 (second quote). See also Schmitz, *Tet Offensive*, 143–7.

107   Quoted in Clark Clifford with Richard Holbrooke, *Counsel to the President: A Memoir* (New York: Random House, 1991), 507. Johnson's promise to cease bombing "around the principal population areas, or in the food-producing areas of North Vietnam" was an inadvertent admission that the US was violating the Geneva Conventions, which outlawed attacks on civilian populations. Quoted in *Pentagon Papers*, 4: 597.

institutions that had been captaining the war policy wanted to stay the course. The military high command had just reiterated its call for a 40 percent increase in US soldiers. The CIA and State Department offered unwavering support for this demand, claiming that the Tet Offensive had in fact represented the last gasp of a terminally weakened adversary.[108] State elites in general stood to reap benefits from continued escalation. The constantly increasing investment in the war meant institutional prosperity for the CIA, State Department, and Pentagon, along with their corporate partners in the military-industrial complex. Even after Tet, their posture remained the same.

The only changes in the equation of forces within the administration had been the near-defeat of Johnson in the New Hampshire primary on March 12 and the sudden shift by the Wise Men. It is possible that the New Hampshire outcome influenced the thinking of the Wise Men, but it had relatively little impact on Johnson's own thinking. Johnson himself said privately on March 26 that "I don't give a damn about the election." The *New York Times* later quoted an anonymous "close observer" who said that the Wise Men had "more weight than something like the New Hampshire primary" in determining Johnson's change in policy.[109] Most insider accounts of Johnson's decision consider the Wise Men to have been the instrumental force.[110]

The dynamics in this critical moment raise two questions: Why did the Wise Men alter their position when the other key elite actors were determined to continue escalating? And why did their opinion prevail over the contrary recommendations of the military, the CIA, and the State Department? Townsend Hoopes, a Pentagon official who chronicled the March meeting in detail, answered the first question by pointing to the much broader perspective of the Wise Men as compared to the military leaders and civilian officials who were conducting the war. The Wise Men "brought to the meeting a wider, better balanced view of America's world role" and a "breadth and depth of relevant experience" that was lacking among the other key decision-makers.[111] That is, they had an appreciation for the larger economic and geopolitical interests of

---

108   This assertion was refuted in May, when the second of three major offensives by the NLF and North Vietnamese forces began.

109   Clifford with Holbrooke, *Counsel*, 515 (Johnson quoted); Smith and Beecher, "'68 Shift on Vietnam."

110   See for example Hoopes, *Limits of Intervention*, 214–21; *Pentagon Papers*, 4: 591–3; Clifford with Holbrooke, *Counsel*, 511–19.

111   Hoopes, *Limits of Intervention*, 218.

the elites at the top of US society, and were less encumbered by parochial institutional interests than were leaders in the State Department, the Pentagon, the intelligence agencies, and the private defense contractors.

Johnson's new Defense secretary, Clark Clifford, became the key representative of this broader business elite within the administration. Clifford was a longtime corporate lawyer who had represented diverse top corporations in Washington, and was therefore "intimately aware of what members of the business and legal establishment were thinking."[112] He thus shared the Wise Men's panoramic concern for the interests of the ruling elite. Vietnam, he argued, "had to be viewed in the context of our overall national interest," and could not be allowed "to impair our ability to achieve other, and perhaps even more important, foreign policy objectives" in other parts of the world. He too had been a long-time supporter of war policy, but his view changed once he took office just after the Tet Offensive and became privy to the realities on the ground.[113] In his own recounting, Tet and subsequent offensives demonstrated that "there appeared to be no diminution in the will of the enemy." The economic costs of indefinite war would be too high to accept; he feared that inflation and a weakened dollar would elicit "stringent controls" by government on future business activity. He also worried about the political and economic consequences of the escalating "domestic unrest," including mounting resistance to the draft. His own fears were echoed by his contacts in top corporations. After Tet, he wrote, the country's business leaders were "no longer with us." His "friends in business and law across the land . . . now feel we are in a hopeless bog."[114] In his role as the new Secretary of Defense, Clifford proposed to President Johnson that he convene the Wise Men, knowing that they would recommend a change in Vietnam policy. He hoped that their leverage as representatives of the pinnacle of the corporate world would neutralize the strength of the forces favoring further escalation.[115] He was right.

The fact that the Wise Men's opinion prevailed provides telling lessons in how executive-branch policymaking works. For one, it shows

112   John Acacia, *Clark Clifford: The Wise Man of Washington* (Lexington: University Press of Kentucky, 2009), 279.

113   Clark M. Clifford, "A Viet Nam Reappraisal," *Foreign Affairs*, July 1969: 612 (quotes); Acacia, *Clark Clifford*, 254–5.

114   Clifford, "Viet Nam Reappraisal," 612 (first quote); Acacia, *Clark Clifford*, 279 (second); Gabriel Kolko, *Anatomy of a War: Vietnam, the United States, and the Modern Historical Experience* (New York: Pantheon, 1985), 317 (third).

115   Clifford with Holbrooke, *Counsel*, 507.

that a unified and motivated corporate elite can impose policy on even the most recalcitrant state agencies by invoking the threat of economic disruption. If the war continued and business profits kept declining, it could have led corporations to withdraw investments from the US economy. For business leaders, the economic costs of continuing the war came to outweigh the rewards of continuing it. De-escalation became the lesser evil.

The episode also demonstrates how mass movements can push the corporate elite to use their leverage over government to force policy change. Vietnamese resistance to the war had been a key contributor to US elites' economic worries. By showing that there was "no diminution in the will of the enemy," Tet convinced corporate leaders that "we are in a hopeless bog," in Clark Clifford's words. As in the case of the civil rights movement, lesser-evil logic led the business elite to force a change of policy on an unwilling political elite.

President Johnson's de-escalation decision did not, in itself, guarantee the US withdrawal from Vietnam, nor even foreclose a renewed escalation when Richard Nixon took office. The Johnson and Nixon administrations would continue the war for five more years, adding hundreds of thousands of deaths to their already prodigious body count. The new strategy, christened "Vietnamization," involved transferring on-the-ground military responsibilities to the fragile South Vietnamese government with the expectation that the insurgency could be contained; in the meantime, Washington continued massive bombing of the villages and sought to negotiate a settlement that would preserve US influence in the region. However, the negotiations stalled and the situation continued to deteriorate. Even Nixon's reescalation of aerial bombing of North Vietnam and his savage attacks on Cambodia and Laos did nothing to extract the US from the "hopeless bog," nor to alter his own assessment as he entered office that "it was no longer a question of whether the next President would withdraw our troops, but of how they would leave and what they would leave behind."[116]

On this key question of what the US "would leave behind," policymakers would again see their ambitions thwarted. The hope as of 1968 was to preserve a client state in South Vietnam that could be a beachhead for US initiatives in the region in the future. But this hope, like the

---

116   Nixon quoted in Lewis Sorley, *A Better War: The Unexamined Victories and Final Tragedy of America's Last Years in Vietnam* (New York: Harcourt Brace & Company, 1999), 128.

hope of "total victory" in earlier years, was frustrated by mass resistance. The primary resistance came from the Vietnamese, but it was augmented by dramatically increased protest from US citizens. This protest involved the well-known antiwar movement inside the United States and, more importantly, growing resistance among US soldiers.

Here again, the Tet Offensive played a critical role. In addition to changing the stance of the corporate elite toward the war, it also catalyzed a decline in morale and discipline within the US military. Over the next four years, that decline matured into an existential threat to the viability of the armed forces. Antiwar sentiment had been diffusing into the military for several years as antiwar protests grew in the mid-1960s. Tet became the turning point, leading large numbers of soldiers and potential recruits to question the war. Desertion rates quadrupled between 1966 and 1971, while re-enlistment rates for first-term soldiers dropped to an all-time low of 12 percent in 1970.[117] Individual soldiers and even whole units in Vietnam increasingly resisted orders to fight. By 1971, surveys of stateside enlisted personnel found that 47 percent had engaged in "dissent or disobedience."[118] Such activity took many forms: organizing meetings, circulating antiwar newspapers, writing petitions, filing lawsuits against superiors, challenging officers to justify their orders, collective evasion of combat in the field, outright refusal to fight, and even more dramatic measures. By conservative estimates, there were at least 788 instances of armed attacks *within* the US military in Vietnam, most by soldiers against their commanding officers, often using fragmentation grenades. Two former military officers wrote with alarm that "there appear to be no historical analogies for large-scale 'fragging'" like that seen in Vietnam.[119] Dissenting soldiers and veterans also formed national organizations. In 1971 one panicked former Marine colonel warned of "at least 14 GI dissent organizations" and "at least six antiwar veterans' groups which strive to influence GIs."[120]

117 David Cortright, *Soldiers in Revolt: GI Resistance during the Vietnam War* (Chicago, IL: Haymarket, 2005 [1975]), 9, 13.

118 Cortright, *Soldiers in Revolt*, 270.

119 Kolko, *Anatomy of a War*, 364; Cortright, *Soldiers in Revolt*, 43–7; Richard A. Gabriel and Paul L. Savage, *Crisis in Command: Mismanagement in the Army* (New York: Hill and Wang, 1978), 43 (quote), 183.

120 Ret. Col. Robert D. Heinl Jr., "The Collapse of the Armed Forces," *Armed Forces Journal*, June 7, 1971: 31–2. On soldier and vet resistance see Cortright, *Soldiers in Revolt*; Richard R. Moser, *The New Winter Soldiers: GI and Veteran Dissent during the Vietnam Era* (New Brunswick, NJ: Rutgers University Press, 1996); Ron Carver, David Cortright, and Barbara Doherty, eds., *Waging Peace in Vietnam: US Soldiers and Veterans Who Opposed the War* (New York: New Village Press, 2019).

Outside the military, potential recruits and draftees in the United States increasingly refused to join the armed forces, greatly exacerbating the manpower crisis. From 1969 to 1975 the number of active-duty forces fell by almost 40 percent, "largely because of recruiting shortfalls," according to a Navy Vice Admiral.[121] Enrollment in the Reserve Officer Training Corps (ROTC)—the main source of officers—declined by 68 percent during the height of the war, with thirty-eight ROTC programs canceled due to campus protest and declining enrollment. In 1970, 60 percent of ROTC enlistees said they would not voluntarily fight in Vietnam.[122] By early 1971, around one hundred thousand draftees across the country had refused to report. Applications for conscientious-objector status skyrocketed. In 1972, conscientious objectors actually outnumbered draft inductees. *Fortune* magazine reported that "dangerous shortages of men prevail in every branch of service, seriously impairing combat capability."[123]

The "Vietnamization" process compounded these problems, since US soldiers now expected to be withdrawn from combat and thus had even less motivation to risk their lives. By 1971, many officers in the field found themselves unable to order dangerous operations due to soldier resistance. As former Army captain Shelby Stanton wrote later, "Morale and discipline caved in on an escalating basis, and combat performance declined."[124] The result was a deepening crisis that imperiled the military's ability to continue functioning as an institution. According to the Chief of Naval Operations, "We have a personnel crisis that borders on disaster."[125]

In the March 1968 debate over de-escalation, the business elite had won out over the military leadership, which had advocated further escalation in response to Tet. Only very reluctantly did the Joint Chiefs and General Creighton Abrams, the top commander in Vietnam from 1968 to 1972, consent to Johnson's October 1968 de-escalation of the bombing of North Vietnam and the Vietnamization policy begun by Nixon.[126] But,

---

121   David Bagley quoted in Cortright, *Soldiers in Revolt*, 4. This admission refutes the assertion of some military officers that the manpower shortage was due to draft restrictions imposed by politicians.

122   Kolko, *Anatomy of a War*, 360; Shelby L. Stanton, *The Rise and Fall of an American Army: U.S. Ground Forces in Vietnam, 1965–1973* (Novato, CA: Presidio Press, 1985), 294.

123   Cortright, *Soldiers in Revolt*, 5, 9 (*Fortune* quote, 1971).

124   Stanton, *Rise and Fall*, 365.

125   Heinl, "Collapse of the Armed Forces," 31, 36 (Adm. Elmo Zumwalt quoted).

126   Clifford, "A Viet Nam Reappraisal," 615; Sorley, *A Better War*, 86–7; David L. Prentice, "Choosing 'the Long Road': Henry Kissinger, Melvin Laird, Vietnamization, and the War over Nixon's Vietnam Strategy," *Diplomatic History* 40, no. 3 (2016): 456–7.

as the Vietnamese resistance failed to subside and the rebellion within the ranks grew, military leaders' commitment to the war began to erode. Top military commanders began to advocate for accelerated US withdrawal. In January 1971, *Time* reported that "disintegrating discipline" among soldiers "is disturbing the highest echelons of the Pentagon," with General William Westmoreland and other top officials "arguing that they are not being pulled out fast enough." Once the initial withdrawals further reduced US military capacity and morale, generals started to argue that they should "get everyone out as fast as possible."[127] General Abrams himself came to believe that "I need to get this Army home to save it."[128] Withdrawal—and the humiliation of military defeat—became the lesser evil compared to the disintegration of the armed forces.

This chronicle of events contradicts most mainstream accounts of the withdrawal. Analysts usually highlight the impact of citizen antiwar protests and/or public opinion on Congress and the White House.[129] More recently, this viewpoint has influenced the strategies of organizers seeking to end US wars in Iraq and Afghanistan. According to one national antiwar leader, the Vietnam War withdrawal had begun when activists exerted pressure on legislators, who then voted in increasing numbers "to withdraw funding." In response to mounting pressure from the public and Congress, President Johnson "began bringing the troops out." The implication for the movement against the Iraq War was clear: "we must build a bipartisan peace bloc in Congress" which would "force Bush and the Pentagon to end the occupation."[130]

This conventional narrative holds some truth. Some members of the foreign policy establishment did cite public opinion and civilian protests

127   "The War within the War," *Time*, January 25, 1971: 44 (last quote from unnamed "Pentagon general").

128   Sorley, *A Better War*, 289 (Abrams quoted); Cortright, *Soldiers in Revolt*, 269. The same logic led to the abandonment of the draft, which was ended in 1973 with the consent of most of the Army high command. See Robert K. Griffith Jr., *The U.S. Army's Transition to the All-Volunteer Force, 1968–1974* (Washington, DC: U.S. Army Center of Military History, 1997).

129   Paul Burstein and William Freudenburg, "Changing Public Policy: The Impact of Public Opinion, Antiwar Demonstrations, and War Costs on Senate Voting on Vietnam War Motions," *AJS* 84, no. 1 (1978): 99–122; Doug McAdam and Yang Su, "The War at Home: Antiwar Protests and Congressional Voting, 1965 to 1973," *ASR* 67, no. 5 (2002): 696–721.

130   Quotes from Judith LeBlanc of United for Peace and Justice, in Joanna Walters, "Infighting Splits US War Protesters," *Observer*, June 3, 2007: 36, and Judith LeBlanc, "Peace Movement at a Turning Point," *People's Weekly World*, September 24–30, 2005: 13. In fact Johnson only ended troop increases; withdrawal began under Nixon in summer 1969.

as factors in their decision-making. They worried that public disapproval would set outer limits on their freedom to continue the war. At one crucial moment, the domestic antiwar movement seems to have helped stop a renewed escalation. The major mobilizations of fall 1969 appear to have helped pressure Richard Nixon to shelve his plan to escalate aerial bombing.[131]

Even so, public opinion, civilian antiwar protests, and Congress were just three factors among many, and much less important than the views of the state and corporate officials who had long established foreign policy. Congress never turned against the war in the way that other elites did. Despite growing rhetorical opposition within both houses, legislators never refused requests for increased war funding. And Clark Clifford spoke to the limited relevance of public opinion when he argued for continued war in November 1967: "No matter what we do, this will never be a popular war. No wars have been popular, with the possible exception of World War II." Clifford, National Security Advisor Henry Kissinger, and other top officials treated public opinion as malleable rather than a barrier to what the policy architects wanted to do. In both the Johnson and Nixon eras, comments scholar Melvin Small, "what was noted and taken seriously as meaningful public opinion depended upon the mood in the Oval Office and the sort of opinion for which the president was looking." The president himself could often swing a major chunk of the public to his position, whatever it was, through appeals to patriotism and loyalty. Following Johnson's March 31 speech, public support for the bombing reduction went from 40 percent to 64 percent. Nixon enjoyed a 77 percent approval rating and strong congressional support in the aftermath of his November 1969 "silent majority" speech, the central thrust of which promised continued war.[132]

While citizen pressure on elected officials had some impact, other factors were much more significant in ending the war. The principal factor was the resistance of the Vietnamese people. The strength and resilience of this movement generated economic disruption that led US business leaders to demand de-escalation. Then, as continued

---

131 Prentice, "Choosing 'the Long Road,'" 470–2.

132 Clifford with Holbrooke, *Counsel*, 455; Melvin Small, "Influencing the Decision Makers: The Vietnam Experience," *Journal of Peace Research* 24, no. 2 (1987): 187; Jeffrey Kimball, *Nixon's Vietnam War* (Lawrence: University Press of Kansas, 1998), 172, 174, 388n6; Prentice, "Choosing 'the Long Road,'" 451, 468–9; Schmitz, *Tet Offensive*, 157–69.

Vietnamese resistance and the domestic US antiwar movement led to growing resistance within the US military, the military leadership began to favor withdrawal as a lesser-evil option. The defeat of US intervention in Vietnam is a perfect case of disruptive protest activating corporate and institutional elites to dramatically revise US foreign policy.

The central role of popular resistance in compelling business and military officials to advocate withdrawal has important implications for antiwar organizers today. It suggests that the most powerful strategy for ending a war is to weaken the commitment of corporate and military leaders by threatening their institutional viability. From the viewpoint of domestic resistance to foreign wars, impeding military recruitment and supporting resistance within the military may be the two most effective approaches. Much civilian activism of the Vietnam era was directed toward these ends, with major impact. It was quite logical for the hawkish Colonel Robert Heinl to condemn the "intense efforts on the part of elements in our society to disrupt discipline and destroy morale" in the military.[133]

History and Movement Strategy: Some Conclusions

Strategic disagreements among activists often stem from different readings of history, readings that rest on different attributions of power and agency. Did workers win the right to unions because of Democratic Party leaders' efforts, or because of their own ability to threaten capitalist profits? Were gains in black legal equality and expanded social services due to the Democratic Party's intervention, or due to black activists' ability to threaten capitalist profits? Did the United States withdraw from Vietnam because of a growing "peace bloc" in Congress, or because resistance from an occupied people and the disintegration of the military's fighting capacity made the war's continuation deeply undesirable to business and military elites? One's answers to these questions have important strategic implications for today's social movements.

Our own reading of these historical processes leads us to several general conclusions about strategy. One is that activists are most effective at shaping policy when they inflict sustained disruption on the institutions that control implementation—be they businesses, branches

---

133   Heinl, "Collapse of the Armed Forces," 35.

of the state, or other powerful institutions. Disruption is most possible when it involves people whose cooperation is central to the functioning of those institutions. When workers, consumers, and soldiers withdraw their cooperation, they exercise their structural capacity to stop those institutions from running. Elections have some bearing on the way policies are created and implemented, and targeting politicians with disruption is sometimes helpful. But even if politicians are sympathetic to a movement's goals, they can do little unless the dominant corporate and state institutions relax their resistance to change. And even when politicians are not sympathetic to the movement, those institutions can usually "pull them around" if they become committed to doing so. Thus, targeting the institutions that wield power over politicians will usually be a better use of movement energies than electing, lobbying, and protesting politicians.

A corollary of this lesson is that successful disruption does not require that a majority of politicians or the public be convinced. It only requires that a large portion of a strategically placed and structurally powerful constituency, such as black residents of Birmingham or US soldiers in Vietnam, be willing and able to exercise their structural power of disruption. Many activists fear that radical goals or tactics will alienate potential allies. They thus devote enormous energy to cultivating a "moderate" image, and to convincing more militant activists to forego disruptive actions. This strategy might make sense if we accept the traditional narratives of the New Deal, the civil rights era, and the Vietnam withdrawal, which stress the role of elections, shifts in public opinion, and Democratic politicians. But the case studies in this chapter suggest that those factors were of only secondary importance. Countless liberals, including some of Martin Luther King Jr.'s own advisers, had called his 1965 proposal for an Alabama boycott "stupid," warning that it "could cost King much of the active white middle-class support that Selma had produced."[134] King responded by arguing that the tradeoff was worthwhile. "I don't think in a social revolution you can always retain support of the moderates," he said. If the newfound allies of the movement were alienated by confrontational tactics, they were unlikely to be of much value to the movement anyway. "I don't think that a person who is truly committed is ever alienated completely by tactics."[135]

---

134   Garrow, *Bearing the Cross*, 415 (first quote, Bayard Rustin), 418. They would later say the same about his growing denunciations of capitalism and US imperialism.
135   Quoted in Garrow, *Bearing the Cross*, 418.

Winning over politicians and the public can help a movement, but not if it means foregoing disruptive tactics.

Finding the *right* disruptive tactics can be a challenge. Different groups of elites are vulnerable to different kinds of disruption. Because the most effective tactic is not always obvious, successful movements often proceed by trial and error. Decentralization within a movement can facilitate this process by allowing local organizers to experiment and then communicate their experiences to organizers elsewhere. By contrast, ossified and top-down organizations tend to persist with failed strategies far longer than is appropriate—in some cases, many decades after their failure has become apparent.

Successful disruption is no easy task; it is much easier to write about it than to do the hard organizing work. Most of the instances of mass disruption examined in this chapter involved long-term organizing, planning, outreach, education, community-building, and agitation before they could even begin. Rosa Parks's 1955 act of defiance and the Montgomery bus boycott that ensued were preceded by years of organizing and preparation.[136] The boycott itself required painstaking coordination and endurance over the span of 381 days. All of the cases examined in this chapter were monumental mass efforts that would have failed without hard work and perseverance. But without this sort of disruption, most of the popular victories in modern US and world history would have come much slower, if at all.

136   Morris, *Origins*, 51–63.

Conclusion: A Different Substance

John Dewey was right: elected politicians are "the shadow cast on society by big business"—and, we would add, by powerful state institutions like the military and law enforcement agencies. While politicians do exercise a degree of autonomy, the general parameters of their activity are determined by those larger institutional forces, the roots and dynamics of which we have sought to explain in these pages.

The dominance of corporations, we argue, derives first and foremost from their control over the investment of capital. This gives them enormous economic, political, and social power, since they can disrupt, or threaten to disrupt, the functioning of the entire society by withholding capital. Other large institutions like the military and law enforcement agencies have narrower domains of influence, but they too can exert leverage over government policy in areas where they have the ability to withhold needed resources or participation.

Dewey was also right that changing "the shadow will not change the substance." Putting different politicians into office does not alter the structure of political power. Imagine, for a moment, that in 2016 the Democratic Party leadership had cared more about defeating Donald Trump than about maintaining the party's pro-corporate orientation, and that Bernie Sanders had been elected instead of Trump. President Sanders would have been severely handcuffed, not only by two hostile parties in Congress but, more importantly, by the need to avoid disinvestment by the corporate elite and the disruptive noncompliance of unelected state institutions. He would have been compelled to retreat from many of his progressive campaign promises, lest capitalists unleash the awesome power of the capital strike.[1]

The same would apply to any other progressive candidate, and even the most dedicated radical leftist, in today's neoliberal capitalist world. The experience of social democratic and leftist governments in Cuba, Chile, France, Greece, Venezuela, and elsewhere since the 1960s highlights the power of the capital strike in action. Even the prospect of a leftist's electoral victory is often enough to send investors fleeing.[2]

US policymakers often encourage capital strikes as a way of coercing other governments: through sanctions, through the denial of credit from US-dominated bodies like the World Bank and International Monetary Fund, and through other signals to investors. After the 1959 Cuban Revolution, the State Department decided that "every possible means should be undertaken promptly to weaken the economic life of Cuba," including a complete embargo and other policies designed to "make the greatest inroads in denying money and supplies to Cuba, to decrease monetary and real wages, to bring about hunger, desperation and overthrow of government."[3] More recently, one of Obama's ambassadors described sanctions as a means to "go after companies and individuals to put pressure on them" in order to "get their government to change."[4] He was thus articulating a main theme of this book: if you want to change public policy, you have to threaten the functioning of the institutions with real power to influence the government.

Political leverage for the general population rests on a similar approach. The normal equation of forces can be altered by a mass movement that threatens the elite institutions that typically call the shots. The best way to counter the political power of those institutions is to disrupt their profits or their functioning. Institutional chaos can force their leaders to look more favorably upon reform, and/or force politicians to support reforms that will bring the chaos to an end. The route to real progressive reform goes through the corporations and state agencies

---

1   For a similar counterfactual see Grover and Peschek, *The Unsustainable Presidency*, 142–3.

2   See for instance "France: The Leftist Threat Prompts an Exodus," *BW*, November 22, 1976: 76.

3   "Memorandum from the Deputy Assistant Secretary of State for Inter-American Affairs (Mallory) to the Assistant Secretary of State for Inter-American Affairs (Rubottom)," April 6, 1960 (Document 499), in *Foreign Relations of the United States, 1958–1960* (Washington, DC: U.S. Government Printing Office, 1991), 6: 887.

4   Former ambassador to Russia Michael McFaul, interviewed on MSNBC's *The Beat with Ari Melber*, July 30, 2018.

that exercise power over the politicians. In the absence of this kind of mass disruption, any progressive reforms to government policy will be weak and easily reversible, as the Obama era demonstrates.

This argument challenges the conventional wisdom in liberal and progressive circles, where electoral strategies remain hegemonic. The Democratic Party necessarily promotes this electoral orientation, since the party's viability relies on the illusion that Democratic candidates will solve our problems. But electoralism is not limited to the Democrats: forces to their left often buy into the notion that electoral campaigns hold the key to change. After all, there are major differences in the platforms and rhetoric of the political parties, and the two major parties work together to portray all their policies as reflective of their voting bases. In the absence of large disruptive mass movements, it may seem easier to work on an electoral campaign than to build a movement from the ground up.[5]

To be sure, many progressive activists do not follow the electoral logic. Beginning around 2010, the US witnessed an upsurge in organizing targeting the "substance" of corporate power. Climate organizers launched a mix of disruptive direct actions and lawsuits against fossil fuel infrastructure projects. In 2018, the executives of pipeline companies complained that "since the rise of the 'Keep It in the Ground' movement, projects were being delayed by a rising tide of protests, litigation and vandalism. 'The level of intensity has ramped up,' Kinder Morgan CEO Steven Kean said . . . 'There's more opponents, and it's more organized.'"[6] Nationwide protests targeted the companies and investors behind the Keystone XL and Dakota Access pipelines. More quietly, local protests and legal action helped halt the construction of scores of coal-fired power plants during the Obama years, and had a bigger impact on combatting climate change than anything the administration itself did. Numerous fossil fuel divestment campaigns also took root across the country, targeting campus endowments, city and pension-fund investments, and bank lending practices. If these efforts continue to grow, they could shift more investment to cleaner energy sources and help force fossil fuel companies to alter their own behavior. Movement

---

5   For a classic discussion of the limits of electoral strategies and social democracy see Robert Brenner, "The Paradox of Social Democracy: The American Case," in *The Year Left: An American Socialist Yearbook, 1985*, eds. Mike Davis, Fred Pfeil, and Michael Sprinker (London: Verso, 1985), 32–86.

6   James Osborne, "Pipeline CEOs Lament Anti-Oil Movement Slowing Pipeline Construction," *Houston Chronicle* online, March 8, 2018.

pressure may also help push non-energy businesses—many of which face threats from climate breakdown—to turn against fossil fuel interests.[7]

Recent history also contains examples of mass disruption forcing non-corporate institutions to change their behavior, leading to progressive change in government policy. The 2011 withdrawal of US soldiers from Iraq illustrates how mass action targeting the US military can weaken military leaders' commitment to war, influencing in turn the decision-making of elected officials.[8] As in Vietnam, the most important disruptive force was the uncontrollable violent and nonviolent resistance within the occupied country. Iraqi resistance forced the Status of Forces Agreement upon the Bush administration in 2008 and the final withdrawal upon the Obama administration in 2011. Internal dissent did not undermine the US military's viability to the same extent as in Vietnam, but significant resistance did develop. Organized resistance coalesced around groups like Iraq Veterans Against the War (later renamed About Face: Veterans Against the War), which mobilized antiwar soldiers and veterans to speak out against the Iraq and Afghanistan wars, and Courage to Resist, which supported soldiers who refused to fight. As in Vietnam, however, the most consequential soldier resistance was unorganized, expressed in declining enlistment rates, plummeting morale, and escalating soldier suicides. Black youth enlistment dropped 58 percent from 2000 to 2007. Just a few months after the March 2003 invasion, officers in Iraq reported that morale levels had already "hit rock bottom" and noted some interesting strategies of resistance: "In some units, there has been an increase in letters from the Red Cross stating soldiers are needed at home, as well as daily instances of female troops being sent

---

7   Michael Schwartz and Kevin Young, "A Winning Strategy for the Left," *Jacobin* online, May 18, 2015; Kevin Young, Tarun Banerjee, and Michael Schwartz, "Who's Calling the Shots?" *Jacobin* online, February 6, 2017. There is growing concern about climate chaos among economic elites. In a survey of attendees at the 2018 World Economic Forum in Davos, Switzerland, respondents listed "extreme weather," "major natural catastrophe," and "failed climate change mitigation" as three of the five "biggest global risks" to their interests. "What They're Worried About," *BW*, January 22, 2018: 43. But that concern has not yet translated into business confrontation of the fossil fuel industries.

8   Information in this paragraph comes from Kevin Young and Michael Schwartz, "A Neglected Mechanism of Social Movement Political Influence: The Role of Anticorporate and Anti-Institutional Protest in Changing Government Policy," *Mobilization* 19, no. 3 (2014): 250.

home due to pregnancy."[9] The problems multiplied thereafter, with later polls finding that 40 percent of active-duty soldiers disapproved of the war and that large majorities favored immediate or near-term withdrawal. While the decisive mass action came from Iraqis, this internal resistance undoubtedly entered into the thinking of both military and civilian officials.

The most efficacious US labor mobilizations of the 2010s also deemphasized electoral activism and lobbying politicians, relying instead on strikes and other job actions. Most notable were the teachers' strikes in Chicago in 2012 and in West Virginia, Oklahoma, Arizona, Virginia, Colorado, Los Angeles, Oakland, and Chicago (again) in 2018–19. By directly disrupting the school system—usually with robust support from parents and students—these strikes forced substantial funding and pay increases, smaller class sizes, and other concessions from state and city governments.[10] Leftists within the labor movement, as opposed to most top union leaders, have long understood the importance of workplace organizing and disruption. Rebuilding and reinvigorating the labor movement must be central to progressive organizing strategies in the years ahead.

The Limits of Disruption and Reform

Mass disruption has accomplished a great deal: unionization rights for workers, civil rights for black people, an end to foreign wars, and many other things. But each of these cases also highlights the inadequacy of reforms. Even when disruptive mass movements forced major changes in government policy, the changes did not fundamentally disrupt the decision-making privileges of elite institutions.

---

9   Ann Scott Tyson, "Troop Morale in Iraq Hits 'Rock Bottom,'" *The Christian Science Monitor*, July 7, 2003: 2.

10   For information on the strikes see Eric Blanc, *Red State Revolt: The Teachers' Strike Wave and Working-Class Politics* (New York: Verso, 2019), plus various issues of *Labor Notes* magazine and labornotes.org. Teachers' strikes also create economic chaos because parents stay home, arrive late to work, bring their kids to work, and otherwise disrupt "business as usual" because their kids are not in school. During the 2019 Los Angeles strike, California governor Gavin Newsom seemed to allude to this problem when he lamented that "this impasse is disrupting the lives of too many kids and their families"—including, presumably, the family members' workplaces. Quoted in Ralph Ellis and Holly Yan, "The Los Angeles Teachers' Strike Has Cost $125.1 Million. Now Both Sides Are Negotiating Again," CNN.com, January 18, 2019.

Rather, the movements utilized points of leverage in the existing structure of political decision-making to their temporary advantage. Workers and nonwhites gained important rights by disrupting corporate profits, but the relative handful of people who controlled society's investment capital retained their power to decide how resources would be invested. The Vietnam War ended, but the Pentagon and a handful of other unaccountable agencies retained the power to inflict violence and oppression with impunity.

Even the most robust policy reforms are vulnerable to the continued power of corporate and institutional elites. When mass disruption recedes, elites tend to rethink the concessions they have granted and try to erode them. Only a few years after the 1935 Wagner Act, Congress and the courts responded to business pressures by modifying labor law to undermine unions and by giving the National Labor Relations Board an increasingly pro-business orientation. Today employers routinely engage in intimidation against employees seeking to organize, replicating the bad old days before mass disruption had compelled business to accept workers' right to unionize.

Similarly, the impact of the landmark civil rights legislation of 1964–65 was soon circumscribed by new legislation and court rulings. As early as 1973, the Supreme Court—which had issued important decisions on behalf of civil rights not long before—legalized inequality in public education by validating local property taxes as the primary source of public school revenues. During the ensuing decades, the courts became the site of a sustained attack on the anti-discrimination policies won in the 1960s, culminating in the 2013 Supreme Court decision that nullified the core of the 1965 Voting Rights Act.[11]

The erosion of the civil rights movement's gains is just one indicator of the systematic oppression still faced by black people. Today, blacks in the US own just a tiny fraction of the wealth that whites do. They live shorter and more precarious lives, due to a combination of poverty and racism.[12] And class inequality irrespective of race is now more extreme

---

11   *San Antonio Independent School District v. Rodríguez*, 411 U.S. 1 (1973); Adam Liptak, "Justices Void Oversight of States, Issue at Heart of Voting Rights Act," *NYT*, June 26, 2013: A1.

12   US Department of Health and Human Services, *Health, United States, 2016* (National Center for Health Statistics, 2017), 16–17; Linda Villarosa, "Why America's Black Mothers and Babies Are in a Life-or-Death Crisis," *NYT Magazine*, April 15, 2018: MM30.

than at any point since before the Great Depression.[13] These grim realities point to the limitations of mass disruption and policy reform for achieving justice.

Mass disruption is further limited by the fact that the people most harmed by an institution are often not essential to it, and therefore have a harder time disrupting it. Structural power is most easily exercised by people whose cooperation is necessary for an institution to function, such as workers, consumers, or soldiers. But the people most directly affected by US military violence and weapons sales have no structural leverage over the institutions that formulate and implement those policies. The future generations who will suffer most from climate disasters have no way to disrupt the fossil fuel industry. In such cases, the oppressed are forced to find other means of exerting pressure or to rely on allies with more leverage.

The only genuine remedy for the misery caused by dominant institutions is a radical democratization of US and global society. In the economic realm, that would involve an end to private capital and markets, and thus an end to private control over economic decision-making. Since the political power of business derives from its control over economic resources, any arrangement that allows business owners to retain economic power will guarantee them immense political influence. Neutralizing their political power requires eliminating their power of economic disruption.

A genuine solution would also require the dismantling of illegitimate hierarchies in other areas of social life, from the exclusionary citizenship regimes of nation-states to patriarchy within the household. We must replace inherently oppressive institutions with different structures of decision-making and rules that incentivize cooperation and solidarity rather than competition, greed, violence, and ecological destruction. We need a fundamentally different substance, not just a different shadow. Until that happens, reforms may bring reprieve from the worst human suffering, and must be pursued for that reason, but they will not solve the root of the problem.

---

13 Angela Hanks, Danyelle Solomon, and Christian E. Weller, *Systematic Inequality: How America's Structural Racism Helped Create the Black-White Wealth Gap* (Center for American Progress, 2018); Facundo Alvaredo, Lucas Chancel, Thomas Piketty, Emmanuel Saez, and Gabriel Zucman, *World Inequality Report 2018* (World Inequality Lab, 2018).

Disruption and Revolutionary Movement-Building

We will not try to sketch out what revolutionary institutions should look like, nor give any blueprint for how they might be built and expanded. Various radical organizers and authors have taken important steps in that direction, and their work merits close attention.[14] In closing, we simply want to make the case that targeting corporations and non-electoral state institutions must be central to any long-term revolutionary strategy. Building militant grassroots movements that focus our analysis, energy, and anger on the substance of the problem can contribute to revolutionary change in a way that focusing on the shadow of elected government cannot. That is true even if those movements are primarily fighting for immediate reforms, as any successful mass movement must.[15]

There are at least three reasons why. First, an anticorporate message has wide resonance among working-class people, even those who will not vote for Democrats. The US public's bipartisan distrust of big business is clear from opinion polls. Hostility is greatest toward the most parasitic sectors, notably the fossil fuel, finance, and health industries that make gargantuan profits while imposing horrific costs on the public. Most people also think corporations have too much political influence. Even most Republican voters think the minimum wage is far too low, as indicated by the recent success of wage-raising ballot measures in Republican-dominated states.

Second, movements that target corporations and non-electoral government institutions are less susceptible to the cycle of misplaced faith and consequent disillusionment that tends to characterize party-based political activism. Every few years, millions of liberals and progressives rally around Democratic politicians, expecting electoral victory to bring meaningful policy change. When the anticipated

---

14   See for instance Robin Hahnel, *Of the People, by the People: The Case for a Participatory Economy* (Oakland, CA: AK Press, 2012); Michael Albert, *Parecon: Life after Capitalism* (London: Verso, 2004); CounterPower/ContraPoder, *Organizing for Autonomy* (Brooklyn, NY: Common Notions, 2020).

15   Part of this section is adapted from Schwartz and Young, "A Winning Strategy for the Left." (The title of that piece was not our choice—we did not intend our argument as a comprehensive strategy.) For helpful analyses of the relationship between reform and revolution see André Gorz, *Strategy for Labor: A Radical Proposal*, trans. Martin A. Nicolaus and Victoria Ortiz (Boston, MA: Beacon, 1967); André Gorz, *Socialism and Revolution*, trans. Norman Denny (Garden City, NY: Anchor/Doubleday, 1973); Robin Hahnel, *Economic Justice and Democracy: From Competition to Cooperation* (New York: Routledge, 2005).

reforms do not materialize or are far weaker than hoped for, disillusioned voters get angry at Republican obstruction, and perhaps also at the Democrats, and watch in despair as Republican demagogues capitalize on popular anger in the next election.

Cycles of optimism and demoralization are less likely when a social movement empowers people to challenge their real enemies: the corporations and other unaccountable institutions that govern so much of our lives. People tend to hold fewer illusions about these targets than they do about politicians; they do not expect them to produce any positive change without constant pressure. Perhaps partly for this reason, activism targeting corporations also tends to use more disruptive tactics.[16]

Finally, by targeting these entities we focus both our activism and our analysis on the institutions at the heart of capitalism, racism, patriarchy, and war. A strategy of targeting politicians is much more likely to get clouded by personalities and rhetoric, and to obscure the fundamental causes of problems. Once people become accustomed to confronting oppressive institutions and winning reforms, they will become more aware of the inherent limitations of reforming those institutions, and will push for more radical transformation. The process of confrontation is thus educational, in that it prepares people for future revolutionary struggles.

Targeting our real enemies can also have positive impacts in the electoral realm. The electoral victories of progressives have typically come on the heels of significant mass struggle *outside* the electoral realm—from the widespread Socialist victories of the early 1900s, to the New Deal Democrats of the 1930s, to the social democrats elected in the 1970s and 1980s. Robert Brenner notes that it may be "quite possible to translate the power accumulated through mass struggle into electoral victories and reform legislation; but the reverse is rarely if ever conceivable."[17] In the absence of mass struggles, the working class (whites, most of all) become susceptible to the appeals of the far right, represented today by Trumpism in the United States and by numerous

---

16   Edward T. Walker, Andrew W. Martin, and John D. McCarthy, "Confronting the State, the Corporation, and the Academy: The Influence of Institutional Targets on Social Movement Repertoires," *AJS* 114, no. 1 (2008): 35–76.

17   "The Paradox of Social Democracy," 68. Most of the victors then sought to forge alliances with business in the interest of boosting corporate profitability and employment, exemplifying the "paradox of social democracy" that Brenner illuminates so well.

other demagogues the world over. The only way to combat that dema-goguery is through participatory mass movements that empower work-ers and demonstrate that fear, racism, and individualism are dead-end strategies that only empower the true oppressors.[18]

The challenge for those seeking genuine alternatives to oppressive systems has always been to fight for reforms in a way that is revolution-ary: to lay the basis for systemic transformation through the day-to-day work of particular reform battles. We believe that targeting the substance of elite power is an indispensable part of that effort.

---

18   See also the analysis—still agonizingly incisive decades after its publication—by Johanna Brenner and Robert Brenner, "Reagan, the Right and the Working Class," *Against the Current*, Winter 1981: 29–35.

Appendices A–C

Appendix A. Data and Sources Used in Antipoverty Study

We drew on 3 types of data:

1. *CAA data:* CAA funding data relate to the first four years of OEO funding, 1965–1968, and come from US National Archives and Records Administration, Record Group 381, OEO, Office of Operations, Policy Research Division, Grant Profiles, 1965–1972, Boxes 3–4 and 14–16.

2. *Movement data:* Our data on protest activity are derived from the Dynamics of Collective Action (DOCA) dataset.[1] The dataset includes all protest events reported in *The New York Times* from 1960–1995. To gauge the impact of movement activism, we identified protests that made a civil rights or related claim over the five-year period preceding OEO funding (1960–1964), organizing these by the county in which they occurred. While limiting protests to those covered in *The New York Times* likely omits many protest events, we presume it to be a reliable indicator of overall trends, and follow prior studies in using it as a measure of movement activism.[2]

1 Sarah A. Soule, Doug McAdam, John D. McCarthy, and Susan Olzak, "Dynamics of Collective Action" (n.d.), web.stanford.edu.

2 For example, see Doug McAdam and Yang Su, "The War at Home: Antiwar Protests and Congressional Voting, 1965–1973," *ASR* 67 (2002): 696–721; Sarah A. Soule, *Contention and Corporate Social Responsibility* (New York: Cambridge University Press, 2009); Edward T. Walker, Andrew W. Martin, and John D. McCarthy, "Confronting the State, the Corporation, and the Academy: The Influence of Institutional Targets on Social Movement Repertoires," *AJS* 114, no. 1 (2008): 35–76; Dan J. Wang and Sarah A. Soule, "Social Movement Organizational Collaboration: Networks of Learning and the Diffusion of Protest Tactics, 1960–1995," *AJS* 117, no. 6 (2012): 1674–1722.

3. *Census data:* Remaining data come from the Bureau of the Census,[3] and include a variety of demographic, political, and economic data.

Appendix B. Summary Statistics for Data Used in Antipoverty Study

	Mean	SD	Min	Max
Antipoverty outcomes				
CAA funded	0.666	0.472	0.000	1.000
CAP funding ($ per person in need)	22.009	28.820	0.000	282.657
Black movement features				
Movement present	0.139	0.346	0.000	1.000
Movement strength (protests per 1000 people)	0.013	0.061	0.000	1.165
Movement targeted government	0.026	0.159	0.000	1.000
Movement targeted business	0.099	0.299	0.000	1.000
Demographic features				
Population (logged)	9.948	0.955	7.537	13.748
Urban (%)	25.406	24.169	0.000	96.600
Black (%)	24.824	20.608	0.000	83.400
Poor (%)	49.416	13.880	12.500	80.800
Government features				
Local government revenue ($1000 per capita)	0.127	0.034	0.015	0.316
Local tax (% of revenue)	28.976	10.134	8.800	63.300
Welfare expenditures ($ per 1000 people)	3.597	7.005	0.000	46.958
Local government debt outstanding ($1000 per capita)	0.116	0.082	0.000	0.571
Federal government penetration (federal employees per 1000 people logged)	1.707	0.681	0.677	6.021
Economic features				
Manufacturing capital expenses ($ per 1000 people logged)	2.658	1.448	0.000	7.632
Retail establishments (number per 1000 people)	10.104	2.311	1.153	25.105
Bank deposits ($1000 per capita)	0.631	0.334	0.000	2.928
Savings capital ($1000 per capita)	0.183	0.279	0.000	2.158

Note: (i) N=736. (ii) Some variables logged to conform to model specifications.

3   US Bureau of the Census, *County and City Data Book [United States] Consolidated File: County Data, 1947–1977* (Ann Arbor, MI: Inter-University Consortium for Political and Social Research [distributor], 2012), icpsr.umich.edu.

Appendix C. Statistical Modeling Strategy and Results for Data Used in Antipoverty Study

To isolate the impact of movement pressure on OEO funding decisions, we conducted zero inflated negative binomial (ZINB) models. These models assessed the impact of movement presence, strength, and targeting strategies on the likelihood of a county being funded and the amount of funding received.[4] Each model in the table below is divided into two parts, with the first predicting the likelihood of a CAA in a county being funded and the second predicting the amount of funding received per poor person in the county.[5]

Table C.1. Zero-inflated negative binomial predictors of CAP funding

	Model 1		Model 2		Model 3	
	CAA funded	CAP $ funding	CAA funded	CAP $ funding	CAA funded	CAP $ funding
Black movement features						
Movement present . . .	0.435	0.247				
	1.545	1.281				
	0.307	0.108				
Movement strength (protests per 1000 people) . . .			0.221	0.641		
			1.248	1.899		
			1.372	0.773		
Movement targeted government . . .					2.161	0.241
					8.678	1.272
					1.067	0.163
Movement targeted business . . .					0.310	0.248
					1.364	1.282
					0.355	0.125
Demographic features						
Population (logged) . . .	0.113	0.061	0.175	0.104	0.090	0.062
	1.119	1.062	1.191	1.110	1.094	1.063
	0.158	0.058	0.152	0.055	0.159	0.059

---

4   While we considered traditional negative binomial models, a dual-model approach is needed because the amount of funding a county receives need not be explained by the same factors that explain whether a county is funded in the first place. Further, a test for over-dispersion showed that another option—Poisson models—was not appropriate. Finally, as the outcome variable included a number of counties that did not receive any funding (246 counties or 33.4 percent), we conducted a Vuong test, which indicated a zero-inflated model was appropriate. In all models, standard errors are clustered by the state in which the county fell.

5   While ZINB models present the former as the predictors of a case remaining a "certain zero" (i.e., of not receiving funding), we reversed the signs in the model to make it more intuitive. Positive coefficients for the first part of each model therefore indicate a county is more likely to see a CAA funded.

Urban (%) . . .	0.014	-0.001	0.015	0.000	0.013	-0.001
	1.014	0.999	1.015	1.000	1.014	0.999
	0.007	0.002	0.007	0.002	0.007	0.002
Black (%) . . .	-0.017	0.000	-0.016	0.000	-0.017	0.000
	0.983	1.000	0.984	1.000	0.983	1.000
	0.005	0.002	0.005	0.002	0.005	0.002
Poor (%) . . .	0.031	0.012	0.032	0.013	0.030	0.012
	1.032	1.012	1.033	1.013	1.030	1.012
	0.010	0.003	0.010	0.003	0.010	0.004
Government features						
Local government revenue	-3.067	1.510	-2.509	2.129	-3.229	1.488
($1000 per capita) . . .	0.047	4.526	0.081	8.404	0.040	4.429
	3.096	1.307	3.074	1.291	3.109	1.312
Local tax (% of revenue) . . .	-0.012	0.015	-0.011	0.016	-0.013	0.015
	0.988	1.015	0.989	1.016	0.987	1.015
	0.012	0.004	0.012	0.004	0.012	0.004
Welfare expenditures ($ per	0.025	0.013	0.025	0.013	0.025	0.013
1000 people) . . .	1.025	1.013	1.025	1.013	1.025	1.013
	0.015	0.004	0.014	0.004	0.015	0.004
Local government debt	-4.112	1.593	-4.201	1.435	-3.862	1.598
outstanding ($1000 per	0.016	4.918	0.015	4.198	0.021	4.944
capita) . . .	1.415	0.556	1.420	0.556	1.418	0.557
Federal government penetration	0.444	0.016	0.468	0.029	0.433	0.014
(federal employees per 1000	1.559	1.016	1.597	1.029	1.542	1.014
people logged) . . .	0.149	0.044	0.148	0.044	0.150	0.044
Economic features						
Manufacturing capital expenses	0.147	-0.020	0.142	-0.023	0.154	-0.021
($ per 1000 people logged) . . .	1.158	0.981	1.152	0.977	1.166	0.979
	0.065	0.025	0.065	0.025	0.066	0.025
Retail establishments (number	-0.041	-0.053	-0.049	-0.056	-0.046	-0.053
per 1000 people) . . .	0.960	0.949	0.953	0.946	0.955	0.948
	0.043	0.015	0.042	0.015	0.043	0.015
Bank deposits ($1000 per	0.298	-0.145	0.348	-0.130	0.336	-0.149
capita) . . .	1.348	0.865	1.416	0.878	1.399	0.861
	0.368	0.124	0.367	0.126	0.370	0.127
Savings capital ($1000 per	0.401	-0.153	0.353	-0.191	0.417	-0.152
capita) . . .	1.493	0.859	1.424	0.826	1.517	0.859
	0.452	0.148	0.449	0.147	0.453	0.149
Constant	-1.888	2.102	-2.586	1.537	-1.513	2.095
N	736		736		736	
Initial / final log likelihood	-2705.193		-2705.193		-2705.193	
	-2485.730		-2490.056		-2484.212	

Note: (i) The first number is the unstandardized coefficient, the second the incidence rate ratio, and the third the standard error.

(ii) Statistical significance not appropriate/presented as model comprises population of counties.

Index